COMPLETE
DIVING MANUAL

NEW
HOLLAND

COMPLETE
DIVING MANUAL

Jack Jackson

First published in 2005 by New Holland (Publishers) Ltd
London • Cape Town • Sydney • Auckland
www.newhollandpublishers.com

Garfield House
86 Edgware Rd
London W2 2EA
United Kingdom

80 McKenzie St
Cape Town
8001
South Africa

14 Aquatic Drive
Frenchs Forest NSW
2086
Australia

218 Lake Rd
Northcote
Auckland
New Zealand

Publisher Mariëlle Renssen
Publishing managers Claudia Dos Santos
and Simon Pooley
Commissioning editor Alfred LeMaitre
Concept design Robert Last

Designer Geraldine Cupido
Editor Anna Tanneberger
Illustrations James Berrangé
Picture researcher Karla Kik
Production Myrna Collins
Proofreader Sandra Cattich

ISBN 1 84330 870 3

Reproduction by Unifoto Pty Ltd
Printed in Malaysia by Times Offset (M) Sdn. Bhd.

1 3 5 7 9 10 8 6 4 2

This book contains a wealth of information backed up by the author's experience over three decades of
diving. However, no book is a substitute for experience itself. No reputable diving shop or diving operation
will refill your scuba cylinder or allow you to hire diving equipment unless you are qualified or are
accompanied by an instructor. It is recommended that this book be used in conjunction with training by a
recognized recreational diving training agency.
The author and publishers have made every effort to ensure that the information contained in this book
was correct at the time of going to press. They accept no responsibility for any loss, injury or inconvenience
sustained by any person using this book or the advice given within it.

To all those who have dived with me.

Opposite: *Anthias and mixed corals, including branching and plate fire corals at Râs Muhammad, Egyptian Red Sea*
Previous Page: *The Umbria wreck is in shallow, well-lit water off Port Sudan, Sudanese Red Sea.*

CONTENTS

GETTING STARTED

Once thought to be the domain of macho men, diving has progressed by exemplary training, reliable equipment and stylish apparel to become one of the fastest-growing adventure sports in the world.

The profusion and colour of fish and invertebrates found in both tropical and temperate waters surprises most people. More amazing, unlike on the plains of Africa, you can get very close to the wildlife. Diving is like visiting an aquarium and getting into the water with the animals. Few marine animals will swim away, some will even be curious enough to come and inspect you. From tiny plankton to the largest animals in the world, divers can often get within touching distance of them. Equally absorbing are kelp forests, the eerie atmosphere of shipwrecks and the myriad of tiny creatures found living on others and the piles of jetties.

Top Centre: *Snorkellers get close to the colourful beauty of coral reefs, but diving will get you close to even more wonders of the marine environment.*

The underwater world

In the first 10m (30ft) there is a remarkable amount of colour. Below that some colours of the light spectrum are filtered out, but they can still be seen when using an underwater light.

Contrary to popular belief, the underwater world is far from silent. If you stop and listen close to a reef, the sounds of animals eating or trying to frighten off others, can be quite loud. If you get close to whales or dolphins, their shrieks, whistles and groans can be felt as well as heard.

Thanks to modern diving equipment the underwater world has become accessible to almost everyone. People from the age of 12 to over 90 are enjoying the sport. Children from the age of eight can 'try it out' with an instructor in protected surroundings. However, diving is equipment-intensive and takes place in an environment alien to the human body, so detailed training is essential.

Initially, the amount of information that you need to assimilate may seem daunting, but once you understand the theory, the practice becomes common sense.

What matters is that you do enough training for the correct reaction to be instinctive if anything goes wrong. Most people are naturally apprehensive when they start diving, so you should begin in protected shallow water or a swimming pool. Most training agencies offer referral courses where you complete your initial training in the classroom and swimming pool and your open water training in an exotic location where the warm, clear water, beautiful corals and colourful fish command your attention, helping to overcome any apprehension that you might have.

Below: *One of the greatest attractions of diving is how close you can get to the wildlife, in this instance a curious Bottlenose Dolphin.*

Above: Having good buoyancy control enables a diver to hover beside a coral reef without damaging it, while viewing its beauty.

Try it first

You do not have to be a strong swimmer to enjoy diving. Some poor swimmers even improve when they no longer hold their head up to breathe. If you feel relaxed in the water, can swim for 200m (200 yards) and tread water for ten minutes, that is enough so long as you are in average health. Average health means that your heart and lungs are normal, your blood pressure is normal and you do not have asthma, diabetes, epilepsy or any other disease that might incapacitate you in the water and cause you to drown.

Training agencies have different policies, but will question you on any existing medical condition before allowing you to train and may ask you to obtain clearance from a doctor. If your problem is borderline, you will be referred to a medical 'referee' – a doctor with specific knowledge of the problems associated with diving. Women should not dive while pregnant.

A minority of people do not enjoy diving. They may feel claustrophobic, anxious, breathe heavily or never manage to clear their ears or sinuses. Make sure that diving is right for you before heading for an exotic destination for the purpose. All recognized diving training agencies run introductory pool sessions where an instructor familiarizes would-be divers with the equipment and some of the techniques before letting them try it in shallow water under supervision.

These introductory sessions are normally enough to give a feeling for the sport. Buy the minimum of equipment and hire the rest from your training agency until you are sure that you wish to continue with the sport. Divers slowly develop their experience and skills, so that they can handle themselves in different or more challenging conditions. Just as your character is influenced by the sum of your personal experiences, your prowess as a diver is influenced by the sum of your dives: you will learn from good dives as well as those where mistakes have been made. As with all adventure sports there is an element of risk, but this is reduced to acceptable limits by good training.

Training agencies

(*See the list of better-known diving training agencies on page 184*)
There are a lot of diving training agencies in the world and most of them have high standards – so is one better than the others? All agencies meet similar minimum standards for the first (entry) level of certification. All these courses include diving theory and practical skills. Some agencies require a minimum number of hours of instruction, others require a minimum number of hours of practice, including the hours in the water – swimming pool or other protected environment, as well as open water. Some agencies want students to meet performance standards, but leave the number of hours of theory and practice up to the instructor.

Individual instructors can exceed an agency's minimum standards and many do. Your best chance of getting the best instruction is not to worry about the agency, but to ask around for the best instructor. Good instructors must not only have the diving experience, but be good communicators, good leaders and have empathy with their students. The macho male may obtain good results with macho men, but not get on with more sensitive men and women. Many women and children will have more respect for a caring, female instructor.

In some countries there are two possibilities for learning to dive: schools and clubs. Diving schools

SOME EQUIVALENT DIVING GRADES

There are many different international diving training agencies and some are specific to one country. This list only includes some of the more commonly recognized diving training agencies.

The British Sub-Aqua Club recognizes the following qualifications by other diving training agencies to be roughly similar:

ENTRY LEVEL
BS-AC Club Diver/
   Ocean Diver
CMAS One Star Diver
NASDS Open Water Diver
   and Advanced Open
   Water Diver
NAUI Scuba Diver and
   Advanced Scuba Diver
PADI Open Water Diver
PADI Advanced Open
   Water Diver and
   AOWD Plus
Royal Navy Ships Diver
SAA Open Water Diver
SSI Open Water Diver
   and Advanced Open
   Water Diver
These Qualifications do
   not usually include
   rescue training.

SECOND LEVEL
BS-AC Sports Diver
CMAS Two Star Diver
HSE Commercial Diver:
   HSE scuba Diver/HSE
   Surface Supply Diver/

HSE Surface Supply (Top
   Up) Diver/HSE Closed
   Bell Diver (formerly HSE
   Diver Part 4, 3, 1 and 2
   respectively)
NASDS Rescue Diver
NAUI Scuba Rescue Diver
PADI Rescue Diver
SAA Club Diver
SSAC Third Class Diver
SSI Advanced Open Water
   Diver with 'Stress and
   Rescue' Speciality
Army Compressed
   Air Diver
These qualifications must
   include rescue training.

THIRD LEVEL
BS-AC Dive Leader
NASDS Dive Supervisor
NAUI Divemaster
PADI Divemaster
SAA Dive Leader
SSAC Second Class
   Diver/Master Diver
SSI Dive Control Specialist
These qualifications
   must include dive
   leadership training.

HIGHER GRADES
BS-AC Advanced Diver
Any higher level of
   qualification than listed

above such as CMAS
Three Star Diver and SAA
Dive Supervisor

Because of the variation allowed in the training for higher diving qualifications awarded by American and other diving training agencies, the BS-AC is unable to recognize them as being of a similar standard to BS-AC Advanced Diver.

LEGEND
BS-AC British Sub-Aqua Club
CMAS Confédération Mondiale des Activités Subaquatiques (World Underwater Federation)
HSE Health and Safety Executive
NASDS National Association of Scuba Diving Schools

NAUI National Association of Underwater Instructors
PADI Professional Association of Diving Instructors
SAA The Sub-Aqua Association
SSAC Scottish Sub-Aqua Club
SSI Scuba Schools International

obviously have a vested interest in getting you qualified in the shortest possible time and in getting you interested enough to want to take further 'speciality courses' for which they can charge you again. The advantage of this system is that all the equipment is available for hire, the course itself is concentrated into a short, but continuous time and the instructors have good reason for wanting to get you through the course and on to the next one. In the short term, or for those who only want to dive on holiday and will always rent equipment at their destination, this is the cheapest option. On the minus side, divers may pass a minimal course with flying colours, but have done it too quickly to really absorb the necessary skills for poorer conditions – they may never have experienced strong currents or rough water.

Diving clubs offer camaraderie, but the original training takes longer because it is spread over nights and weekends and some or all equipment may have to be bought. Depending on where you learn and with which club, you are likely to be taught some of the extras that would be considered part of 'speciality courses' at the schools, and you are likely to experience a wider range of water conditions.

Statistics indicate a strong correlation between dive accidents and lack of experience, but no correlation between accidents and the training agency. The names of some training agencies may seem to crop up often, but this is more likely to be because they are larger agencies and train more divers. Individual divers and individual instructors differ more than agencies do, so ask around for a good instructor.

Above: *Although the Caribbean is less colourful than the Indo-Pacific, this mixture of Lilac Stove Sponges and the corals in Bonaire is still beautiful.*

The marine environment

Viewed from space the oceans dominate the earth. Covering 70% of our planet they provide us with food, a large area for recreation and they regulate the climate. Mankind has treated the oceans as a rubbish pit for centuries, but modern agricultural and industrial pollution is much more damaging. Combined with overfishing, often by detrimental methods, the cumulative effect had been damaged reefs and collapsing fish stocks. Heavy metals poisonous to man, such as mercury, accumulate in shellfish and older fish such as Humphead (Napoleon) Wrasse, sharks, dolphins and whales. Tunicates concentrate Vanadium and Niobium, oysters accumulate Zinc and lobsters accumulate Copper. Ships taking on organisms in seawater ballast in one region and discharging it in another upset the ecology in many areas. Sometimes exotic fauna and flora are released from aquariums into seas where they have no natural predators.

In the natural course of events coral reefs are occasionally damaged by storm-driven wave action, the effects of El Niño or aggregations of Crown-of-Thorns Starfish. However, some human activities such as blast and cyanide fishing, bottom-trawling, coral mining, siltation from construction work, imported sand for artificial beaches, landfill, dredging or logging and the indiscriminate collection of corals for sale are just as destructive. Overfishing depletes fish life and upsets the food chain. When the number of herbivorous fish are reduced the corals become overgrown with algae.

With the growing popularity of diving, environmentalists are becoming concerned by the damage done by careless divers and boatmen to live corals. Some diving operators in warm waters have

Below: Colourful Anemonefish, also called Clownfish, such as this Allen's or Skunk Clownfish are divers' favourites as they scamper about non-stop in the safety of their chosen anemone.

Above: This Gorgonian Sea Rod forms a colourful display at Jessie Beazley Reef in the Philippines Sulu Sea.

industry in an ecologically sustainable manner. The capital investment necessary to develop ecotourism is minimal, much-needed employment becomes available to the local population and, in the long term, the profits exceed those of logging or overfishing.

Many divers, dive operators and diving resorts lead the field in protecting marine ecosystems, but we all need food and shelter and thus have an impact on the environment. A small resort without a waste-treatment system may not seriously harm nearby reefs. However, pressure of numbers make controls necessary.

Coral reefs are not the only places affected by divers. There is also concern over some divers' behaviour where larger animals congregate, but education can control this.

There is a danger in overregulation too, however. If the rules in one area are too strict, divers and snorkellers may lose interest and go elsewhere. If divers and snorkellers are not around regularly to keep an eye on the animals or coral reef and the local people do not gain employment from tourism, there is more chance of fishermen killing the animals or using damaging fishing methods.

There are two schools of thought on fish-feeding. Some believe that, while it may seem harmless, it can upset the animals' normal feeding patterns, provoke aggressive behaviour and affect the animals' health. However, others say that so long as the food is part of the animals' natural diet, selected fish-feeding has produced theme dives that make them worth more alive than dead as tourist diving attractions. The publicity ensures conservation of animals that would otherwise be fished out and brings work and other benefits to the local economy as more divers visit the area.

The ecological sustainability of diving areas depends on divers too:

- Coral is killed by divers touching it while trying to adjust their buoyancy – master buoyancy control.
- Ensure that you are properly weighted and have all equipment tucked in to prevent any of it touching marine organisms.

banned the use of gloves except on wrecks in an effort to stop divers from holding onto live corals.

The growing awareness of environmental issues has given rise to 'ecotourism' – tourism with an ecological conscience. Ecotourism is often summed up with the slogan 'take nothing but photographs, leave nothing but footprints'. However, any form of touching is harmful to corals. A better approach is to manage the tourist

- If you must settle on the seabed to practise diving techniques or adjust equipment, do so in a sandy area away from the reef.
- If you are about to collide with the reef, steady yourself with your fingertips on a part of the reef that is already dead.
- Do not use deep fin-strokes next to the reef. The surge of water stresses delicate organisms; and sand that is stirred up settles on and smothers corals.
- In warm waters, not wearing gloves (except on wrecks) will help avoid the temptation to hold onto live corals.
- Do not move organisms around to photograph or play with them nor hitch rides on turtles, Manta Rays or Whale Sharks. It causes them considerable stress.
- Never touch corals, basket or barrel sponges.
- Limit the number of people in underwater caverns and caves, and do not stay long. Exhausted air is trapped under the roof of the cave and creatures living there 'suffocate' in air.
- Do not collect or purchase marine souvenirs.
- Before booking a trip on a boat, ask about the company's environmental policy. Avoid boats that cause unnecessary anchor damage, have bad oil leaks, or discharge sewage near reefs.
- On any excursion, whether with a dive operator or privately organized, make sure you take your garbage back for proper disposal on land.
- Do not participate in spear-fishing for sport, selective killing of larger fish upsets the reproductive chain. If you are living on a boat and rely on spear-fishing for food, familiarize yourself with local fish and game regulations and get the necessary licenses.
- During night dives, avoid pointing bright lights directly at fish. This dazzles and confuses them.

Above: *This Tubastrea Cup Coral at Panganaa Island in the Philippines forms a brilliant flower-like display in shady places with its polyps extended to feed.*

THE SCIENCE OF DIVING

It may seem daunting to have to complete classroom work, involving chemistry and physics, for a sport that is fun. However, for the sport to be safe divers must understand how water and gas pressures affect the human body. Some of the laws may initially sound complicated, but they are actually quite straightforward.

We are used to living in air. When we venture underwater our perception of weight, colour, distance, size and sound are different. Water quickly conducts heat away from our bodies and in particular the pressure at depth acting on the gases we are breathing, the blood and tissues carrying these gases and the air spaces within the body, all have physiological effects on the diver.

Buoyancy

Archimedes' Principle states: 'Any object that is wholly or partially immersed in a liquid is buoyed up by a force equal to the weight of the liquid displaced by that object'. Put simply, if the object is less dense than the liquid it will float (positively buoyant) and if it is denser than the liquid it will sink (negatively buoyant).

A diver's total weight can be increased by adding lead weights. A diver's volume can be adjusted in a small way by the depth of breathing and in a larger way by varying the amount of air in the buoyancy compensator device (BCD).

Neutral buoyancy is achieved when the diver's overall density is the same as that of the surrounding water. By adding air to the BCD, the diver will ascend and by venting air from the BCD, the diver will descend, (*see weight systems p50 and BCDs pp53 and 103*).

The more dense the liquid, the more buoyant it will be. Saltwater contains salts in solution, which make it denser than freshwater and therefore more buoyant.

Most exposure suits increase the diver's buoyancy. However, because many consist of bubbles of gas in neoprene, these bubbles will compress and the suit become less buoyant as the diver descends. The bubbles will expand to become more buoyant as the diver ascends. The same thing happens with the air (gas) in the BCD. The scuba cylinder, on the other hand, is rigid and the air (breathing gas) within it can not expand or be compressed further by differences in the outside water pressure. However, as air is used up, its total weight, and therefore density, becomes less, so it becomes more buoyant.

All these buoyancy situations can be adjusted for by adding or removing air (breathing gas or Argon if carried) to or from the BCD.

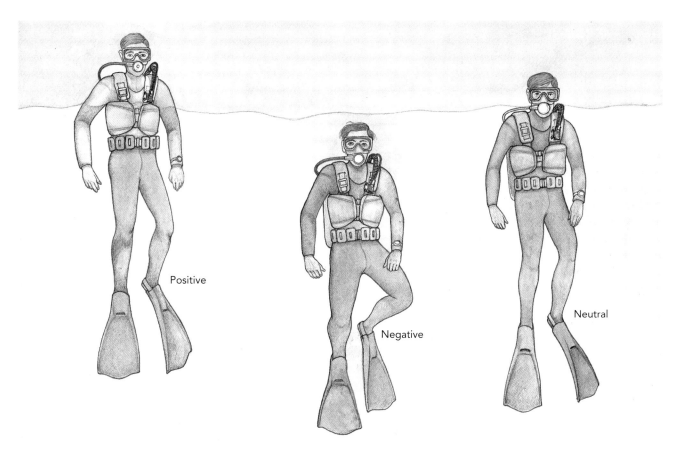

Positive

Negative

Neutral

Above: *Finding and maintaining the right buoyancy is a question of weight and breath control, and takes time to learn.*

Above: A correctly weighted diver will float comfortably with the mouth just above the surface of the water.

Air

Most sport divers breathe compressed air, a mixture of colourless, odourless and tasteless gases. The composition of air in the atmosphere is approximately 78% Nitrogen, 21% Oxygen and 1% other gases.

OXYGEN

O_2 is required to convert food into energy and heat. However, under enough pressure it becomes toxic. The resulting convulsions are particularly dangerous underwater.

CARBON DIOXIDE

CO_2 is made up of two atoms of oxygen attached to a single atom of carbon. It is a by-product of the conversion of food and oxygen into energy and is a major constituent of exhaled air. Sensors in the body measure the amount of carbon dioxide as it builds up. If the quantity becomes too high signals are sent to the brain that tell it either to initiate breathing or to increase the rate of breathing.

NITROGEN

N_2 is the major component of air, but the human body cannot make use of it. At sea level, the amount of N_2 inhaled is the same as the amount exhaled. Our bodies cannot hold any more or less of the gas unless the pressure on the tissues is altered. Under the increased pressure of diving, more air is inhaled because it is at

Some dry suits are made from materials that are not compressible and rely on undergarments for warmth. As divers wearing this type of suit descend, the increase in water pressure causes the undergarments to compress and the suit to press uncomfortably onto the skin (squeeze). Adding air to the suit itself will help, though

this must be released on ascent. Most such suits have an automatic exhaust valve, but the angle of the body in the water can affect its efficiency. Air may have to be released by inserting a finger under the neck seal or the wrist seal of a raised arm. The diver's main buoyancy is best adjusted with the BCD.

a higher pressure, and thus denser, than at sea level. The extra nitrogen, for which the body has no use, dissolves in the blood and tissues. If we dive deeply enough it interferes with the central nervous system causing nitrogen narcosis – the effects of which resemble drunkenness. This extra dissolved nitrogen is released from solution in the blood and tissues as the diver ascends. If the diver ascends too quickly, however, nitrogen is released too rapidly and can form bubbles that become too large for the human body to release safely. These bubbles can block blood vessels or disrupt tissues. If bubbles block the flow of blood to the brain or heart, permanent injury, paralysis or death, can result. (*See decompression pp39, 40 and 114.*)

Many advanced divers now breathe Enriched Air Nitrox, air with extra oxygen to reduce the nitrogen content and therefore reduce the risk of decompression sickness. (*See Enriched Air Nitrox p149.*)

CARBON MONOXIDE

Carbon monoxide (CO) is made up of one atom of carbon attached to a single atom of oxygen. It combines with the haemoglobin in the blood, which then prevents the haemoglobin from carrying the oxygen we require for life. Carbon monoxide is formed by incomplete combustion.

It gets into divers' breathing air through bad compressor maintenance or by positioning the compressor air intake where it can pick up exhaust fumes from a nearby internal combustion engine such as one driving the compressor, or the boat's engine.

HELIUM

Helium (He) is an odourless, inert (unreactive) gas used in place of some or all the nitrogen and some of the oxygen to avoid the narcotic effect of nitrogen and the toxic effect of oxygen in deep diving. However, it distorts the voice, conducts heat away from the body more quickly than air and requires extra decompression schedules (*see p151*).

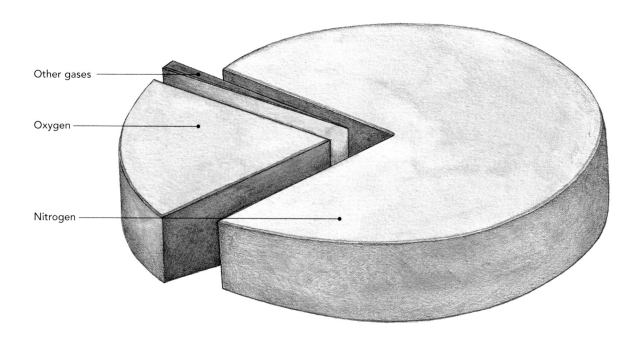

Other gases

Oxygen

Nitrogen

Above: *The composition of the air we breathe.*

The gas laws

Gases are substances that will expand to fill all of the space available to them, they can also be compressed into a smaller volume. To understand the behaviour of gases underwater, divers must have some knowledge of the gas laws.

Boyle's Law states that 'so long as the temperature remains constant, the pressure is inversely proportional to the volume.'

This means that as the pressure on a gas increases, the volume of the gas decreases and vice versa.

Another way of explaining Boyle's Law is that for a fixed quantity of gas, so long as the temperature does not change, then the pressure multiplied by the volume is constant. This is expressed as:

$P \times V = K$
where P = absolute pressure;
V = volume; K = constant
If P and V vary, then
$$P_1 \times V_1 = K$$
and also $P_2 \times V_2 = K$
So combining the two equations
gives: $P_1 \times V_1 = P_2 \times V_2$

If a fixed quantity of gas is pumped into a rigid container such as a scuba cylinder then, because the volume of that cylinder

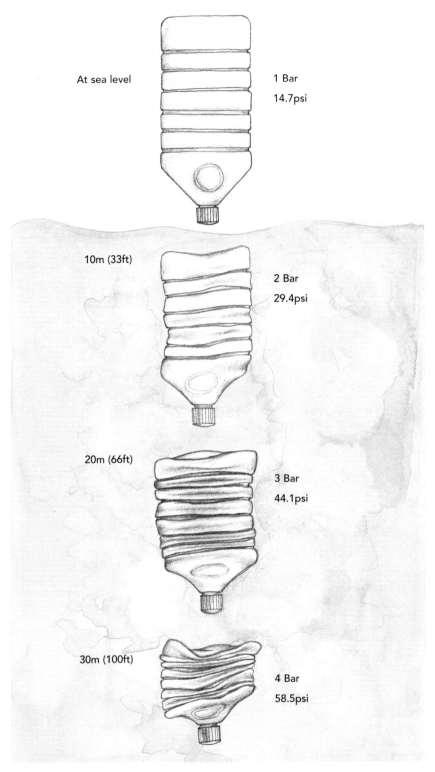

At sea level — 1 Bar 14.7psi

10m (33ft) — 2 Bar 29.4psi

20m (66ft) — 3 Bar 44.1psi

30m (100ft) — 4 Bar 58.5psi

Above: *The effects of pressure change with depth shown with a plastic bottle. As the pressure on a gas increases, its volume decreases, and vice versa.*

cannot change, it will determine the pressure of the gas inside. If the same quantity of gas is pumped into a flexible container such as a balloon, it will expand to keep the pressure inside equal to the pressure of the gas outside. Here the pressure determines the volume of the balloon.

At sea level the atmosphere exerts a pressure of 1 bar (14.7psi). At 10m (33ft) below the surface of the water, this pressure is doubled to 2 bar (29.4psi) and for each further 10m (33ft) in depth the pressure is increased by another bar (14.7psi).

Imagine an inverted open glass bottle, full of air at the surface. At a depth of 10m (33ft), where the pressure is 2 bar (29.4psi) the air in this bottle will have been compressed into half its original volume. At 20m (66ft) the pressure will be 3 bar (44.1psi) and the air will have been compressed into a third of its original volume. At 30m (100ft) the pressure will be 4 bar (58.8psi) and the air will have been compressed into a quarter of its original volume.

While the pressure and volume of a gas are inversely proportional, its pressure and density are directly proportional. Therefore when we increase the pressure of a gas, thus reducing the volume, the space between its molecules is reduced and the gas becomes denser. At twice atmospheric pressure, a given volume of gas is twice as dense as at the surface and so on. This is why divers use up their air supply more quickly at depth. A full breath of air at twice atmospheric pressure takes in twice the number of air molecules as at the surface. Therefore at three atmospheres the cylinder will only last one-third as long as at the surface.

A diver must breathe air at a pressure equal to that of the surrounding water. This allows for expansion to the lungs' normal volume, regardless of depth. A diving regulator is a system of valves that reduce the pressure of the compressed air in the scuba cylinder to the same pressure as that of the water at the same depth as the diver's lungs. Divers do not wish to waste the air in their cylinder so the diving regulator is designed to supply air only when they demand it, hence the alternative name, 'demand valve' (see *diving regulators, p71*).

On every dive there are several gas-filled items such as the devices worn to control buoyancy (see *BCDs p53 and dry suits p60*), cylinders, masks and the small bubbles in wet and neoprene dry suits. The body also has gas-filled cavities – sinuses, ears, stomach and lungs (see *p41*). Except for rigid cylinders, these spaces contract as we descend or expand as we ascend. On ascent, divers must get rid of the air expanding in their lungs and equalize their ears and sinuses to avoid pain and tissue damage known as barotrauma (see *p41*). (This has nothing to do with decompression stages or stops – they are another subject.)

Current thinking is that the rate at which gases expand in a diver's body during ascent is particularly high in the top 10m (33ft) of the dive, so divers should forcibly exhale while ascending slowly from that depth to the surface.

COMPOSITION OF SEAWATER

Common salt (sodium chloride), is the most dominant chemical among those that give seawater its salty taste. On average seawater contains about 3% salt, although it varies from about 1% in the polar seas to 5% in enclosed waters such as the Mediterranean Sea and Red Sea. Salt obtained by the evaporation of seawater contains 77.76% sodium chloride, 10.88% magnesium chloride, 4.74% magnesium sulphate, 3.60% calcium sulphate, 2.46% potassium chloride, 0.22% magnesium bromide, and 0.34% calcium carbonate.

THE CONSTANT-VOLUME LAW

If the volume of a fixed mass of gas is kept constant, then the pressure is directly proportional to the temperature.

Thus if the temperature is increased, so is the pressure. Similarly, if the pressure is increased, so is the temperature. This is the reason why full scuba cylinders, which have a constant volume, should not be stored near a source of heat or in direct sunlight, as the expanding gas could cause them to explode. Another example is that when a diver enters water that is colder than the air temperature at which the scuba cylinder has been stored, the pressure within the scuba cylinder drops. As a rule of thumb for every 1°C of temperature change, the pressure in a full diving cylinder will change by 0.6 bar. Or for 1°F of temperature change the pressure in a full diving cylinder will change by 5psi.

CHARLES' LAW

If a fixed mass of gas is kept at a constant pressure, then the volume is directly proportional to the absolute temperature. In other words, if the temperature is increased, then the volume will also increase.

This law is also known as Gay-Lussac's Law after the Frenchman who first formulated it but it is now known to be only approximately true.

Boyle's Law, Charles' Law and the Constant-Volume Law can be combined as:

$$\frac{P \times V}{T} = K$$

where
P = absolute pressure; V = volume;
T = absolute temperature;
K = constant
This gives us the mathematical equation:

$$\frac{P_1 \times V_1}{T_1} = K$$

But if things vary then also:

$$\frac{P_2 \times V_2}{T_2} = K$$

Combining the two equations gives us a mathematical equation for the general gas law:

$$\frac{P_1 \times V_1}{T_1} = \frac{P_2 \times V_2}{T_2}$$

When filling or emptying a diving cylinder both V_1 and V_2 are identical, so they cancel each other out and the equation becomes:

$$\frac{P_1}{T_1} = \frac{P_2}{T_2}$$

In practice these laws and formulae are only true for a perfect gas, but they are close enough for use by divers. It is impossible to avoid altering all three parameters together. For example, when a scuba cylinder is filled from a compressor, the air is heated by the compressor and this warms the scuba cylinder.

DALTON'S LAW

In a mixture of gases, the pressure exerted by any one of the gases is the same as it would exert if it alone occupied the same volume.

Thus the total pressure exerted by a mixture of gases is equal to the sum of the pressures of each of the gases making up the mixture. Put simply, each individual gas within a mixture of gases acts independently of the other gases.

When gases are mixed, although their molecules vary in size and molecular weight, the molecules are in constant motion so they will mix easily. In a mixture of gases, each gas exerts a pressure proportional to the percentage of that gas in the total. The individual pressure exerted by an individual gas within a mixture of gases is referred to as the partial pressure (pp).

For example, if we assume that air is made up of four-fifths nitrogen and one-fifth oxygen, then the nitrogen molecules will exert four-fifths of the pressure and the oxygen molecules will exert one-fifth of the pressure. If the total pressure is one atmosphere then the partial pressure of the nitrogen will be four-fifths of an atmosphere and the partial pressure of oxygen will be one-fifth of an atmosphere.

Mathematically Dalton's Law can be expressed as:

TOTAL P = ppA + ppB + ppC etc.
or
ppA = TOTAL P x % volume A
where A, B and C are the individual gases in the gas mixture.

As a diver descends, the pressure of the water increases and the pressure inside the lungs increases. The lungs are flexible so to maintain their original volume, they take in more gas through the regulator. While the individual gas percentages within a gas mixture remain constant, the number of gas molecules within a given volume increases with the pressure. This means that we take in considerably more of the individual gases with each breath at depth, than we would normally do at the surface. Taken in enough quantity, even normally safe gases such as oxygen become toxic.

For example, if a poorly sited compressor fills a diving cylinder with 0.5% by volume of carbon monoxide, we are unlikely to suffer much more than a headache by breathing it at the surface. However, if the diver descends to 40m (130ft) the partial pressure of the carbon monoxide will have increased enough to be the equivalent of breathing 2.5% by volume of the gas at the surface – a toxic level.

ENRICHED AIR NITROX AND DALTON'S LAW

Nowadays many divers breathe Enriched Air Nitrox (EAN) – where extra oxygen has been added to replace some of the nitrogen (*see EAN diving p149*). When compared with divers breathing normal air, divers breathing Enriched Air Nitrox absorb less nitrogen for a given depth and duration so they have a longer no-decompression time or a shorter decompression time. However, above a partial pressure of 1.4ata (atmospheres absolute), oxygen toxicity becomes unacceptable. When diving on normal air, this partial pressure of oxygen would only occur when diving deeper than sport-diving depths, but with Enriched Air Nitrox it occurs within those depths. Divers must observe depth limits according to the percentage of Oxygen in the mix (*see Enriched Air Nitrox diving p149*).

HENRY'S LAW

This is one of the laws involved in the absorption of gases by liquids.

At a given temperature, the amount of gas that will dissolve in a liquid with which it is in contact, is proportional to the partial pressure of that gas.

Thus there are at least two factors that affect the solubility of a gas in a liquid – pressure and temperature.

The spaces between the molecules that make up a liquid are greater than those in a solid, but less than those in a gas. There is enough room between the molecules of a liquid to accommodate some gas molecules. When this happens, the gas is said to be in solution, or dissolved within the liquid. Gas molecules in solution retain their gas properties. Although they are completely surrounded by the liquid molecules, the gas molecules still exert a pressure within the liquid; this is known as 'gas tension'.

Let us use an example of a container of liquid that initially has no gas dissolved in it. In this state the gas tension is zero. The molecules of a gas will flow from high pressure to low pressure. Therefore if this liquid comes into contact with a gas, the gas molecules will penetrate into the liquid because it has a lower gas tension. Gas will continue to enter the liquid and the gas tension will continue to rise until the gas pressure within the liquid is equal to the pressure of the gas in contact with the liquid. The liquid is then saturated, gas molecules will continue to pass into and out of solution but there will be no net exchange of gas.

The difference between the partial pressure of the gas in contact with the liquid and the gas tension within the liquid is called the pressure gradient. When the pressure gradient is high the rate of absorption of the gas into the liquid will be high.

If the pressure on the gas in contact with the liquid is reduced, the pressure gradient is reversed. The liquid is now supersaturated; it contains more gas than it can retain in solution at the new pressure. Consequently gases will flow out of solution until the gas tension within the liquid is again in equilibrium with the pressure of the gases in contact with it.

If the pressure is reduced quickly, the gas will come out of solution more rapidly than it can diffuse into the gas in contact with the liquid. In this situation the gas within the liquid will form bubbles. This is what happens when the sealing cap from a carbonated (fizzy) drink bottle is removed and bubbles of carbon dioxide can be seen escaping from solution. This illustrates what happens when a diver ascends too rapidly, reducing the pressure on the body quickly.

When we dive to different depths, different tissues absorb or release nitrogen at different rates. This also depends on variables such as blood circulation, temperature and the amount of exercise performed. When gas is being diffused into the diver's tissues, we call this 'ingassing' and where gases are diffusing out of the tissues, we call it 'outgassing'. So long as the diver ascends slowly enough, the body will continue to release nitrogen in a safe manner even after reaching the surface. However, if the diver has not ascended correctly, then nitrogen may be outgassed so quickly that large enough bubbles are formed in the tissues to result in decompression sickness (*see pp82, 113 and 118*).

Above: *If pressure is reduced quickly, the gas comes out of solution more rapidly than it can diffuse into the gas in contact with the liquid, and the gas in the liquid will form bubbles.*

Diving tables and diving computer algorithms are based on estimated rates of ingassing and outgassing for different tissues in young men. Some tissues may actually still be ingassing at shallow decompression or safety stops, though not at a rate that will cause problems when the diver surfaces. Older people and people working hard underwater are at greater risk and should dive conservatively.

Other factors that affect diving

DRAG

Because of the higher density, the molecules of water are much closer together than those of air. Thus the diver experiences a much greater resistance to movement in water than in air. Drag varies with the viscosity of the water, the speed of swimming and the size and shape of the diver with equipment. Drag is increased by increased density of the water, the size of the diver with equipment and the irregularity of the total shape. Twin scuba cylinders have more drag than a single scuba cylinder of the same capacity and older divers will have noticed that the modern but bulky jacket-style BCD has more drag than the older minimal 'horse-collar' BCDs.

Above: *The horse-collar BCD has less drag than a modern jacket-style one, but the large video housing increases drag.*

WATER

Water is made up of two atoms of hydrogen attached to a single atom of oxygen (H_2O). Unfortunately, the human body can no longer separate out the oxygen from this for breathing.

At normal temperature and pressure water is a liquid and within the pressures involved in diving, liquids can be considered incompressible. However, the weight of water over deep ocean basins is so great that the water column is estimated to be compressed by nearly 30m (100ft). This number is small when compared with the depth concerned, but it is significant in terms of sea level relative to the continents.

Most materials expand when heated and contract when cooled. Water contracts when cooled

Above: *A diver kitting up with one of the old-fashioned horse-collar BCDs (see p53).*

down to 4°C (39°F), but below this temperature it begins to expand again. When it begins to freeze it expands dramatically, increasing in volume by some 9%. This is why water pipes burst in freezing conditions and why ice floats. If this did not happen, ice would be denser than water and sink. Since it floats on the surface, ice acts as an insulator, slows down the cooling of water and therefore the freezing process. Another remarkable property of water is its ability to store heat. Only ammonia has a greater heat capacity.

The land absorbs and loses heat relatively quickly. If the earth's surface was all land, the world would be hot by day and below freezing at night. The vast volume of the world's oceans acts as an enormous heat-controlling engine, absorbing and losing heat slowly and, because of the great ocean current systems, absorbing heat in one region and releasing it in another. These two physical properties have a fundamental effect on the planet's weather.

The third remarkable property of water is its capacity to dissolve more substances than any other liquid. Unfortunately this includes many pollutants. From the diving perspective the most important elements dissolved in seawater are sodium and chlorine, which when combined produce common salt (sodium chloride). Ocean salinity varies with depth, temperature and evaporation. It also varies between enclosed basins, land-locked seas and areas where there are large or few river outlets.

Every day huge quantities of seawater are drawn off by evaporation and over a quarter of this is precipitated onto the continents as mist, fog, rain, sleet, snow, or hailstones. Sometimes this water is made slightly acidic by gases and solid particles. This can be from natural sources such as carbon dioxide, forest fires, volcanic emissions or from man-made pollution. Some of this water may evaporate back into the air before reaching the ground or from hot surfaces in a dry region, from freshwater lakes, or by transpiration through the leaves of plants. The remaining water attacks the rocks of the earth's surface and combines with

temperature, wind and man to erode the land. Rivers carry suspended or dissolved minerals and organic compounds down to the coast and collect domestic and industrial pollution en route before finally completing the cycle by flowing back into the sea.

THE TRANSFER OF HEAT IN WATER

Conduction, the transmission of heat by direct contact, is very poor in air, hence its use as an insulator in duvets and down clothing. Water is denser than air and conducts heat nearly 25 times more efficiently. An unclad diver may be quite comfortable in air at 21°C (70°F), but at the same temperature in water, the body will lose heat faster than it can generate it and will become cold.

Heat is also transmitted by convection; the water in contact with the diver's body heats up and becomes less dense. If this water is not kept in position by an exposure suit (wet or dry suit), it will rise and be replaced by heavier, cooler water. There is always colder water cooling a diver, even when he or she is not moving about.

The amount of heat loss by radiation underwater is minimal. However, some heat is used to warm the air in the lungs, which is lost on exhalation, adding to the chill factor.

HUMIDITY

The process of compressing air into scuba cylinders dehumidifies it. When breathing this air, moisture from body tissues will rehumidify it, leading to partial dehydration of the body. Divers should make an effort to drink between dives, but be aware that alcohol and caffeine dehydrate the body instead of rehydrating it.

In very cold conditions, moisture from exhaled breath can cause the scuba regulator to freeze so divers should make sure that they are properly trained in the use of equipment in the cold before diving in these conditions.

Left: Even in the warmth of the Sudanese Red Sea, a diver will appreciate a lycra-skin keeping warm water next to the body (see exposure suits pp 56–63).

THE TRANSFER OF LIGHT IN WATER

Because air, glass and water have different densities, light travels at different speeds in each. Light travels around 25% slower in water than in air. Light rays will be refracted (bent) as they cross the interface between each medium unless they hit that boundary at a right angle. As light crosses the water/glass/air boundary of a diver's mask, this causes a false impression of distance by a ratio of approximately 4:3 and magnification by a third. If an object is 4m (4 yards) away, it will appear to be 3m (3 yards) away and about one-third larger (the degree of magnification depends on the object-to-faceplate and eye-to-faceplate distances). If the index of refraction of the water is 1.33 and that of air is 1.00, the factor 1.33 is the maximum possible magnification. Also, it is only at small mask-to-object distances that objects appear to be closer than they are. For various reasons, at larger mask-to-object distances divers tend to overestimate the distance.

Of the electromagnetic spectrum (from the longest radio waves to the shortest gamma radiation) only a small range can be

Right: The amount of light refracted into the water depends on its angle to the surface, how much that surface is disturbed and how much the light is diffused.

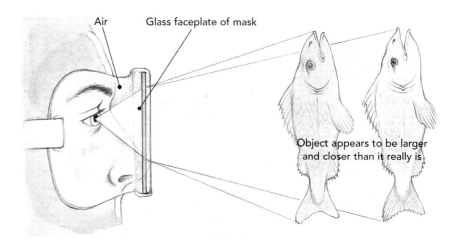

Air   Glass faceplate of mask

Object appears to be larger and closer than it really is.

Above: *Light refraction. Rays passing from the water to air are refracted or 'bent'.*

recognized by the human eye. Differences in these wavelengths are perceived as colours.

When light strikes an object, the object absorbs some wavelengths and reflects others. The eye perceives the colour of the object from the visible wavelengths that are reflected. If all the visible wavelengths are reflected, the eye perceives the object as white; when very few of the visible wavelengths are reflected the eye perceives it as black. Some objects are stimulated by shorter wavelengths to emit longer visible wavelengths, this is termed fluorescence. Apart from its use in diving equipment for maximum visibility, fluorescence can be observed in some plankton, anemones and corals at night.

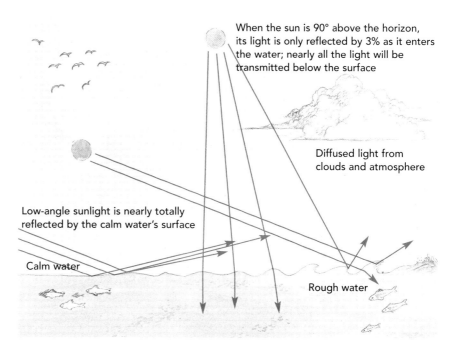

When the sun is 90° above the horizon, its light is only reflected by 3% as it enters the water; nearly all the light will be transmitted below the surface

Diffused light from clouds and atmosphere

Low-angle sunlight is nearly totally reflected by the calm water's surface

Calm water

Rough water

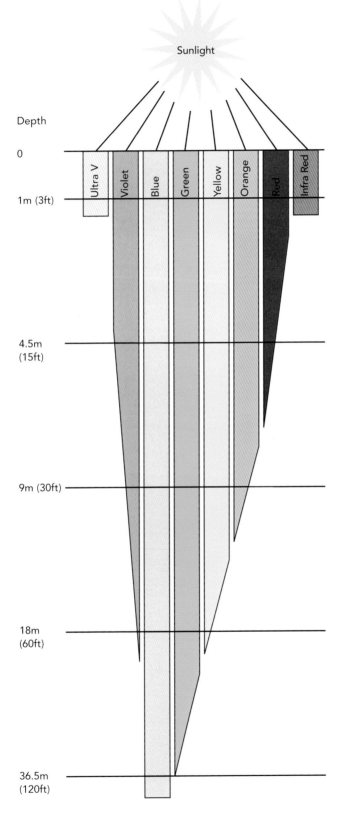

As light penetrates water its wavelengths are progressively filtered out. The first to go are those with the least energy – the reds in the visible spectrum – followed by orange and yellow, then green and finally blue. At depth, red, orange and yellow objects appear grey/black unless lit by an underwater light

Wavelengths perceived by the human eye as blue penetrate water by the maximum distance in any direction. Suspended matter in the water, both organic and inorganic, cause turbidity and in turbid water the maximum penetration shifts to wavelengths perceived as yellow-green. So clear water is dominated by blue and turbid water is dominated by yellow-green.

Top: *Shallow coastal waters such as at the Bay of Pigs in Cuba, appear yellow-green.*

Above: *Deep ocean water, such as at Elphinstone Reef in Egypt, appears blue.*

PERSONAL VISION

Most recreational divers take up the sport because they enjoy observing the underwater environment. Poor personal vision decreases their enjoyment and compromises their safety. In the lower light conditions underwater, uncorrected vision becomes even worse.

Divers who have a problem reading instrument displays, should consider investing in optical lenses fitted to the diving mask or wearing contact lenses.

Diving masks act as magnifiers due to light refracting (bending) as it crosses the water to glass to air boundaries, so divers and snorkellers who are mildly short-sighted will not require help, but long-sighted people or those with astigmatism will gain from using corrective lenses.

Some corrective lenses for the short-sighted can be ground directly into the mask faceplate. More complicated lenses must be ground separately and bonded to the faceplate of the mask; this is the best method of correction as the lens alignment is set accurately for the distance between the centres of each of the diver's eyes. This system allows divers to select their mask solely on fit so long as there is enough space between the face and the faceplate to fit the lenses.

Some twin-lens masks have interchangeable lenses, the supplier stocks a selection of ready-made lenses for either eye that are ground in half-dioptre increments. However these lenses are limited in their coverage of astigmatism and are often not accurately centred with regard to the centre of the individual's eyes. Lenses that are not centred accurately can cause eyestrain, perceptual changes or double vision.

One problem with corrective lenses in a mask is that divers and snorkellers also need spectacles when not wearing the mask. There used to be some fears over the use of contact lenses for diving, but these have now been dispelled so long as they are gas-permeable. Properly fitted rigid gas-permeable contact lenses are rarely lost underwater. When ascending from a deep dive there is sometimes a build-up of microscopic bubbles in the tear-film between the lens and the eye, but these bubbles outgas slowly through the lens and generally clear quickly. Soft lenses fit the eye differently and there are different opinions as to whether they can be lost easily. If a diver's mask floods, or is lost, it is best to open the eyes only partially to prevent the loss of the lenses. Disposable soft lenses are intentionally discarded after use so their loss is not a problem. Some divers use disposable lenses just for diving.

One mask design attempts to correct the distorted vision that occurs with all normal masks, but it seems to be of use only to very short-sighted people.

Even clear water scatters, deflects and polarizes light (termed diffusion) and it reduces shadows and contrast. Because it is easier to see objects that stand out against their background, the selective absorption of colours will determine which colours will contrast with each other. The loss of contrast means that acuity of perception of small details is generally much poorer in water than in air. The deterioration increases with the distance the light travels through the water, largely because the image-forming light is further scattered as it passes through the water between the object and the diver's eyes.

Individual photons of light are deflected or diverted when they encounter suspended particles in the water. The way light diffuses as it interacts with matter, depends on the size of the particles of that matter. In 'Rayleigh Scattering', Lord Rayleigh found that 'The angle through which sunlight in the atmosphere is scattered by molecules of the constituent gases varies inversely as the fourth power of the wavelength.' Thus short-wavelength blue light will be scattered much more than long-wavelength red light. This results in the blue colour of sunlit sky and clear water.

The eye adapts to the dim light underwater and once the pupil is open to its maximum diameter the brain switches to photoreceptors that are more sensitive to light, but less sensitive to colour – so we perceive even less colour. Although divers can spend 15 to 30 minutes in dim light to allow their eyes to adapt before diving, this will not enable them to see more fine detail or colour when underwater.

The amount of light that penetrates into the water also depends on the time of day. When the sun is high in the sky, generally between 10:00 and 14:00 local time, then a greater amount of light will strike the surface at a high angle and penetrate the water. This is the time preferred by underwater photographers to take wide-angle photographs. When the sun is low in the sky, it is at a low angle and much of it will be reflected off the surface. If the sky is overcast even less light penetrates the water.

Divers looking up to the surface from underwater can also see reflections from the water's interface with air. The surface can appear as a bright circle directly overhead while all water outside the circle is darker. This circle through which the sky is visible is called Snell's window. The area around it is backscattered light from deep water.

When the water surface has small ripples, fluctuations of dim and bright light flicker across underwater objects or the bottom (crinkle patterns). These are caused by the waves acting as if they were lenses. The cresting portion of a wave acts as positive dioptre lens (magnifying glass) concentrating light as a bright area. The trough portions of the waves act as negative dioptre lenses, dispersing the light and producing a dim area.

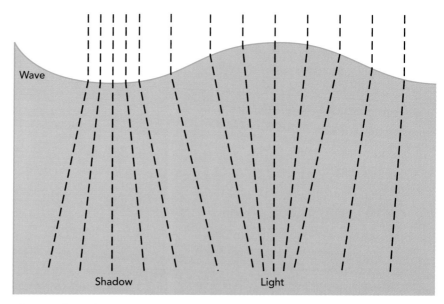

Above: *Light ripples are caused by waves concentrating and dispersing light. Wave crests focus light rays; troughs disperse light rays, causing shadows*

MAGNIFYING GLASSES FOR USE UNDERWATER

As with any lens, rays of light are bent when they cross from the surrounding medium, into the glass or plastic of a magnifying glass and then again when they pass back into the surrounding medium on the other side of the lens. Each medium has its own refractive index and the amount of bending, and hence magnification, depends not only on the shape of the lens, but also on the change of refractive index as the light enters and then leaves the magnifying glass.

In water, the change of refractive index is less than it would be in air so the amount of magnification is less. However, divers and snorkellers already know the answer to this problem as they experience it with the air space trapped behind their face mask. Objects appear to be larger and closer than they actually are because the light travels through water, glass, and air before it enters your eye – (*see p27*). What divers require in a magnifying glass for underwater use is one that is sealed within its own airspace. Some muck divers make their own but they are commercially available.

VISIBILITY

Underwater visibility is defined as the estimated distance at which you can easily discern a diver and it should always be measured horizontally. The theoretical visibility for distilled water is less than 75m (246ft). Under normal ocean conditions, horizontal visibility greater than 60m (200ft) is mythical.

Visibility underwater depends on the amount of light that reaches the depth of the diver and the amount of organic or inorganic matter suspended in the water. Illumination itself depends on the thickness of the water layer (absorption), and on the reflection and scatter of light rays in the water. 18% of the light rays reach a depth of 18m (60ft) and some 1% reach a depth of 100m (330ft). The amount of light reflected into the water depends on the angle between the rays of light and the surface of the water and on the quantity of air-bubbles in the surface layer that have been formed by the motion of the water.

The amount of suspended matter in the water varies with the position of the sun, the state of the moon and tide, recent bad weather and the season. Where organic matter (free-floating or self-propelled) gains from photosynthesis, water temperature and the amount of sunlight are important. Too little or too much

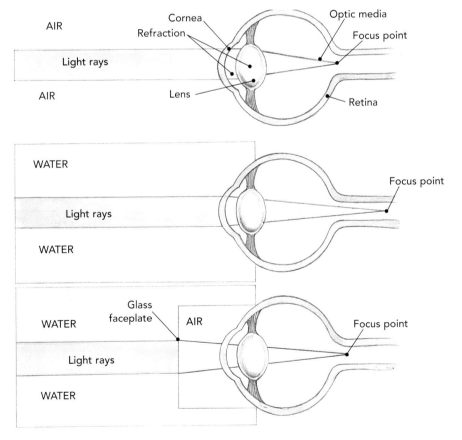

Above: *Focussing of the eye in air and underwater*

sunlight can have an adverse effect. For this reason, these plankton and the animals, tiny or large that feed on them, move up and down the water column during the day to get the optimum amount of sunlight. At night, the plankton layer is often found at the surface and in some lakes, animals that contain chlorophyll (some jellyfish, for example) actually follow the sun across the lake during the day. The state of the moon affects the tide and in some cases, organic matter such as that from coral or other animals spawning. Dive sites close to reefs or beaches will suffer from extra organic and inorganic sediment on ebb tides. Bad weather can stir up the bottom in shallow water, aerate water close to the surface with breaking waves or the wind and wash more inorganic sediments and organic nutrients down rivers into the sea. Heavy rain can accelerate plankton blooms and form a cloudy halocline where layers of freshwater meet layers of saltwater. Plankton blooms are seasonal and in the autumn, more leaves are blown into the water.

Another problem is that the light refraction from water into the human eye is less than it would be from air into the eye. This means that the image is formed far beyond the retina, corresponding to hyperopia (long-sightedness). The diver's face mask provides normal conditions for visibility by introducing a layer of air

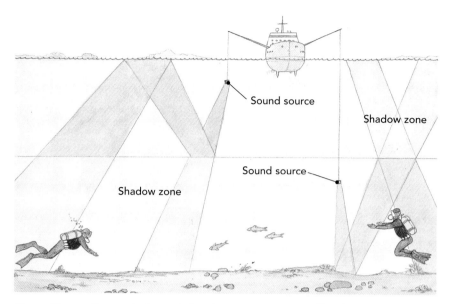

Above: Thermoclines and other variations in water temperature affect the transmission of sound. If a source of sound is near the surface, there will be a 'shadow zone' beyond which the sound is not received.

in contact with the eye. This layer of air is essential for vision; if the face mask is lost, the diver's vision is considerably impaired.

THE TRANSFER OF SOUND IN WATER

Due to its higher density (seawater is 800 times denser than air), sound travels much faster and further in water than in air. Lower frequency sounds such as those from ship's engines, can often be heard when the source is not in sight. The speed of sound in water increases with temperature, salinity and pressure, which increases with depth. Sound transmission is also affected by a thermocline, (a meeting point of two layers of water with different temperatures). The different temperatures

on either side of the thermocline also mean different densities. When sound waves cross an interface of different densities they lose a lot of energy. Sound waves beamed at the thermocline may be refracted partially, or even completely, depending on their angle to the thermocline, producing a sound shadow beneath it. So, if the sound originates in water above a thermocline, it may not be heard easily below it. Sounds made above the water's surface will not be heard in the water and vice versa. Divers' hearing is reduced by the effect of water on the eardrums and the increased speed of the sound confuses the stereophonic reception of human ears. Underwater, sound is conducted to the hearing organs through the bones of the skull rather than through the eardrums as in air. Because of this the delay between the sound reaching one ear and then the other is too short for the ears to differentiate between time and intensity; the sound is not perceived as coming from its source, but from all directions at once.

Systems of measurement

Most countries base their measurements on the metric system. This is easier to use in scientific calculations because it is based on units of 10. Some countries use the imperial system, where there may be differences in certain units such as gallons and miles. Measurements based on 12 are useful in some circumstances, because 12 is divisible by 2, 3, 4 and 6 whereas 10 is only divisible by 2 and 5.

Within the context of diving, 'mass' and 'weight' can be considered the same thing. One kilogram is the weight of one litre of water – approximately 2.2 pounds. One metre is derived from the speed of light in a vacuum and equals 39.37 inches. Pressure can be expressed in kilograms per square centimetre (kg/cm^2), pounds per square inch (psi) or millimetres of mercury (mmHg).

The atmosphere, the air in which we normally live, has its own weight, pressing equally on us in all directions, and on the ground, as 'pressure'. At average sea level this pressure, also called the barometric pressure or one atmosphere, is universally accepted to be 760mmHg or 14.7psi at 0°C (32°F). In the metric system this is usually referred to as one bar. Atmospheric pressure varies with changes in weather conditions and decreases with altitude.

Most pressure gauges read zero at sea level although they should be reading the pressure of the atmosphere. This leads to a difference in the way that true pressure is measured. If a gauge reads 200 bars (2940psi), it really means 200 bars (2940psi) above atmospheric pressure. Known as gauge pressure, it is indicated by a 'g' at the end of the unit measurement, e.g. 1 bar gauge or 14.7psig. If the gauge was calibrated to true zero, as found in a vacuum, it would read 201 bars (2955psi), the extra pressure being the atmospheric pressure. Such a reading is referred to as an absolute pressure and is indicated by adding an 'a' at the end of the unit measurement, for example 1 bar absolute or 14.7psia. When measuring in atmospheres we would use 'ata' for atmospheres absolute.

Depth gauges read pressure and are only accurate when used in the environment for which they were calibrated. Those calibrated for seawater will not be accurate in freshwater and vice versa; and those zeroed for sea level will not be accurate at altitude.

For temperature, the metric system uses degrees Celsius (°C) and the imperial system uses degrees Fahrenheit (°F). Both systems are based on the freezing point (0°C or 32°F) and the boiling point (100°C or 212°F) of pure water at sea level.

To convert from Celsius to Fahrenheit multiply the Celsius figure by 9, divide by 5 and then add 32.

(°C x 9 ÷ 5) + 32 = °F

To convert from Fahrenheit to Celsius, subtract 32 from the Fahrenheit figure then multiply the result by 5 and divide by 9.

(°F - 32) x 5 ÷ 9 = °C

Sometimes calculations use a temperature scale relative to absolute zero, the temperature at which all molecular movement is calculated to cease. In the metric system, this uses the Kelvin scale where 0 Kelvin is -273.16°C and in the imperial system we use the Rankine scale where 0°Rankine is -459.67°F (note that Kelvin measurements do not use the degree sign).
Hence 0°C = 273Kelvin and
0°F = 460°Rankine.

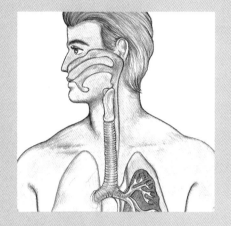 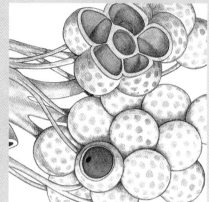 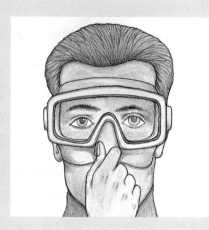

THE PHYSIOLOGY OF DIVING

Scuba equipment allows us to breathe underwater. However, despite the best efforts of diving regulator designers, the regulator does add resistance, thereby increasing our breathing workload. As we descend, the workload also gets progressively larger, with increased external pressures on the lungs causing greater resistance to their expansion and the breathing gases becoming denser. In the same way that an athlete's body adapts with training, a diver's body adapts with regular diving – oxygen consumption is reduced as the body learns to use it more efficiently, and a greater tolerance to carbon dioxide build-up develops.

The cardiovascular system

The circulatory and respiratory systems together are called the cardiovascular system, they provide oxygen (O_2) and nutrients to the body and remove carbon dioxide (CO_2). Food is converted into carbohydrates, which react chemically with oxygen and change into energy, water and carbon dioxide.

Without oxygen (O_2), tissues in the body start to die. This is called hypoxia. To maintain the right levels of oxygen and carbon dioxide in the blood, the brain regulates breathing mainly in accordance with changes in the blood's carbon dioxide content and, to a lesser extent, by sensors perceiving the oxygen level of the blood in the aorta and carotid arteries. The brain signals breathing to start when it detects a build-up of carbon dioxide. This is why hyperventilation for a breath-hold dive can lead to unconsciousness – the lowered carbon dioxide level does not stimulate the respiratory centre despite reduced oxygen.

Cardiovascular system: Oxygenated blood from the lungs (red) enters the left side of the heart and is then pumped through arteries, which branch into smaller arteries and finally into tiny blood vessels called capillaries. In the capillaries the blood exchanges oxygen for carbon dioxide and then returns to the lungs through the veins. Back in the lungs the blood releases its carbon dioxide, takes in fresh oxygen and begins another cycle.

Arteries have thick, elastic walls because they carry blood under considerable pressure. Veins only carry blood at low pressure so they have non-elastic, relatively thin walls. Capillaries have microscopic walls to facilitate gas diffusion.

The tissues of the brain and nervous system consume nearly one-fifth of the oxygen transported by the circulatory system. Deprived of oxygen they begin to die within minutes, while other tissues can survive for hours.

The heart is made up of two receiving chambers (atria) and two muscular pumps (ventricles). One-way valves prevent reversal of flow into the atria when the ventricles contract. The two sides of the heart contract simultaneously but are independent of each other.

The right ventricle develops less pressure than the left because it only has to pump blood the short distance to the lungs. The left ventricle has to produce enough pressure to reach the head, hands and feet.

The rate at which the heart contracts (the pulse rate) varies, but for normal people it is 60–80 contractions per minute when resting and 80–150 when exercising.

The average human body contains 4.5–6 litres (8–11 English pints; 9.5–13 US pints) of blood. Blood consists of plasma – a solution of salts, sugars and proteins dissolved in water – which acts as a carrier for the body's nutrients. Suspended in this plasma are: red corpuscles, which are involved in the transport of oxygen, white corpuscles, which are involved in fighting infection, and platelets, which are involved in preventing bleeding by forming clots.

During exercise, or when the body is under stress, the rate and pressure of circulation increases so that more oxygen can be supplied to the tissues and more carbon dioxide removed. The pressure and volume of the blood supply must not drop so low as to starve tissues of oxygen or rise so high as to rupture arteries.

When relaxed, the normal blood pressure when the heart is contracting (systolic) is 120–140mmHg and during the resting period between contractions (diastolic) it is 70–80mmHg. Blood pressure is normally written as systolic/diastolic, for example 130/80.

Various factors, including decompression sickness (DCS) and near-drowning, can prevent the heart maintaining blood pressure. A large fall in blood pressure is termed shock. At the other extreme, the body reacts to fright or stress by releasing adrenaline into the blood system to stimulate the heart and breathing rate and to constrict blood vessels. Persons with a history of cardiac problems or high blood pressure should consult a doctor specializing in diving, before participating in the sport.

Diving and the body

HYPERCAPNIA

Hypercapnia (also called hypercarbia), is an excess of carbon dioxide. It can have several causes, but most commonly it is due to heavy physical exertion and inadequate ventilation of the lungs.

Under heavy exertion, the muscle tissues can produce carbon dioxide (CO_2) faster than the respiratory system can release it. The high level of carbon dioxide stimulates faster breathing, producing even more

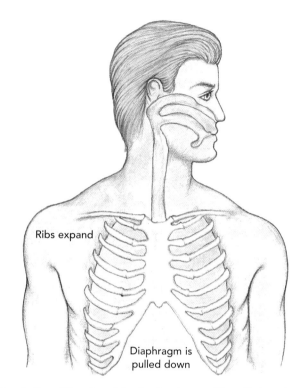

Inspiration: When breathing in, the chest wall is pulled out by the chest-wall muscles and the diaphragm is pulled down. Thus the pressure within the chest and lungs is reduced and air flows into the lungs.

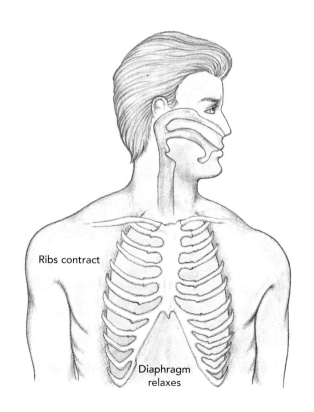

Exhalation: Breathing out is mostly due to the elastic recoil of the lungs and chest wall after expansion. This increases the pressure within the chest and forces exhaled air out of the lungs. No muscular effort is involved unless the diver exhales forcefully.

carbon dioxide and creating a vicious circle that only ceases when the diver stops all activity and allows breathing to return to normal. When we exhale, the last portion of gas breathed out of our lungs only gets as far as the large airways – it is not cleared, but breathed back in with the next breath. We call the passages containing this gas 'dead space'. If this dead space is not being ventilated properly, we could suffer from hypercapnia.

CO_2 contamination and skip-breathing, (breath-holding to increase bottom time or to approach skittish subjects quietly), can also cause hypercapnia. The usual symptoms are headache, mental confusion and dizziness, and sometimes unconsciousness.

HYPOCAPNIA

Hypocapnia (also called hypocarbia), is the reverse of hypercapnia: too little carbon dioxide (CO_2). It is mostly the result of hyperventilation either voluntary (for a breath-hold dive) or involuntary (due to fright or stress). As the CO_2 is not allowed to build up, the brain does not sense the need to breathe and the diver's oxygen level may fall below that required to remain conscious (hypoxia).

At depth the increased partial pressure of oxygen in the lungs (see *pp22-23*) makes it possible for oxygen to continue bonding with haemoglobin in the blood, allowing the body to consume oxygen even after it has dropped below the level that would cause unconsciousness at the surface. As the diver ascends, the partial pressure of oxygen in the lungs falls until it is insufficient to make low levels of oxygen usable. This results in hypoxia and the diver blacks out. This is termed shallow-water blackout or hypoxia of ascent.

CARBON MONOXIDE (CO) POISONING

Carbon monoxide bonds with the haemoglobin in the blood 200 times more readily than oxygen. Therefore where both carbon monoxide and oxygen are present, the haemoglobin will bond with the carbon monoxide in preference to oxygen. These bonds are not easily

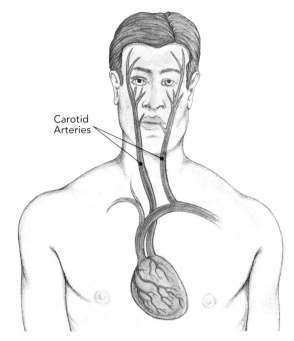

Carotid Arteries

Carotid-sinus reflex: When the carotid-sinus sensor detects high blood pressure, it tells the brain to slow down the heart rate. If the diver has an over-tight dry suit neck seal, wet suit hood or other equipment that presses on the neck, the carotid-sinus sensors can mistakenly interpret this excess pressure as high blood pressure and cause the heart to slow down, resulting in unconsciousness.

broken and it can take 8–12 hours of breathing clean air before all carbon monoxide is eliminated. While haemoglobin is carrying carbon monoxide it cannot carry oxygen, so if the problem goes unnoticed it causes hypoxia.

At diving depths the increased pressure causes enough oxygen to dissolve in plasma in the blood to support the body's needs, delaying the onset of warning symptoms of CO poisoning like headache, confusion or narrowed vision. As the diver ascends there is no longer enough pressure to dissolve sufficient oxygen in the plasma and the diver blacks out (hypoxia of ascent).

When carbon monoxide bonds with haemoglobin it becomes bright red carboxyhaemoglobin, so people with carbon monoxide poisoning have flushed lips and cheeks, but this is not obvious underwater. Otherwise the symptoms are similar to hypercapnia (see *p36*).

OXYGEN (O_2) TOXICITY

Oxygen is a very active molecule. Although the human body requires it for life, it can also form harmful oxidants. It exists briefly as a free radical in the form of monatomic oxygen, a single atom of oxygen (O) not combined with anything. However, it needs to be combined with something for stability. At depth the higher partial pressures of oxygen produce higher levels of oxidants in the body and these levels are further increased by how long the body is exposed to them.

When exercising heavily under pressure we build up carbon dioxide in the bloodstream, dilating the blood vessels in the brain and making the blood more acidic. This causes the haemoglobin to give up oxygen more quickly. The combined result is the increased exposure of the brain to high oxygen levels. The build-up of carbon dioxide also signals to the brain that we should breathe faster, so it is a catalyst for oxygen toxicity. Energetic dives should not be performed on breathing mixtures high in oxygen.

As with nitrogen, exposure to high partial pressures of oxygen has a cumulative effect. This is not a concern in normal recreational diving. However, for deep diving on air, diving on enriched air, or during recompression treatment, we must monitor the 'oxygen clock', and have sensible surface intervals (*see Enriched Air Nitrox p149*).

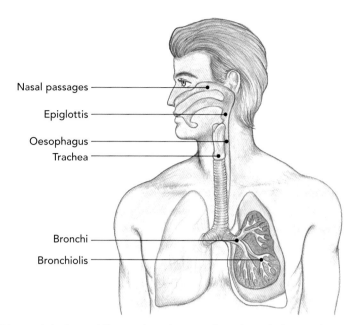

Breathing and the lungs: *When we breathe in, air flows through the mouth, nose and sinuses, past the epiglottis (a flap of skin that stops food from entering the windpipe) and into the windpipe (trachea). This branches into left and right passages (the bronchi) and each of these bronchi divides many times to produce many tiny bronchioles (smaller passages). Each bronchiole ends in an air sac (alveolus), where the gases diffuse across the thin walls of capillaries into or out of the blood.*

There are two types of oxygen toxicity. Low-dosage, long-term, pulmonary or whole-body toxicity (called the Lorraine Smith effect after the researcher who first described it), produces symptoms similar to pneumonia. It results from longer exposures to oxygen than recreational divers normally experience. High-dosage, short-term, central nervous system (CNS) toxicity (the Paul Bert effect), becomes a risk with oxygen above a partial pressure of 1.4ata (*see pp22-23*). When diving on normal air, this partial pressure is reached at a depth of 57m (185ft). There is a caution zone between 1.4ata and 1.6ata. Above 1.6ata is hazardous. On normal air 1.6ata is reached at a depth of 66m (218ft). When diving on Enriched Air Nitrox we reach the 1.4ata limit within recreational diving depths, so detailed training is essential (*see p149*).

Symptoms are unconsciousness or convulsions, both of which would probably lead to drowning if they occurred underwater.

NITROGEN NARCOSIS

Although the body cannot make use of nitrogen it is dissolved in the blood and tissues in direct proportion to the depth until those tissues are saturated. The uptake

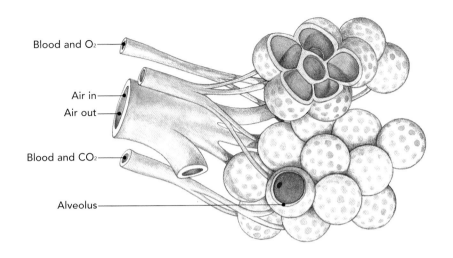

Structure of the lungs: The lungs resemble two large sponges, but despite the huge area available for gas diffusion the lungs only absorb a small percentage of the oxygen (O_2) available in each breath. A large percentage of oxygen remains in exhaled breath, which explains why Exhaled Air Resuscitation (EAR), also known as mouth-to-mouth, contains enough oxygen to sustain life.

Blood and O_2
Air in
Air out
Blood and CO_2
Alveolus

make things worse or cause narcosis at shallower depth. Nitrogen narcosis can mask the symptoms of other problems and reduce the diver's ability to cope with emergencies. It begins quickly, but disappears equally quickly on ascent. Unlike alcohol, there are no after-effects.

In some commercial and technical diving, helium gas (He) is used in place of some or all the nitrogen and some of the oxygen to reduce the problems with nitrogen and oxygen at depth. However, helium has its own problems (*see p151*).

Decompression sickness (DCS) and Decompression illness (DCI)

Decompression sickness (DCS) is caused by dissolved nitrogen being released from solution in the body tissues instead of into the lungs and exhaled. Other decompression-related injuries happen when the lungs expand too much and air enters blood vessels through ruptured alveoli. Air (Gas) Embolism is variously known as arterial gas embolism (AGE), cerebral arterial gas embolism (CAGE), or intravascular gas embolism (IGE). Because the treatment is the same, DCS and air embolism are together referred to as decompression illness (DCI).

Decompression sickness was first observed in French coal miners leaving a pressurized mine in 1841. It was

or release of the gas varies with the type of tissue, the body's temperature and the rate of circulation of the blood. Nitrogen is much more soluble in fat than in water, so body tissues high in fat will absorb more. Tissues served by a large blood flow will absorb or release nitrogen quickly, and are called 'fast tissues'. Tissues with a poor blood flow, cartilage, tendons and stored fat absorb and release nitrogen slowly. These are called 'slow tissues' though they can hold more dissolved nitrogen than fast tissues. As the diver ascends, the nitrogen in the tissues is released.

Almost any gas can cause anaesthesia (general loss of sensation) at high partial pressures. It is thought that nitrogen interferes with the electrical transfer between nerve cells. This affects alertness and coordination. The result is similar to being drunk: a feeling of elation (rapture of the deep) followed by impaired reasoning and apprehension. This is nitrogen narcosis. Individuals vary in their susceptibility: some 'acclimatize' with regular exposure while others just learn to cope. Some can suffer at 30m (100ft) while everyone suffers by 50m (165ft).

Drugs that block transmission between nerve cells, such as alcohol, tranquillizers, sleeping pills, sea sickness remedies, antihistamines and antidiarrhoeals, will

later seen in workers leaving *caissons* (chambers kept watertight with compressed air during the construction of bridge foundations), so it was called Caisson Workers Disease. DCS victims could often ease the pain by keeping the joint bent and immobile so it is also called 'the bends'.

The rate at which nitrogen is absorbed or released by the body depends on the pressure gradient, the individual's rate of circulation, body temperature and the mass of the tissues concerned. After any dive tiny micro-bubbles, too small to cause DCS, exist in the tissues and bloodstream. When there are many of these they combine to form larger ones and, if the pressure gradient is high, bubbles form that are large enough to cause DCS. These bubbles can damage local and surrounding tissues. They press against nerves and also obstruct blood flow. Tissues that are beyond the blockage are starved of oxygen, become hypoxic and may be permanently damaged. Symptoms depend on the location of the bubbles.

EPIDERMAL OR CUTANEOUS DCS (SKIN BENDS)

The skin itches, tingles or has a burning sensation. There may be a patchy red rash.

These symptoms often occur almost immediately on leaving the water. They are not dangerous in themselves and disappear quickly, but may be an indication of more serious DCS problems.

MUSCULAR, JOINT AND LIMB PAIN DCS

The most commonly reported symptoms of DCS are pains around large joints such as knees, elbows and shoulders. This is thought to be caused by bubbles forming around or within tendons, ligaments and related muscles. Although the pain may not appear for some hours after a dive, it should be considered serious.

NEUROLOGICAL DCS

When the blood flow to the spinal cord is restricted there can be numbness, pins-and-needles and paralysis of the lower limbs, difficulty in controlling the bladder or paralysis from the neck down. If bloodflow to the brain is affected there can be blurred vision, headache, confusion, unconsciousness, a stroke or death.

Treatment of decompression illness

A physical injury or a previous incident of DCS makes one more likely to suffer from DCS. The most common symptom is extreme fatigue. The treatment for divers with suspected DCS is to administer pure oxygen and transport them at low altitude to a recompression (hyperbaric) chamber. There the patient can be rapidly recompressed to reduce the size of the bubbles and force them

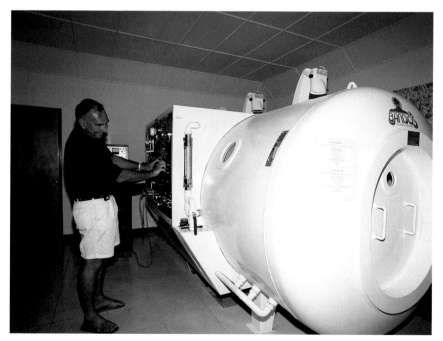

Above: *Divers should always know where the nearest recompression (hyperbaric) chamber is located. However, do not assume that it is the most appropriate one for treatment, so check out local information first.*

back into solution. The diver is then decompressed very slowly while being treated with oxygen, drugs (to reduce blood clotting) and intravenous fluids.

Even at normal atmospheric pressure pure oxygen can cause lung damage when administered continuously for 8–12 hours, so patients require breaks during which they breathe normal air. Young children, people with chronic lung disease or very high blood pressure can be harmed by breathing pure oxygen, but these people are not permitted to dive, so the problem should not arise.

Response to pressure changes in body air spaces

Any gas space in the body can suffer barotrauma (pressure injury). Barotraumas of descent are termed 'squeezes' and those of ascent 'reverse squeezes'.

Most of the body is not compressible within recreational diving depths, but gases are, so those parts of the body containing gases – the ears, sinuses, teeth, lungs, gastrointestinal tract and the facial area covered by the mask – are affected when the pressure on the diver changes.

A similar squeeze on a dry suit can cause pinching and bruising and this is solved by adding air (or gas) to the suit. The extra air must be released during ascent.

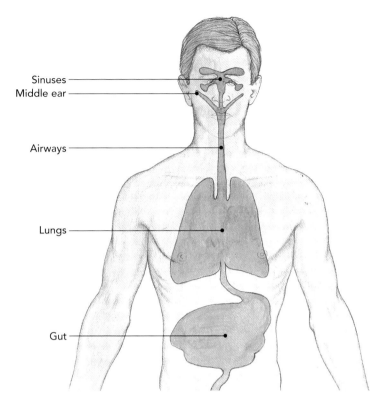

Sinuses
Middle ear
Airways
Lungs
Gut

Above: Some parts of the body respond automatically to changes in pressure.

THE EARS

Some divers have a lot of trouble with equalizing (clearing) their ears. They may find it easier to descend feet first. Water pressure forces the eardrum inward, causing pain in the middle ear because the inside of the eardrum and the middle ear are still at the lesser pressure on the surface. The middle ear is connected to the throat by the Eustachian tube so this inner and outer ear pressure can usually be equalized by swallowing while the nose and mouth are as shut as can be managed with a mouthpiece in place (called the Toynbee manoeuvre). If this fails, pinch the nose closed and try to snort out through the nose (often inaccurately called a Valsalva manoeuvre). Most diving masks have a soft section around the nose for this purpose. Avoid excessive force when snorting for this can do serious damage. The middle-ear spaces must be equalized frequently on descent and ascent. If you fail to equalize your ears, reverse the descent (or ascent) and try again. Equalizing is often easier when looking up – extending the neck tends to open the eustachian tubes.

If the eustachian tubes are congested, usually due to a cold or an allergy, it may be difficult or impossible to equalize. If a diver

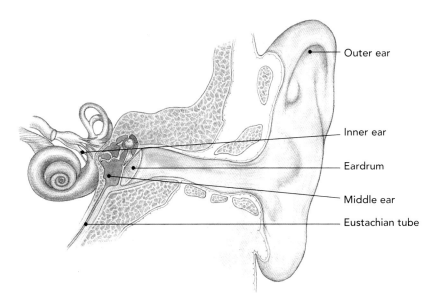

Above: On descent the higher pressure of the water pushes the eardrum inwards, where the air in the middle ear is still at the lower surface pressure.

Above: To equalize the pressures on either side of the eardrum, pinch the nose shut, close the mouth and try to snort through the nose. This should open the eustachian tubes.

continues to descend without equalization, fluids and blood are forced into the middle ear until the eardrum ruptures. The diver will experience pain and vertigo until the water that has entered the ear warms up.

On ascent, expanding air usually vents through the eustachian tubes to the throat without any conscious effort by the diver. A reverse ear squeeze on ascent can happen when the effects of decongestants (taken to facilitate diving with a cold) wear off. In this case your air supply dictates how long you can try to equalize before you are forced to the surface despite the pain. Decongestants are not recommended for diving, but if you do resort to them, use a long-lasting one so that its effects will not wear off during the dive.

SWIMMER'S EAR

A constant pain in the ears whether in or out of the water is not a barotrauma, but an infection of the ear canal that can be caused by different bacteria or fungi. It can be avoided by treating the ears with non-prescription 'drying' agents after each dive (*see p167*).

THE LUNGS

Provided that divers breathe continuously and ascend slowly, they will not have problems with changing pressure in the lungs. The golden rule of diving is 'never hold your breath' (skip breathing). The risk of over-expansion of gases in the lungs on ascent is highest in shallow water, so forcibly breathe out while ascending the last 10m (33ft). Over-expansion of gases within the lungs causes them to

tear, the tears themselves are not serious, the problems occur from air entering the tissues or bloodstream (air embolism).

Arterial gas embolism (AGE), cerebral arterial gas embolism (CAGE) and intravascular gas embolism (IGE) are the result of air entering the pulmonary vein through torn alveoli, to be pumped across the heart to the arterial side from where bubbles can be pumped around the body and block blood flow.

When a lung has torn, air can escape into the part of the chest containing the windpipe and heart where it reduces the efficiency of these organs (mediastinal emphysema) and into the soft tissues at the base of the neck (subcutaneous emphysema). If air gets between the lungs and the chest wall, the outside pressure on the lungs causes them to collapse (pneumothorax). The symptoms are chest pain, shortness of breath and frothy blood at the mouth.

While DCS is often delayed, the symptoms of lung injuries occur immediately on surfacing. If circulation to the heart is blocked, the symptoms are those of a heart attack. If the arteries to the central nervous system are obstructed, there could be poor coordination, dizziness, paralysis, convulsions, unconsciousness or death.

A torn lung is not life-threatening, but can lead to an air embolism, which is. The patient should be treated by a doctor experienced in diving-related conditions. In the short term treat as for DCS, administer pure oxygen and transport the patient to the nearest appropriate recompression chamber.

THE SINUSES

When descending with congestion of the sinuses, water pressure forces blood and fluid into the air cavities and on ascent these fluids are pushed by the expanding air into the nose and usually into the mask.

THE TEETH

Cavities in teeth due to tooth decay or poor fillings may cause pain as air expands inside them on ascent. This is painful but not serious. Consult a dentist.

GASTROINTESTINAL BAROTRAUMA

Abdominal discomfort and colicky pains occur when divers have swallowed compressed gases or recently taken a heavy meal or carbonated (fizzy) drink.

Apart from avoiding these before a dive, it can help if you descend in an upright position and slow or pause on ascent.

THE FACIAL AREA BEHIND THE MASK

This area is another air space that suffers from increases in pressure during descent (mask squeeze). Divers usually equalize the squeeze on their mask without thinking, but it tends to be more noticeable on rapid descents. Breathing out through the nose into the mask solves the problem.

OVEREXERTION

Swimming too hard increases the heart rate and blood pressure, it may also demand more air from your regulator than it can supply. This produces sensations of suffocation and apprehension, which can lead to panic. Ideally you should stop and allow your breathing and heart rate to return to normal.

Most overexertion involves swimming against a current. If the bottom is free of live coral, you will find it easier to pull yourself along the bottom, than to swim.

Hyperthermia

Hyperthermia (higher than normal body core temperature) is the result of one or more of: exercise, exposure to heat, over-insulation and inadequate fluid intake. The body sweats to cool down, but exposure suits impede this process

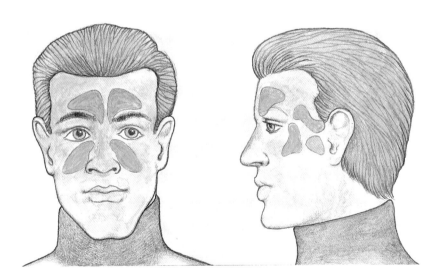

Above: *The sinuses of healthy divers are air-filled, mucous-lined cavities and tubes in the skull that normally equalize automatically when equalizing the ears. Avoid diving with a cold, allergy or nasal congestion.*

and the overheated diver may become incoherent and collapse. When the body's temperature-regulating mechanism fails, the victim has heatstroke.

The casualty should be moved to a cool place, fanned or sponged down. If the patient is conscious, give sweet drinks with half a teaspoon of salt per litre (1.75 English pints; 2 US pints). If unconscious, place the casualty in the recovery position, monitor the airway, breathing and circulation and seek medical help.

Hypothermia

Hypothermia (excessive heat-loss from the body core). Optimum body temperature in humans is 36.9°C (98.4°F) plus or minus 0.5°C (0.9°F).

When cold, apart from shivering, the body restricts blood flow to the extremities by narrowing the blood vessels (vasoconstriction). However, the body does not restrict blood flow to the head in this way and the head also lacks natural insulation, so it loses heat quickly. In water temperatures below 21°C (70°F), it is important to insulate the head. Hands have a large surface area in relation to their volume so they also lose warmth quickly.

Small or thin divers get cold more quickly than larger or more obese ones. (This is not because of body mass, there are many other variables.) Underwater photographers and others who do not move around much will not generate as much heat as those who fin around. There is evidence that women are better protected against the cold than men, particularly in the water. When divers make several dives in a day they feel the cold more with each successive dive. Keep in mind that neoprene wet suits and uncompressed neoprene dry suits compress with depth. Over time they wear out and lose their insulation as the bubbles inside the neoprene collapse.

Warm surroundings and warm non-alcoholic drinks between dives will help to bring your temperature back to normal. Getting cold is very common, but feeling cold enough to want to abort the dive occurs long before hypothermia.

There is a difference between warming the surface of your body, for example by sunbathing, and warming the core of your body. You can feel warm enough even while your core temperature is still low. A diver who returns to the water in this condition, will quickly feel cold.

Above: Hypothermic divers must be warmed up in a sheltered area with blankets or towels and hot drinks.

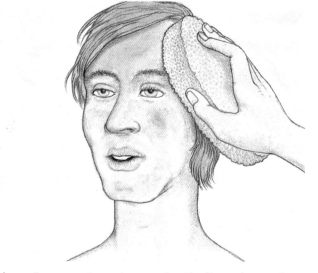

Above: Exposure suits can increase the risk of hyperthermia, those affected should be sponged down with cold water.

One of the first symptoms of hypothermia is numbness of the extremities. Others are loss of coordination and eventually loss of consciousness. The treatment is to warm the person from the outside in. If possible, immerse the diver in hot water, with the legs elevated. Expired air resuscitation and cardiopulmonary resuscitation may be necessary. If the patient is conscious, warm fluids and glucose should be given by mouth. Alcohol should never be given because it increases blood supply to the extremities and makes the condition worse. Where a hot bath is not possible, the best treatment is to lie other, unaffected, divers against the patient's skin in as warm and sheltered an environment as can be found, for example under blankets and out of the wind.

Hypothermia at sea is most likely in survivors picked up after being lost. When someone suffering from hypothermia is lifted into a boat or winched up to a rescue helicopter, the pressure of the water is removed and blood returns to the extremities. However, gravity forces the blood into the legs so that the central volume of blood is reduced and the casualty can become shocked and die. These deaths can be avoided by lifting the casualty in the horizontal position with the legs raised.

Protect against wind-chill on a moving boat by changing into dry clothing and a windproof jacket.

Another danger is when a hot person jumps into very cold water; the thermal shock can stop the heart.

Near-drowning

Near-drowning is when someone has inhaled fluid into the lungs, but survived. Where water enters the lungs, this is termed wet drowning. When inhaled water causes the larynx to spasm, the inevitable coughing prevents us maintaining a breathing pattern; this is a dry drowning. The mechanism of wet drowning is different for saltwater and freshwater, but the result is the same: lack of oxygen to the tissues (hypoxia).

The casualty will be cyanosed (bluish-purple in colour), not breathing and may have bloodstained froth issuing from the mouth and nose. Raise the casualty's legs, give EAR and CPR and keep going until the casualty recovers or is pronounced dead by a doctor. Casualties of near-drowning have recovered after up to 40 minutes of immersion, especially in cold water, so continue attempting to revive them for at least an hour. If the casualty begins to breathe, then administer pure oxygen where possible.

Damage to the lungs may cause secondary drowning hours or even days after revival, so survivors of near-drowning should be admitted to hospital for observation.

With scuba diving accidents it may be impossible to decide the cause. However, near-drowning, lung-expansion injuries and DCS require the same initial treatments: EAR and CPR as required, followed by pure oxygen and transporting the patient to a hospital with a recompression (hyperbaric) chamber.

Cramps

Cramps are painful contractions of the muscle brought about by exercise, cold or abnormalities in body salts. Relief can be obtained by stretching and massaging the muscle. When diving, cramp usually occurs in the calf muscle, so pulling the fin towards the body while straightening the leg should help. If cramps persist, it is better to abort the dive.

Above: Cramp in the calf muscle can usually be eased by holding the tip of the fin and pulling the foot toward the body.

 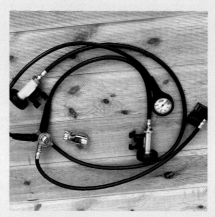 

EQUIPMENT

Over the years diving equipment has become more efficient, more comfortable to wear and more stylish than in the early days of the sport. With the wide variety of equipment available, there is no reason why divers should not enter the water properly equipped for the conditions expected.

Face masks

The human eye cannot focus in water because water has a higher density than air and therefore transmits light in a different way. For clear vision, divers wear a mask to maintain an air space in front of the eyes. This space is affected by water pressure and needs to be equalized on descent. For this reason, the nose should be inside the mask, making it possible to exhale through the nose into the mask. The part over the nose should also be flexible so that the nostrils can be pinched while snorting to equalize ears and sinuses.

Low-volume masks are easier to clear than larger-volume ones, which also have extra buoyancy pulling the mask from the face, affecting the seal. Photographers often have their models wear a single-lens mask, which makes it easier to light up their eyes in photographs, but these masks do not give the best vision.

Above: This diver is wearing the type of mask preferred by underwater photographers for their models. It allows in plenty of light from the flashgun to illuminate the face.

A GOOD MASK OFFERS THE FOLLOWING FEATURES:

• Silicon rubber skirts – these last up to four times longer than neoprene rubber skirts in strong sunlight or in contact with sun protection preparations, diesel or petrol (gasoline). They are comfortable, non-allergenic, maintain flexibility over a wide range of temperatures and allow plenty of light to reach the diver's face. This is more pleasant than the tunnel-vision effect when wearing the old neoprene rubber masks. However, underwater photographers prefer a black skirt because too much extraneous light affects the view through the viewfinder and often produces reflections on the camera eyepiece.

Double skirts give a better seal. The edge of each skirt is feathered, becoming thinner towards the edge to give a more flexible and comfortable fit. Double skirts do not extend to the bottom of the mask, so that water can still be expelled easily.

• Purge valves are one-way valves that allow the expulsion of water from the mask by snorting into

Retaining strap

Soft, flexible skirt

Non-corroding frames

Quick-release strap adjustment

Tempered glass lens

Nose pocket

Above: Features of a good diving mask.

them, rather than by looking up and breaking the skirt-to-skin seal. These days most divers find them unnecessary unless they have limited use of their hands. A purge valve also makes it possible to expel water from the mask with little risk of losing a contact lens.

- A strong retaining strap (head-band) with non-slip adjustment. Always carry a spare.
- Low volume for easy equaliza-tion. With these, breathing out regularly through the nose is enough to keep the mask clear of water.
- Tempered glass – less breakable and more scratch-resistant than plain glass. If it breaks, it shatters into small, less harmful pieces.

Faces vary considerably in shape, so it is important to try several designs for fit and comfort before purchasing. With the retaining strap out of the way, look up and fit the mask lightly to the face. Breathe in through the nose, let go of the mask and shake your head, the mask should remain firmly in place, even when you bend for-ward with your head down, but be ready to catch it!

Check that you can pinch the nose effectively if you need to equalize your ears or sinuses.

Men with moustaches or some-one with a bone injury under the upper lip will never obtain a 100% seal with any mask. Some divers apply petroleum jelly to the moustache or upper lip, but it will attack neoprene.

Innovations in masks include coloured lenses to improve the colour and contrast of divers' vision; deeper and curved faceplates and sides; or panoramic windows for a greater field of view. The most useful innovation is Howard Rosenstein's ProEar mask, which keeps the ears dry, preventing ear infections (*see p167*) and improv-ing hearing – in clarity and direction. It is a traditional mask with silicone and plastic ear-covering cups. The ear cups are connected with tubes to the air space behind the faceplate to facilitate clearing the ears.

New masks often have a film of oil from the production process that causes fogging underwater. There are various ways to keep a cleaned mask from fogging under-water (*see p97*).

Keep your mask around your neck after diving to avoid damage until it can be packed away.

Above: A ProEar mask showing the ear cups and equalisation tubes connecting the ear cups to the air space behind the faceplate.

Left: A diver wearing a ProEar mask. It keeps the ears dry, thus preventing infections.

Snorkels

Snorkels make it possible for divers to swim to and from the dive site without using air from the scuba cylinder.

Design features include purge valves to help clear water that enters the snorkel. There may be an additional valve near the top to stop choppy water splashing down the barrel. Some snorkels have a self-draining barrel or mouthpiece, a one-way valve that allows gravity to drain the portion of the barrel that is clear of the water. However, none of this is essential.

Even when fitted with all these valves, water will enter the snorkel, so one should breathe carefully and blow the water out regularly to avoid inhaling it. Large-bore models with an internal diameter of roughly 25mm (1 inch) are the easiest to breathe through. However, smaller divers may prefer a smaller bore which will be easier to purge and have a smaller mouthpiece. The angle of the mouthpiece must be comfortable in the snorkellers' mouth; some may swivel.

When not in use the snorkel can be tucked away under the knife straps on the diver's leg. When needed, it is attached to the mask strap by a retaining clip or band or is slipped between the mask strap and the diver's head. Those that are permanently attached to a diver's mask can catch on things and cause the mask to leak. They also get in the way if the diver has to refit a dislodged mask.

Fins

The extra thrust provided by fins is needed to overcome the drag of scuba equipment and exposure suits or when swimming against a current. When wearing fins the hands are needed only for minor adjustments of body position or direction.

Fins come in two types: full foot-pocket fins, where the foot fits into a close-fitting shoe attached to the fin, and open-heel foot-pocket fins, where the foot is inserted and retained by an adjustable strap at the heel.

Full foot-pocket fins are used by snorkellers and when not wearing bootees. If the heel tears, the whole fin has to be replaced, so it is necessary to carry a spare set of fins.

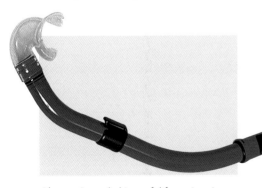

Above: A snorkel is useful for swimming on the surface to or from a dive site without using air from the cylinder.

Above (top to bottom): Force fins are very efficient and make finning easier; open-heel foot-pocket fins with adjustable heel straps can be worn over bootees; full foot-pocket fins are popular with snorkellers.

Open-heel foot-pockets fit over bootees and they have a larger fin area than full foot-pocket fins. The main point of failure with these is the adjustable heel strap, so you need several spares. Unbreakable, coiled-steel fin straps, popular two decades ago, reappeared on the market in late 2003.

Fin blades come in various materials, designs and sizes. The larger and stiffer the blades the stronger the diver's leg muscles need to be. If you are small, or do not dive often enough to keep your leg muscles in condition, then you are likely to get cramp when using large fins with stiff blades. Longitudinal channels of thin flexible material between stiffer plastic allow the fin to capture a larger quantity of water. They increase efficiency, but again require stronger muscles. The channels also weaken with age. Vented fins, (Jet Fins), make finning easier, especially on the upstroke where leg muscles are less powerful. Ribs strengthen the blade and prevent the fin from shimmying from side to side as it travels up and down through the water. Some of the recent blade designs have split fins. These allow water to spill through a split which produces a propeller-like movement. They make it difficult to change direction in the water.

When choosing fins, fit is more important than the design. Fins should not be so tight that they pinch or bruise, nor loose enough to wobble when shaking your feet.

When buying open-heel foot-pocket fins, try them on while wearing hard-soled bootees or the boots attached to dry suits, if that is what you are going to wear.

Weight belts, integrated weight systems and weights

Most people are positively buoyant in freshwater and this buoyancy increases in denser saltwater. Exposure suits, BCDs and nearly empty scuba cylinders increase buoyancy still further so, to remain submerged, divers wear a collection of lead weights.

Several different weight systems are available: a plain belt with block weights; belts with pockets that will take either standard block weights or the more comfortable lead shot; belts with an additional shoulder harness to spread the load; or those integrated with a buoyancy control device.

Whatever system you use, the most important feature is that you (or your buddy) are able to dump (release and discard) the weight belt or weights quickly in an emergency without it snagging on anything. For this reason your weight belt should be put on last and should always be worn with a right-hand release, even if you are left-handed.

If you require several weights, a weight belt can become unwieldy

Above: Unbreakable coiled-steel fin straps. Originally they were too tight, so I stretched them in a vice. They have now done over 5000 dives and outlasted three pairs of fins.

Above: *An athlete's neoprene back support provides an extra cushioning layer under the weight belt and provides support and warmth to the back.*

or uncomfortable. To prevent a standard weight belt from bruising or chafing, wear an athlete's neoprene back support under the exposure suit. This provides an extra layer under the weight belt and extra warmth for the small of the back.

Weight belts are usually made of 5cm (2-inch) wide nylon webbing. Some divers prefer a tensioning system, such as neoprene rubber, which is pulled tight at the surface and then compensates for the compression of their exposure suits at depth. Nylon webbing belts can be cut to length with a sharp knife and the new end sealed with the flame of a match or cigarette lighter. When cutting a weight belt to length, allow extra length for additional weights. These will be necessary to compensate

for the additional buoyancy when wearing an extra thickness of exposure suit for colder water or night dives. The quick-release buckle should be a positive fit, easily adjustable and not likely to snag or release unexpectedly.

With more than 10kg (22lb) on the weight belt, it is best to use a metal buckle. Plastic buckles from all manufacturers wear out and tend to slip apart with too much weight on the belt.

Divers whose waist is wider than their hips will require an integrated or harness weight system. These make the combined BCD and scuba cylinder heavier and the diver's centre of gravity higher when out of the water. They are also more comfortable, improve the diver's trim, reduce the strain on the lower back and are

not affected by exposure suit compression. If your buddy is using an integrated or harness weight system you should familiarize yourself with its release mechanism before entering the water.

Weights are usually simple rectangular 1 or 2kg (2 or 4lb) block mouldings of lead, each with two slots for the belt to pass through. Larger ones are curved, adapting their length to fit on the hip. Cylindrical 'bullet' weights have rounded ends and a single slot so that the belt passes through it only once.

If the weights are not in pockets, they tend to move about on the belt, which can cause the diver to become lopsided. A weight can also slip off the end while the belt is being handed up to the boat. To

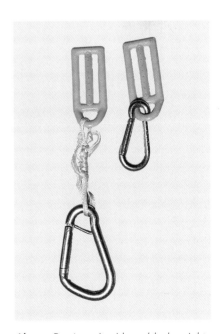

Above: *Retainers (top) keep block weights in position on weight belts. Carabiners (below) are for attaching other items.*

avoid this, the weights are held in place with retainers, which may also include a separate ring for a karabiner (snap-link) so that you can attach other items to the belt.

If the weight belt is long enough, block weights can be held in position by passing the belt through one side of the weight and then twisting it over on itself before passing it through the other side. This may only be required on the weights at either end of the belt.

Weight belts with pockets that take either standard block weights or lead shot are more comfortable and keep the weights in place.

Some divers find small ankle weights useful. Another trick is to strap some weight high on the scuba cylinder. This enables the diver to trim buoyancy for a more comfortable horizontal position while swimming underwater and for a face-up position on the surface.

When flying to a diving destination divers need not take weights or weight belts, as dive operators provide standard belts and block weights. However, it is wise to carry weight retainers and divers who prefer integrated or harness systems will need to fly these, but not the weights.

HOW MUCH WEIGHT?

A properly weighted diver with no air in the BCD, scuba cylinder less than a quarter full and carrying any preferred extras, should float in an upright position with the surface at eye level. When diving in freshwater or using a steel scuba cylinder a diver will require less weight. More weight is needed when using an aluminium scuba cylinder.

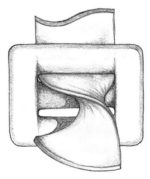

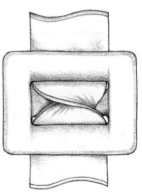

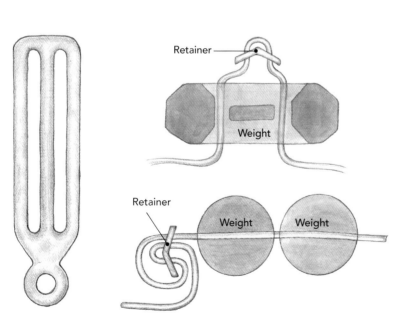

Above: Different methods of holding different kinds and shapes of weights in place on a weight belt.

Above: Thread the loose end of the weight belt through one side of the weight block.
Put a single twist in the belt.
Pass it back through the other side of the weight and pull the belt tight to secure the weight firmly in place.

Buoyancy compensator devices

The basic need for buoyancy compensator devices (BCDs), also called buoyancy compensators (BCs), adjustable buoyancy life jackets (ABLJs) or stabilizing jackets, is because exposure suits and some parts of a diver's body are compressed on descent and expand on ascent. This causes the diver's buoyancy to change. A device is needed to compensate for these changes or the diver will either have to fin constantly to avoid sinking or will float to the surface, risking physiological problems. BCDs contain a gas bladder and divers can compensate for this variation in buoyancy by adding or dumping gas. They can then move about more easily underwater, use up less breathing gas and avoid colliding with a coral reef or wreck.

The original buoyancy aids were just life jackets designed to float a diver face-up on the surface. Improved versions of these were known as front-mounted or horse-collar BCDs.

Today's jacket-style buoyancy compensator device is a multifunctional, multicomponent system to which the scuba cylinder, regulator, alternative air supply, accessories and, in some designs, weights, are attached. It can be put on or taken off as a single unit. Most BCDs also have pockets and D-rings for dive lights and other equipment.

Top: Horse-collar BCDs in use at Sanganeb in the Sudanese Red Sea.

Above Left: Although not designed for convenient inflation by a direct-feed, the older horse-collar BCDs gave less drag when swimming and better face-up support on the surface.

Above Right: A jacket-style BCD and regulator attached to a scuba cylinder. The BCD has Velcro-faced tabs or restraining clips to keep hoses and instruments close to the body where they are accessible and will not snag or damage the reef. The pockets will hold small items and the whole system can be donned as a single unit.

The fit is important to avoid the scuba cylinder sliding or bouncing around on your back. Look for a BCD that fits you in the middle of its adjustment range when wearing your exposure suit. Most manufacturers have BCDs in different sizes and of different buoyancy (also known as lift) and designs suitable for a woman's shape. Most BCDs have adjustable shoulder straps with quick-release buckles.

Back-mounted inflation BCDs, called wings, are popular with technical divers, models, underwater photographers and those who swim long distances on the surface. The gas bladders do not cover the front of the body, leaving it free for other equipment or easier face-down swimming. For a good face-up surface flotation position, a counterweight is organized with a back-mounted integral weight system, or some weight can be attached to the cylinder.

Modern BCDs are fitted with restraining clips or Velcro tabs for keeping hoses and instruments close to the body to avoid snagging on wrecks or making harmful contact with reef animals.

The BCD's gas bladder system can be either single-bladder (the gas container also takes the wear) or twin-bag. The twin-bag system has an inner bladder made of polythene (polyethylene) which can be replaced cheaply if damaged. Since the outer bag does not have to be a bladder, it can be made of a hard-wearing material, easily repaired if torn. Twin-bag BCDs are heavier to wear and fly to holiday destinations, but are more durable and easy to service.

Most modern BCDs have a low-pressure direct-feed (power-inflator)

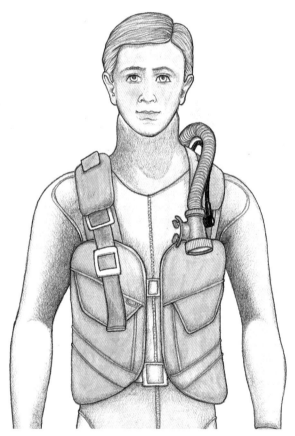

Above: *If the BCD is too small it will not give adequate support (lift). It should fit in the middle of its adjustment range.*

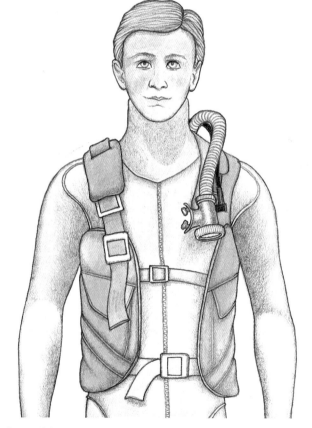

Above: *If the BCD is too large, the cylinder will flop about and the system will not give good head-up support at the surface.*

connected to the regulator, and a method of oral inflation. Some BCDs have a small emergency breathing gas cylinder with an integral yoke-connector (A-clamp) that is filled from a full scuba cylinder before each dive (see *flying scuba cylinders p67*). Other BCDs are fitted with a carbon dioxide (CO_2) cartridge for one-off emergency inflation at the surface only.

These inflation devices should be used with caution to avoid large increases in buoyancy. The low-pressure direct-feed can also be connected to an alternate breathable gas supply, which functions as an extra second stage. This serves the same function as an octopus rig (see *p78*), though it is not ideal for buddy breathing. In an emergency it is better to let the buddy breathe from the second stage, while the diver wearing the short-hosed alternate breathable gas supply, breathes from that instead.

Gas can be released rapidly through a dump valve by pulling either a separate cord or a cord enclosed in the corrugated flexible oral-inflation hose. Another method is to raise the hose above your head and press the purge button on the end.

All BCDs have over-pressure release valves in case you over-inflate the bladder or leave the inflated unit in the sun. These are usually located at the lowest point on the BCD so that if they leak, the

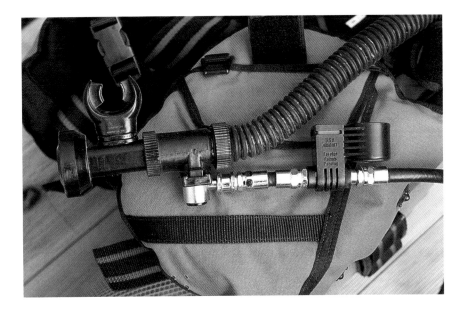

bladder will still hold enough air to be effective, if the diver is not constantly head-down. Dump valves should be disassembled regularly and salt crystals or sand grains flushed away with freshwater.

Before packing away a BCD, flush out the inside of the gas bladder with freshwater containing

Top: *The direct-feed from the scuba cylinder feeds the BCD and a power whistle.*

Above: *BCDs with a single gas bladder, rather than a twin-bag system, are lighter to fly to holiday destinations, but not as hard-wearing. They are more difficult to service and the single bladder takes all the wear.*

disinfectant and wash the outside. Fill the gas bladder to one-third with freshwater through the oral-inflation hose and shake the jacket around to remove as much saltwater as possible. Drain it in the upside down position with the hose hanging free and the purge button held open with a matchstick. When dry, inflate it fully and leave for an hour, away from sunlight. It should remain inflated. If not, reclean and regrease all the valves. If it still deflates when tested, have it serviced.

BCDS WITH CARBON DIOXIDE (CO₂) CARTRIDGES

CO_2 cartridges can only be used once, so you should carry spares. To check it, unscrew the CO_2 cartridge and check that it has not been used (the cartridge should not have a hole made by the firing pin). While the cartridge is removed, operate the firing mechanism and check that it is working properly. Replace the cartridge.

BCD COLOUR

Divers surfacing after a drift dive are more easily spotted if they wear an orange or yellow BCD. As a boat captain (and not suffering from colour blindness), I had difficulty picking out divers in black or blue BCDs at a distance. In fact, if the divers were not using a surface marker buoy, the glint of the sun on a mask or a sunburned face was often more obvious.

Exposure suits

A diver's comfort underwater depends on body-shape, metabolism, activity during the dive, water temperature and the number of dives undertaken that day. Exposure suits protect against abrasion, cuts, animal stings and heat loss in the water. Water conducts heat away from the body faster than air. In general, the colder the water the thicker the suit and the more of the body is covered. Most manufacturers make foam neoprene wet and semidry suits in standard sizes as well as to measure.

Wet suits should be as tight a fit as is comfortable. The best fit will feel slightly restrictive when out of the water, but fine when in the water. A well-fitting suit may be difficult to put on when dry. Running water through the suit before donning it can make it much easier.

All exposure suit materials will deteriorate if they come into contact with oil or diesel oil on the surface of the water, which is common in harbours.

Right (top to bottom): Wet suits protect divers from sun and cold water. Hoods are used in very cold water. Nylon gloves protect against abrasion. Hard-soled bootees are easier to walk in.

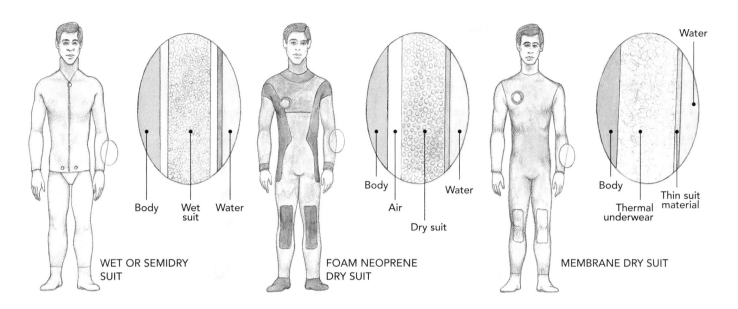

Body Wet Water
suit

WET OR SEMIDRY
SUIT

Body Water
Air
Dry suit

FOAM NEOPRENE
DRY SUIT

Water

Body Thin suit
Thermal material
underwear

MEMBRANE DRY SUIT

LIGHTWEIGHT BODY SKINS, LYCRA, SPANDEX, THERMOPLASTIC

For very warm water, lightweight one-piece full-body suits, or Lycra-skins, are often enough. They are highly elastic and neutrally buoyant. Unfortunately, they deteriorate rapidly in strong sunlight.

Lycra is a trademark of the DuPont Corporation for a spandex fibre, an elastic fibre that is mainly a synthetic polymer of polyurethane. The word spandex is derived from the word expand.

Most Lycra body suits have stirrups at the ankles to stop the legs from riding up and loops that slip around the thumbs to keep the sleeves fully down. Body skins are worn for protection or under wet suits for added insulation or to make the wet suit easier to don or doff. Because of their high elasticity Lycra-skins are sold ready-made in standard sizes.

Another type of warm-water suit has either a thin layer of heat-retaining thermoplastic sandwiched between two layers of spandex or a plush lining. A thermoplastic suit can be worn under a neoprene suit for extra warmth. They are neutrally buoyant and have the advantage of being windproof.

Top: Thermal insulation is achieved by different methods in different types of diving suit.

WET AND SEMIDRY SUITS

The commonest form of protection is a wet suit. Wet and semidry suits are made from closed-cell

Above: Brightly coloured Lycra-skins are lightweight and highly elastic, give good protection in warm water, but the material breaks down quickly in strong sunlight.

foam neoprene, a polymer made from acetylene and hydrochloric acid that has been expanded either chemically or with nitrogen gas bubbles. These bubbles are trapped in the rubber, but separated from each other so the suit does not absorb water. It provides insulation while having elasticity.

The fragile neoprene is sandwiched between a colourful abrasion-resistant nylon fabric on the outside and a fleece-like plush lining or titanium fabric on the inside. The jury is still out on the thermal effectiveness of titanium linings. The suits are made from several sections that are glued end-to-end. The resulting seam is blind-stitched through the reinforcing fabrics to strengthen them

without piercing the wet suit. Wet and semidry suits vary in thickness between 2mm (1/16 inch) for warm water and 9mm (11/32 inch), for very cold water. Although they are flexible, swimming in a 9mm (11/32 inch) suit can be tiring. The suits may have extra thick foam neoprene pads at areas that get cold easily, such as against the spine. Some use thinner material on the arms and/or legs for more flexibility. Thinner material on the legs also minimizes buoyancy that would cause the legs to float up.

'Shorty' wet suits only cover the upper legs and torso. One-piece suits provide thermal and abrasion protection from wrist to ankle. With thicker neoprene, two-piece wet suits are the most popular

because they are easier to don and doff. The most popular of these is the 'Farmer John' bottom which covers the body from the ankles to just below the shoulders. This is covered by a jacket which usually includes a long zip to make it easier to put on and take off. This provides a double layer of thermal protection over the torso.

Water does get between a wet suit and the body, but as long as it is not being continuously flushed out again it is heated by the diver's body and helps to provide insulation. If the suit is a loose fit, water will flush through and reduce the suit's thermal effectiveness.

Although the neoprene may be windproof, the suit as a whole is not. It contains water that will evaporate so a diver may get chilled between dives, especially on a moving boat, unless a windproof overgarment is worn.

SEMIDRY SUITS

Semidry suits are wet suits with tight-fitting neoprene seals at the ankles and wrists preventing water from flushing through. A small amount of water will still enter at the neck, but cannot be flushed through the seals. These are one or two-piece suits and can have a hood. Some recent semidry suits are much like a dry suit with a cross-shoulder zip and a neck seal that is inverted. These suits are not completely dry, but work well.

Above: *Flotation of the wet suit material can cause the legs to float upwards.*

MOULD AND BACTERIAL GROWTH ON WET OR SEMIDRY SUITS

A tight-fitting wet or semidry suit is an ideal environment for mould and bacterial growth, especially for women. Regularly wash the suits with freshwater inside and out and occasionally add a small amount of disinfectant to the final rinse.

Above: Divers kitting up with wet and semidry suits on a live-aboard boat. One-piece suits provide thermal and abrasion protection from wrist to ankle.

ACCESSORIES FOR WET OR SEMIDRY SUITS INCLUDE

- Hoods – attached or separate.
- Vests – an extra layer of insulation worn under the suit in cold water, some have a hood.
- Bootees – preferably with hard soles for traversing rough ground on land.
- Gloves – of nylon for protection against abrasion on wrecks in warm water or of neoprene for warmth in cold water. Do not wear gloves near coral as you will be more tempted to grab it.
- Spine-pads – an extra layer of thick neoprene where the natural curvature of the spine allows water to flow through.
- Kneepads – protect against abrasion if the diver kneels on a wreck and reduce the damage

caused by a bended knee stretching the neoprene on the outside of the curve.
- Pockets – can be general or shaped for specialized articles.
- Zips – at wrist and ankle make the suit easier to don or doff.
- Heat packs – can be slipped into integral suit pockets or strap-on exterior pouches. These packs contain a non-toxic, reusable chemical that heats up to about 54°C (130°F) for roughly 30 minutes while crystallizing out. Under normal conditions in an open container, sodium acetate will change from a liquid to a solid at 54°C (130°F). However, by putting this into a sealed container, the solution can be supercooled well below this temperature. Flexing a piece of stainless steel

inside the super-cooled liquid causes a single molecule of liquid to crystallize and begin a chain reaction that causes the entire solution to change from liquid to solid. The process produces heat. The packs can be reused by placing them in boiling water until all the crystals have disappeared, and then allowing them to cool.

STORAGE OF WET AND SEMIDRY SUITS

Wash and disinfect a wet or semidry suit and dry it out of the sun. Do not store it folded as the creases formed will have less insulation. Hang it on a broad coat hanger in a cool, dark place away from vehicle exhaust fumes. Do not store in a garage.

DRY SUITS

Unlike wet suits there are several things that can go wrong when diving with a dry suit, from uncontrolled ascents to feet-first ascents when air migrates to, and is trapped in, the suit's legs. All training agencies run courses on dry suit diving.

Dry suits only come in one style – a suit that fully encloses the body with seals at the neck, wrists and, occasionally, ankles. Where differences do exist these are in the materials of construction, the seals, types of hood and boot, braces (straps supporting the lower half of the suit from the shoulders), and the position and strength of the waterproof zips.

Foam neoprene dry suits are manufactured from the same material as wet suits. They tend to be the most comfortable, have inherent insulation properties, but lose buoyancy and insulation as the diver descends and the neoprene is compressed. If the suit is pierced, and floods, the neoprene will continue to provide some buoyancy and insulation. The diver can become positively buoyant by inflating the BCD or dumping weights. These suits can either be manufactured as a tight fit like a wet suit or as a slack fit to be worn over warm undergarments.

Membrane (shell) dry suits rely on a waterproof membrane to keep out the water. They have no insulation properties, so the diver needs to wear warm undergarments. They used to be made of vulcanized rubber, but these have almost disappeared from the recreational diving market. Modern membrane dry suits are made of either a urethane-coated mate-

Right: The material of this dry suit is a tri-laminate of vulcanized rubber sandwiched between two layers of hard-wearing synthetic material. As with crushed neoprene these suits have no insulation properties of their own, but rely on warm undergarments.

rial, or a tri-laminate of vulcanized rubber sandwiched between two layers of hard-wearing synthetic fabric, or foam neoprene that has had the gas bubbles crushed or compressed to reduce their bubble size. All these have fewer buoyancy problems than foam neoprene. Coated and tri-laminate materials do not have any stretch so they have to be loose-fitting

ALLERGY TO NEOPRENE

Allergy to neoprene is quite common. It is usually a reaction to one of the chemicals used in the production of neoprene, but it may just be chaffing. You can be tested for allergies to the many chemicals used, but then you could rarely be sure that the chemical concerned is not present in another make of suit. Other than using an anti-chaffing compound such as KY Jelly, divers can only get a suit made from another compound.

and large enough for the neck and shoulder section to slip over the diver's head. Some suits have internal braces to keep the leg section up and some have methods of folding over the excess material and securing it. The loose fit can allow gas to move around inside the suit, depending on the diver's attitude in the water, body shape and equipment worn. This movement of gas can force the diver's body into unwanted attitudes, such as rolling to one side. In extreme cases gas migrates to the legs and feet, creating a head-down position in the water, possibly expanding the boots and causing the fins to burst off. Divers should learn how to correct this before diving with a membrane dry suit. It can be minimized by a suit that fits the body as closely as possible, while still allowing the diver to crouch down.

Compressed and crushed foam neoprene suits have more stretch than those made from material containing a fabric. Compressed neoprene has been compressed to reduce the gas-bubble size before it is cut by the dry suit manufacturer. Crushed neoprene is crushed while heated after the suit has been put together, toughening the material and tightening up the bonding and stitching at the same time. There is some distortion, but the final product has a reputation for being hard wearing.

URINATING WHEN WEARING DRY SUITS

Having struggled into a dry suit you may want to go to the toilet. Some dry suits have zips around the crotch for use when not in the water, but these are only suitable for men.

When the body temperature drops, blood vessels in the extremities constrict, causing the central blood volume to increase. Sensors detect this and signal the kidneys to remove water to return the blood volume to normal. The bladder fills up even if the diver has just gone to the toilet. The worst thing that a diver can do is to refuse to drink since this increases the risk of decompression sickness. Men and women can wear adult incontinence pads – remember to wash out the suit and disinfect it after use.

For men there are pee-valves with an automatic pressure equalization valve. The valve is connected to the penis with a male condom-style catheter. Pee-valves can be balanced or unbalanced. The diver's body is attached to a urination tube, which is a flexible container. Extreme depths may cause the volume in this tube to decrease, causing a squeeze. This is alleviated by balanced valves which equalize the pressure difference between the valve system and the ambient water pressure. Absolute hygiene is essential with these devices. At the end of a day's diving they should be disassembled and disinfected.

Nowadays most dry suits have attached boots. Some have built-in hoods, while others use a wet suit hood. Membrane dry suits are also made of lightweight materials for use in warm waters.

Dry suit zips must be kept clean and the recommended lubricant used. Traditionally they are positioned across the shoulders where they will encounter the least bending. Other zips start around the back of the neck and run diagonally down the front so that the diver can don these suits unaided.

DRY SUIT VALVES

The air in a dry suit is compressed as the diver descends, causing loss of buoyancy and discomfort as creases forming in the material of the suit are squeezed against the body. This can be compensated for by having a low-pressure direct feed similar to that on the BCD, to feed breathing gas through a valve into the suit. This valve is usually positioned on the chest where it will not interfere with any of the fittings on the BCD. On ascent this gas expands and it must be dumped, or the diver will accelerate to the surface. Breathing gas is less dense than water so it will rise to the highest point if allowed to. Many suits have automatic dump valves at the cuff and divers can raise an arm to make it the highest point when required. However, this is not a good valve position for a diver who must raise an arm for other reasons, as the gas will then automatically empty out. For these divers the dump valve can be positioned just below the shoulder. When the diver needs to dump gas, the shoulder with the valve must be raised and revolved to position it at the highest point. Undergarments that produce fluff can jam these valves or their material may press against them. For this reason many divers wear undergarments of open weave material or simply cut it away around the valve.

Although a dry suit's buoyancy can be adjusted, a BCD is still necessary for righting a diver who becomes inverted due to gas migrating to the legs. A BCD is also needed in the event that the suit is torn and no longer gas-tight. On the surface an inflated BCD is more comfortable than the pressure on the neck seal when the dry suit is inflated for positive buoyancy.

Divers may require larger fins to fit over dry suit boots and many divers, particularly women, use small ankle weights to keep their legs down in the water.

Dry suit seals

There are two types of dry suit seal, latex and neoprene. The larger the contact area the more likely they are to keep the diver dry. Latex seals can be easily trimmed to fit, they tend to be more efficient than neoprene for the same size, but seem to require replacing more often and some divers develop an allergy to them (see p60). Neoprene seals must be a good fit, but tend to be more comfortable and more resistant to damage. Latex seals are normally left flat against the skin, but neoprene neck seals are usually folded back inside the suit to give a firmer seal as the gas inside the suit presses the seal against the skin. However, when the seal is worn in this way, over-pressurized gas within

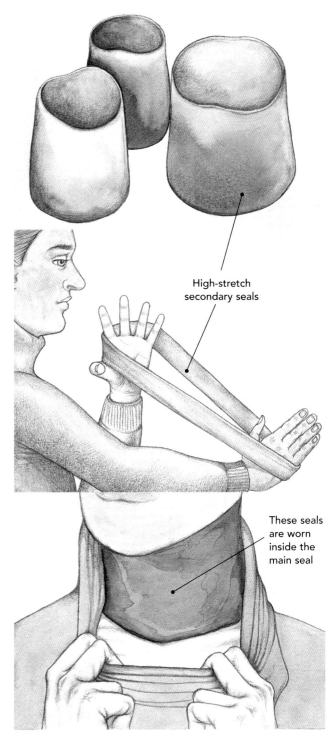

High-stretch secondary seals

These seals are worn inside the main seal

Above: Bio-Seals make high-stretch, self-lubricating secondary seals that are worn between the dry suit seal and the skin to reduce seal friction, allergy to latex and improve on the watertightness of the seal.

the suit cannot easily be vented by forcing the seal away from the skin with a finger.

When a diver grips something, a camera for instance, the wrist tendons are raised, which can cause leaking. Some divers get a rash under the neck seal. Bio-Seals are high-stretch, self-lubricating secondary seals worn between the dry suit seal and the skin to prevent leakage and reduce seal friction on the neck and allergy to latex. These seals do contain oils that can cause early deterioration of latex, but cleaning the latex after each use can help delay this effect.

All dry suits are likely to require replacement seals and one company now has zip-on seals. Flexible urethane rings are attached to the neck and cuffs and mating rings are fitted to the seals. Pressed together they form a strong, interlocking connection. The same company also produces gloves that zip onto the cuffs in place of the zip-on wrist seals. Another advantage is that when hiring a dry suit like this, seals of a suitable size can be fitted.

DONNING DRY SUITS

Before donning a dry suit, dust the seals with unscented talcum powder (scented powder contains chemicals that can degrade rubber). Apply the recommended lubricant on the outer teeth of the zip. Remove anything sharp, such as jewellery, to prevent snags and

---

DRY SUIT WRIST AND NECK SEALS

Dry suits may have a choice of seals for the neck and wrist. Neoprene seals are hard-wearing but relatively thick. They tend to leak where the body contours change abruptly, such as around bony wrists. Neoprene seals require stretching before use. Wrist seals can be stretched over a tinned-food can overnight and neck seals can be stretched over the widest part of a scuba cylinder. Latex seals are thinner and very elastic so they seal better, but are fragile, wear quickly and are torn by sharp fingernails or watches. They should be trimmed until they are 15% smaller than the circumference of the diver's wrist or neck. Latex seals are usually easily replaced, so carry spares.

Neoprene neck seals should be turned in on themselves, like a polo neck sweater in reverse. Then add enough air to the suit to maintain positive pressure.

---

tears. Don the suit with minimum stretching. Never force the zip. Ensure that it runs free and does not trap undergarments. Some divers use liquid soap or KY Jelly as a seal lubricant for donning, but avoid them where there is sand.

DRY SUIT UNDERGARMENTS

Dry suit undergarments can range from easily washed thermal underwear and tracksuits through thicker synthetic pile 'woolly bears' or fleeces to a warmer (but more difficult to launder) mat of very thin artificial fibres (Thinsulate™). It is hydrophobic – will not absorb water – and retains its trapped air even if it gets wet. Despite the term, dry suits are seldom completely dry – leaks and perspiration result in damp undergarments.

Undergarments manufactured from Thinsulate™ should be washed as seldom as possible because if the detergent is not removed thoroughly, it conducts water into the fibres and causes the insulation to flood. Washing by hand is not recommended, as it is difficult to remove dirt without damaging the insulation. Remove salt crystals by washing the garments in water without detergent. If necessary, use very dilute disinfectant, but do not add detergent. Grease can be spot-cleaned with detergent and then machine washed in water without detergent. If the entire garment requires cleaning, use detergent for one wash-cycle, then put the garment through four more cycles without detergent, just water.

To minimize the need to wash a Thinsulate™ garment, wear thermal underwear, made from a synthetic material that wicks moisture, under it.

STORAGE OF DRY SUITS

Thoroughly wash and disinfect the suit, soak the zip and valves. Do not close a dirty zip, clean it with a toothbrush. Wash the seals with soapy water. With the zip open, hang the suit by the feet to dry. When the suit is dry, close the zip and apply the recommended lubricant to the outer teeth. Dust the seals with fragrance-free talcum powder to help the suit slip on easily, reduce chafing and prolong the life of the latex seals.

Store the suit rolled up loosely with the zip on top and valves that might snag on the outside of the roll. Never use silicon spray on any part of the suit. Store the suit in an airtight bag in a cool, dry place away from vehicle exhaust fumes.

The Main Scuba Cylinder

Scuba cylinders, also called tanks or bottles, are manufactured in various sizes and pressure ratings. They can be used singly, as twin sets (two units linked to feed a single regulator) or, for more demanding situations, two or more units where each cylinder is fitted with its own regulator. The higher the pressure rating, the greater the capacity of a cylinder of a given size. However, this assumes that the compressor available can fill the cylinder to the pressure required and this is not always the case. Another problem with high-capacity cylinders is that there is a greater change in buoyancy as the diver consumes the breathing gas. A small diver will find that a twin set made up of two small cylinders is more comfortable to wear and less likely to strike the wearer's neck than a single large cylinder, but twin sets have more drag than a single cylinder of equivalent size.

For redundancy, single scuba cylinders can be fitted with two completely separate regulators on an 'H' or 'Y' scuba cylinder valve. Alternatively, twin scuba cylinders can be connected by a manifold with a centre isolation

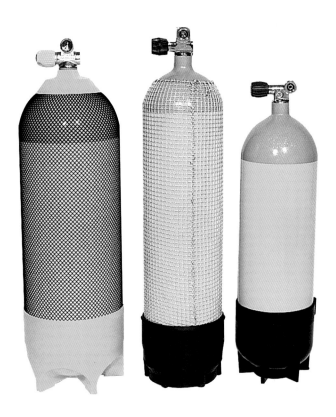

Above: Scuba cylinders range in size from 6 to 18 litres (49 to 148 cu ft) water capacity and come in various lengths to suit each diver's height. In warm water they are used singly, though small divers may find a twin set (two smaller cylinders) more comfortable to wear than a single large cylinder. In cold water it is common to use a twin set made up of two larger cylinders.

New European Union regulations for 2005 say that any scuba cylinder containing a percentage of oxygen greater than that found in normal breathing air should have an outlet connection to the regulator first stage that is a DIN-fitting, but with a different thread diameter from that of the DIN-fitting first stages already in use. This includes all gas mixes from 22% O_2 to 100% O_2. Therefore Nitrox regulators will have to be dedicated to Nitrox scuba cylinders.

ARGON

Technical divers often use argon gas to inflate dry suits and maintain body temperature. Denser than air, and much denser than helium, argon is a better insulator for retaining body heat when used to inflate the suit enough to eliminate body-squeezes.

The argon is carried in a separate small cylinder, but it is particularly important to make sure that only the correct inflation hose is connected between the cylinder and the dry suit so that the gas cannot be breathed by mistake. Some divers use a standard regulator which, as well as having a suit-inflation hose, still has a regulator second stage attached. The Argon cylinder does not contain any oxygen, so if the diver switched to the wrong second stage by mistake, the result would be fatal.

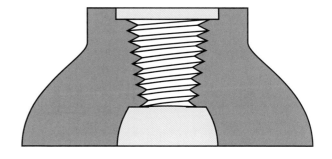

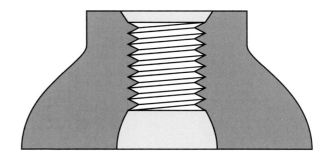

Above: Steel cylinders (top) have taper threads sealed with plumber's PTFE sealing tape. Aluminium cylinders (above) have parallel threads and are sealed with an O-ring.

valve and have separate regulators on each scuba cylinder valve. With this set-up, in the event of a failure in one cylinder, you still have access to the contents of both scuba cylinders through one scuba cylinder valve. If there is a failure of one scuba cylinder O-ring then that scuba cylinder can be isolated from the other by closing the isolation valve. Twin scuba cylinders are best mounted with the manifold uppermost, so that you can reach over your shoulder and turn your own valves on or off while in the water. This ensures that you can use the manifold's full functionality at all times.

Single scuba cylinders are fitted to BCD backpacks with webbing cam bands. However, these are inadequate if the scuba cylinders are connected by a manifold as movement stresses the connections between the manifold and the scuba cylinder valves. There are a number of stainless steel bands and stainless steel or aluminium alloy backplates available instead.

Recreational scuba cylinders are made either of steel or of aluminium alloy. Steel cylinders are more resistant to abrasion damage and have good buoyancy characteristics, but without proper care

they may rust inside and out. If water gets inside a steel cylinder, the higher pressure means that there is more oxygen to fuel corrosion. Galvanizing (coating with zinc) inhibits rust on the outside, but it cannot be used on the inside because it affects the purity of the air. Aluminium cylinders are more easily damaged by abrasion and require thicker walls to take the same internal pressure. They are heavier, but more positively buoyant than an equivalent capacity of steel cylinder. Although aluminium corrodes, the thin coating of aluminium oxide formed inhibits further corrosion.

This is an important factor for those running sport diving operations where clients often breathe their cylinder dry, so that a small amount of moisture enters the cylinder and may not be noticed until the next inspection. Aluminium cylinders are more prone to electrolytic reaction with the brass on/off valve. The threads will seize if the valves are not removed regularly and put back using the correct thread compound.

The internationally accepted colour-coding systems for all gas cylinders are ignored by sport diving suppliers in favour of attractive colours, except for cylinders containing Enriched Air Nitrox (see p149).

Some manufacturing problems have become apparent over the years and some cylinders have been banned, so it is important to buy cylinders only from recognized scuba equipment dealers.

CARE OF SCUBA CYLINDERS

Due to the high pressure, scuba cylinders are dangerous. All first world countries require regular inspections. The dates of these inspections and other details required by law such as the working pressure, the type of metal used and the government agency concerned, are usually stamped on the neck of the cylinder where the cylinder wall is thickest. A technician will check these details before agreeing to fill the cylinder.

Above: *All necessary detail required by law are stamped on the neck of the scuba cylinder, inlcuding the type of metal used, working pressure and the date of the last technical inspection.*

FOR DIVER SAFETY (AND THAT OF WHOEVER FILLS THEM) SCUBA CYLINDERS SHOULD

- be handled carefully
- be tested regularly – visually and hydrostatically
- never be filled to more than their certified working pressure
- be rinsed outside with freshwater after use in saltwater
- be filled with air slowly, while placed in a water bath to conduct away some of the heat produced
- be kept away from strong heat, including the sun
- be carefully secured for safe transportation
- never be breathed dry underwater. (If a cylinder has been breathed dry underwater, it must be washed out with freshwater and allowed to dry, before being refilled, in case the ambient pressure has forced water into it.)
- be thrown away if they have been in a fire
- be stored upright with 10–20 bar (145–290 psi) of breathing gas pressure inside them. This reduces the concentration of oxygen and therefore any oxygen-related corrosion.

WATER CAN ENTER THE CYLINDER DUE TO

- poor compressor maintenance, including overdue filter changes
- leaving the valve open where there is condensation or high humidity.

SCUBA CYLINDER ACCESSORIES

- Boots. Steel cylinders have round bases so they cannot be stored upright unless fitted with plastic or rubber cylinder boots. Aluminium cylinders have flat bases. Boots for either type of cylinder must drain the water easily. They are sometimes squared off on the sides to stop them rolling around when transported on their sides.
- Sleeves. Nowadays usually man-made fibre netting, they can help to protect the exterior of the cylinder from scratches.
- Smaller cylinders containing spare air or Enriched Air Nitrox for decompression.
- Battery-packs for lights can be attached to the main cylinder.
- Attachments to help carry the cylinder when out of the water, or to act as a wheeled trolley.

TRANSPORTING SCUBA CYLINDERS

There is no need to fly cylinders when diving with an operator. Occasionally cylinders do have to be flown, but some airlines will not allow scuba cylinders at all; others will, as long as the on/off valve is removed so that they can be sure that the cylinder is empty. The same applies to the emergency air cylinder fitted to some BCDs. It can be removed without affecting the BCD's ability to hold air. If you have a direct-feed then the emergency air cylinder is not required.

Top: Aluminium scuba cylinders have flat bases so they can be stored in the upright position without the need to fit an extra boot (steel scuba cylinders have round bases).
Above: A pony (smaller) bottle that is filled with Nitrox for decompression, attached to a diver's main scuba cylinder.

SCUBA CYLINDER VALVES

Scuba cylinders have on/off valves screwed into the neck of the cylinder. Modern scuba cylinder valves are balanced and give few problems. The one valve is used both for filling the cylinder and for connection to the regulator. However, you can use an H- or Y-valve, which gives them two separate regulators on one scuba cylinder. You can also convert single cylinder systems to a twin cylinder system with a connecting manifold and isolating valve. For critical cave, wreck or cold water diving, two or more cylinders with completely separate valves and regulators are preferred in case one malfunctions.

Valves for steel scuba cylinders have taper threads and are fitted with plumber's polytetrafluoro-ethylene (PTFE) sealing tape. Aluminium cylinder valves have parallel threads and are sealed with an O-ring. Inside the cylinder the valve has a narrow pipe about 25mm (1 inch) long. This is designed to prevent moisture or scale from restricting the airflow through the valve when the cylinder is inverted. The valve is opened (turned on) by turning the valve handle in an anticlockwise direction. Care should be taken when closing the valve because the sealing seat is made of relatively soft material that is damaged by over-tightening. Scuba cylinder valves have a 'burst disk' – a thin copper disk that

bursts and vents off the gas if the cylinder is overfilled by about 40%, or left under conditions of extreme heat. Burst disks corrode over time and require replacing. They are manufactured to 'burst' at different pressures, so make sure that the replacement has the correct pressure rating. Similarly, when changing a valve to another cylinder, ensure that the burst disk has the correct pressure rating for the new cylinder.

Valves incorporating a spring-loaded reserve system used to be popular. (Early scuba equipment brochures referred to them as item J – hence the name J-valves.)

However, divers often forgot to set the reserve and a diver with strong lungs could easily breathe past the resistance of the spring and use up the reserve air without realizing it. Nowadays divers use submersible pressure gauges. Valves for use in gas mixes high in oxygen use special O-rings and other items in oxygen-compatible materials.

Some scuba cylinder valves have almost universal regulator fittings, the valve has a screw-type DIN socket (Deutsche Industrie Norm is the German standards organization), and a removable yoke-connector (A-clamp) insert is screwed into the DIN socket with a

Female part of DIN fitting valve

DIN to yoke-connector insert fitted

Above: The top part of this illustration shows the female part of the DIN fitting valve and a DIN to yoke-connector adapter plug. The lower part of the illustration shows a DIN to yoke-connector adapter insert screwed into position. The valve can then be fitted with the first stage of a yoke-connector regulator.

Above left and right: This universal regulator first stage has a male DIN fitting, which can either be screwed directly to a female DIN fitting valve or by using the female DIN fitting of the yoke connector shown on the right, fitted to a yoke-clamp valve.

hexagon key (Allen Key). DIN screw fittings are more stream-lined than yoke-connector fittings so they are less likely to get snagged, or damaged by contact when used on the side-mounted scuba cylinders favoured by many technical and cave divers.

The size of the recess machined into the valve that houses the locat-ing groove for the cylinder-to-regulator O-ring, and mates with the yoke-connector, varies between imperial and metric units. Travelling divers have to carry two different sizes of yoke-connector if their

regulators will accept them. Some regulators do not have inter-changeable yoke-connectors, so that some metric-sized regulators will not fit imperial-sized valves and vice versa.

Yoke-connectors and 5-thread DIN screw fittings are used for pressures up to 200 bar (2900psi). For higher pressures 7-thread DIN screw fittings are used.

The cylinder valve-to-regulator O-ring seal relies more on the air pressure for a seal than the pres-sure created by tightening the yoke-connector or DIN screw fit-tings. These O-rings deteriorate, especially in sunlight, and will not seal if there are salt crystals or nicks on the surface. Always wipe these O-rings with a wet finger before

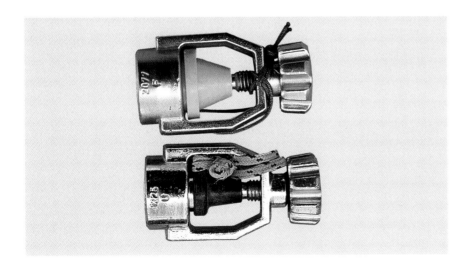

Left: Two different sizes of DIN to yoke-connectors. These have different diameters where they mate with the scuba cylinder valve

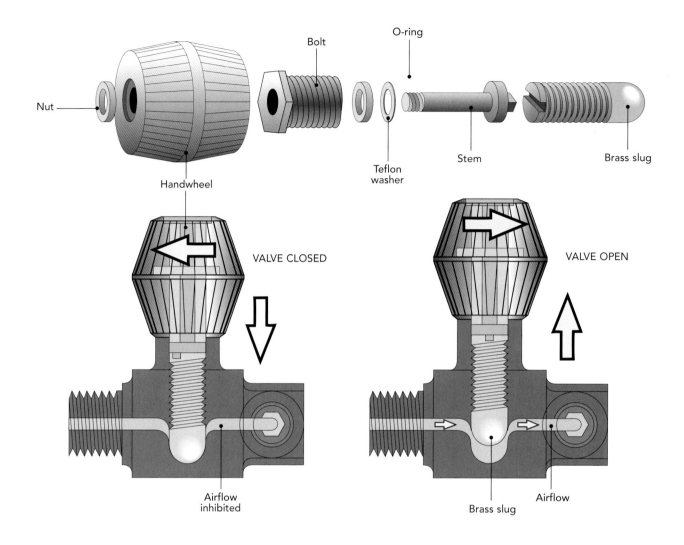

Nut

Handwheel

Bolt

O-ring

Teflon washer

Stem

Brass slug

VALVE CLOSED

Airflow inhibited

VALVE OPEN

Brass slug

Airflow

fitting the regulator first stage. Dive operators and dive boats are often short of these O-rings so always carry your own spares.

Never use force to close the valve and when opening it, turn it anticlockwise until it is fully open and then close it again by a quarter turn. This will prevent it from seizing in the open position.

After rinsing or soaking in freshwater after a dive, there will still be some water around the valve ori-fice. If the cylinder is filled before this water has evaporated, some water could enter the scuba cylin-der, so open the valve a little before connecting it to the com-pressor or breathing gas bank. This will force the water away from the orifice.

A protective cap or sleeve is useful to keep the O-ring in place, protect it and its locating groove from damage and keep out dust. Fitting this protection in place

Above: The standard scuba cylinder valve is a simple on-off valve screwed into the neck of the cylinder. Early scuba equipment brochures referred to these valves as 'item K' so some people call them K-valves.

with adhesive tape will then also indicate that the cylinder has been filled.

Scuba cylinder valves should be serviced regularly and always when the cylinder goes in for inspection.

Regulators (demand valves)

The regulator is also called a demand valve because it delivers breathing gas when a diver demands it by inhaling. The size of the mouthpiece varies as does pressure toward one side or up and down in the mouth so always try it for fit before purchase. Regulators used for breathing gas mixtures high in oxygen have special O-rings and other oxygen-compatible materials to minimize the risk of ignition.

Regulator first stages have a number of openings called ports. Those that connect the scuba cylinder directly to a gauge that shows the pressure in the scuba cylinder (*see SPG p80*) require a connection that can withstand high pressure. High-pressure ports have a different-sized thread to that of the low-pressure ports to avoid equipment being connected to the wrong port. The other ports are for connecting to low-pressure

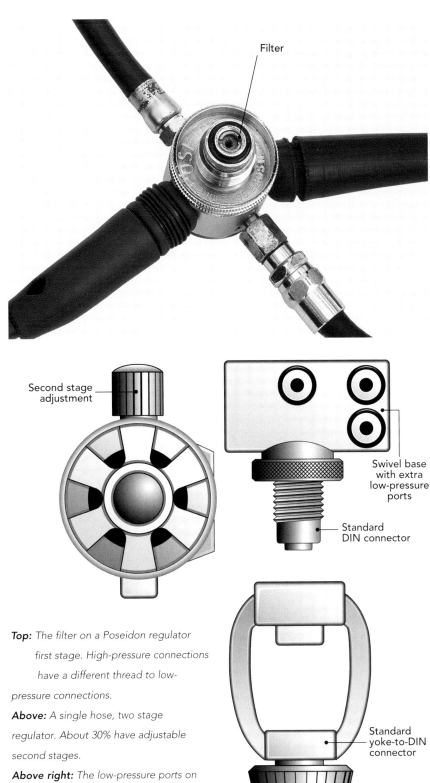

Filter

Second stage adjustment

Swivel base with extra low-pressure ports

Standard DIN connector

Standard yoke-to-DIN connector

Above: When connected to a direct feed, depressing the top lever of this device produces a blast of breathing gas for drying equipment on the surface or filling lifting bags underwater.

Top: The filter on a Poseidon regulator first stage. High-pressure connections have a different thread to low-pressure connections.

Above: A single hose, two stage regulator. About 30% have adjustable second stages.

Above right: The low-pressure ports on the regulator are used for inflating BCDs and dry suits; for power tools; and as an extra second stage (or octopus rig).

items – the second stage, an alternate breathing gas source (also known as alternate second stage or octopus rig), and for inflating BCDs, dry suits, breathing gas blowers and driving power tools and other applications.

Basic regulators do not produce a large amount of breathing gas on demand, have a limited number of low-pressure ports and have a fixed single-size yoke-connector. On the plus side they are relatively simple, rarely malfunction and stand up to a lot of abuse so they are popular with training schools and divers who only dive occasionally in warm water.

Regulators must connect to the scuba cylinder on/off valve. Most regulator first stages are fitted with yoke-connectors (called A-clamps in some countries). More expensive regulators may have a fixed DIN screw fitting compatible with the maximum useable pressure, which can either be fitted directly to a cylinder valve or to various sizes of yoke-connector.

The diameter depends on whether the yoke connector is manufactured to imperial or metric measurements. Travelling divers may have to carry two yoke-connectors if their regulators will accept both sizes. Yoke-connectors and 5-thread DIN screw fittings are used for pressures up to 200 bar (2900psi) but 7-thread DIN screw fittings are used for higher pressures.

The more expensive regulators will usually have more low-pressure ports and can easily supply the extra breathing gas required. Some regulator second stages have a lever to control the valve's tendency to allow free-flowing breathing gas on the surface. Others have a manually-adjustable breathing-resistance control that can change the effort necessary. It enables the supply of more breathing gas at depth and can be adjusted back to normal as the diver ascends. They are not a good idea for divers who are likely to have their hands full with other equipment. Contrary to popular belief, divers have a lower rate of air consumption if their second stages are tuned for the least breathing resistance.

Above: *A diver using a regulator with an adjustable second stage.*

Nowadays the standard unit is a single-hose, two-stage regulator. Single-hose refers to the basic breathing unit (excluding the low-pressure hoses that feed other devices and the high-pressure hose that connects to the submersible pressure gauge). Two-stage refers to the breathing gas pressure being reduced in two stages to a pressure at which the diver can breathe it.

FIRST STAGES

The first stage of a regulator is attached to the on/off valve of the cylinder. It must reduce the pressure of around 200 bar (2900psi) to a level that the low-pressure hose and the second stage can handle, but still high enough to overcome ambient pressure on the lungs at depth. For most regulators this is about 10–13bar (145–189psi). First stages used to come in two basic types (piston or diaphragm), but Poseidon have now introduced a first-stage using a ball as the seal.

First stages can be balanced or unbalanced. In a balanced design, the amount of breathing gas available at the second stage is not affected by depth or cylinder pressure. This makes for easier breathing at depth; a good supply of breathing gas to other items; and for two divers sharing through the main and alternate source (alternate second stage) at the same time. Unbalanced first stages become harder to breathe from as the pressure in the cylinder falls.

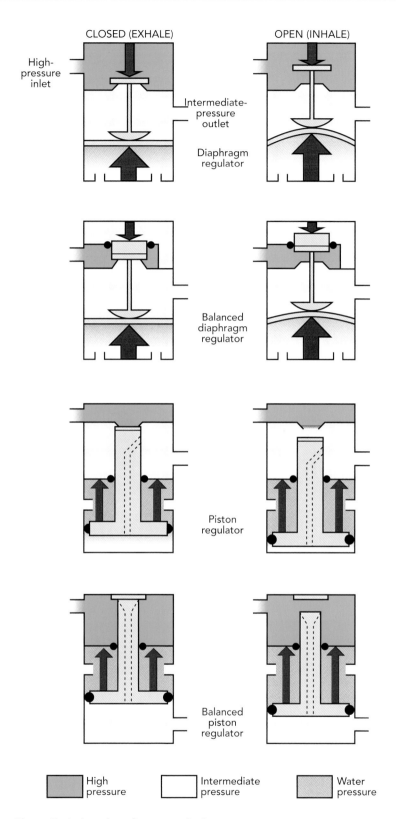

Above: Typical regulator first stages. Red arrows represent spring pressure.

Black dots represent O-rings.

Piston first stages are cheaper to manufacture and service, but harder to adjust in the field. Their open design means that water and sediment can enter the main body and cause malfunction. The internal O-ring seals can be damaged by salt crystals or sediment.

Diaphragm first stages have more moving parts, but do not allow water or sediment into the main body, thus reducing internal corrosion and contamination. They are better for use in polluted water and easier (for qualified people) to adjust in the field.

Piston first stages have a high-pressure sealing valve operated by the opposing forces of the intermediate pressure and the regulator's main high-pressure spring. When a diver inhales, the intermediate pressure is lowered. This allows the main spring to move the piston towards the low-pressure side, moving the valve off its seat and allowing breathing gas from the cylinder to enter. The pressure of the breathing gas from the cylinder increases the intermediate pressure until it overcomes the main spring pressure, thus moving the piston in the opposite direction and closing the valve. Unbalanced piston first stages have small orifices so that breathing resistance is increased as the pressure in the cylinder drops.

With diaphragm first stages, when a diver inhales, a diaphragm flexes inward, pushing on a rod that causes the high-pressure valve to open and breathing gas to enter. When the diver stops inhaling, the diaphragm returns to its normal position and the high-pressure spring closes the valve.

The valve stem of a balanced diaphragm first stage extends through the high-pressure chamber into the intermediate pressure chamber. This helps to balance the forces acting on the valve so that the breathing gas from the cylinder cannot exert a closing force.

All first stages are supplied with a dust cap, which is fitted to the inlet port to protect it from knocks and keep out dust and moisture when the regulator is not fitted to a cylinder valve. For cold water diving, some first stages can be environmentally sealed with a flexible chamber so that only a silicone or alcohol-based fluid comes into contact with the piston or diaphragm. This transmits the ambient water pressure to the first stage, while preventing water from entering the system and freezing.

The increased popularity of technical diving and its requirement of gas integrity in the first stage has led Poseidon to design the Xstream, which minimizes the use of O-rings and gaskets and uses a stainless steel ball to seal the high-pressure valve. The Xstream has continuous positive pressure yet does not free-flow, is self-balancing and has built-in antifreeze protection. The earliest Xstreams were manufactured with a minimal number of outlet ports with the intention that technical

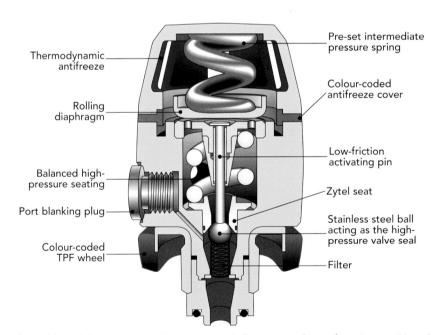

Thermodynamic antifreeze

Rolling diaphragm

Balanced high-pressure seating

Port blanking plug

Colour-coded TPF wheel

Pre-set intermediate pressure spring

Colour-coded antifreeze cover

Low-friction activating pin

Zytel seat

Stainless steel ball acting as the high-pressure valve seal

Filter

Above: *Normal designs are sensitive to wear, misalignment and manufacturing precision. A ball always finds its correct seating.*

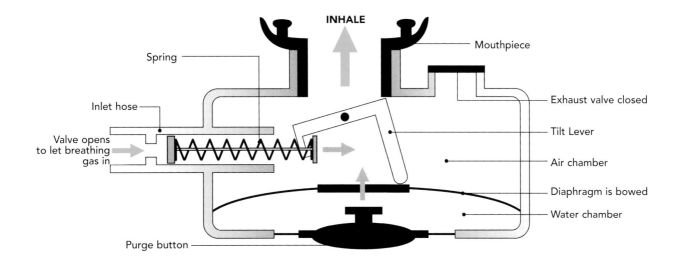

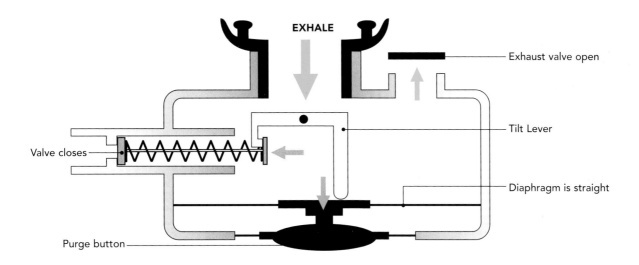

divers would have a separate regulator for each gas mix, but the design has proved so popular that further models with extra ports are now available. Some divers do not like the small purge button on the second stage, which can be difficult to press when wearing gloves.

SECOND STAGES

The second stage contains the mouthpiece for inhalation, an exhaust valve to release the gases

Above: Modern second stages have downstream inlet valves. In cold water, some metal construction (while heavier than plastic) absorbs heat from exhaled breath to reduce freezing.

breathed out and a purge valve (a button is pressed to open the second stage inlet valve and allow breathing gas to flow freely). It is used to test that the regulator is working and to clear water and debris from the second stage before putting it in your mouth. A diver must also press the purge button to release the pressure inside

the regulator before disconnecting it from the scuba cylinder.

The most common type of second stage has the low-pressure hose passing over the diver's right shoulder. There is a purge button on the front and an exhaust valve at the rear, which directs exhaust bubbles to either side of the face. This design has a top and bottom

Left: A diver using a regulator with a lightweight second stage where the outer shell is made of plastic.

Some modern second stages use plastic where possible to reduce weight and corrosion, though some metal parts are better for cold water diving. Metal housings conduct heat from the water and exhaled breathing gas to the orifice, minimizing the formation of ice crystals. Some plastic housings have metal heat conductors to bring heat to the orifice and some have synthetic coatings to discourage icing.

Most second stages have 'downstream' inlet valves. When a diver inhales, the diaphragm is sucked inwards and pushes against a tilt lever that is connected to a one-way inlet valve. This causes the valve to open and supply the diver with breathing gas. Because the inlet valve opens away from the gas flow it is termed downstream. This system is fail-safe; if the valve malfunctions then it will remain open instead of closing and cutting off the supply of breathing gas. When a diver inhales, the exhaust valve is sucked into the closed position, when the diver exhales, the inlet valve closes and the exhaust valve is forced open. Other innovations include venturi-assistance, which reduces resistance to the flow of breathing gas in the second stage, and sections inside the second

and must be used the right way up, but some can be altered to fit over the opposite shoulder. If they are too small, this design will emit exhaust bubbles in front of the mask, obscuring your view.

Another type of second stage has the diaphragm and exhaust valve on the opposite side to the low-pressure inlet hose. Often smaller and lighter, this type can be used on either side of the face so that the low-pressure hose can pass over either shoulder and exhaust bubbles are directed clear of the face. It also lets photographers get closer to the camera eyepiece. Since either way is up, it is better as an alternate source of breathing gas (octopus rig), because a stressed diver cannot put it in the mouth upside down.

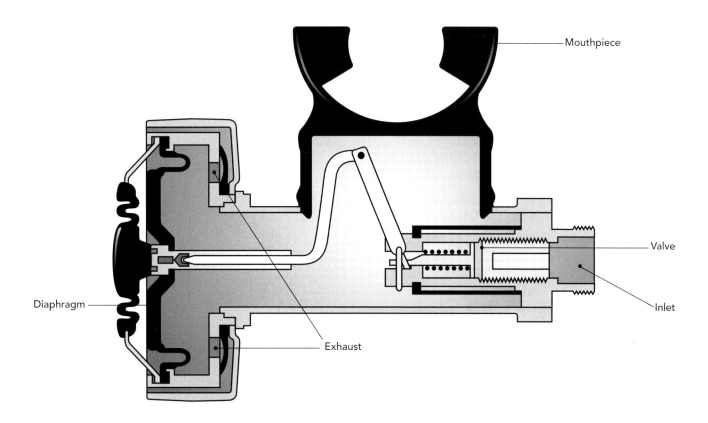

- Mouthpiece
- Valve
- Inlet
- Diaphragm
- Exhaust

Above: With this type of second stage, the exhaust valve is on the opposite side to where the breathing gas enters, so it can be worn over either shoulder. Although the exhaust gases come out at the rear of the second stage housing, they are then channelled round to the front for release to one side of the face.

Above: A second stage that can be worn over either shoulder.

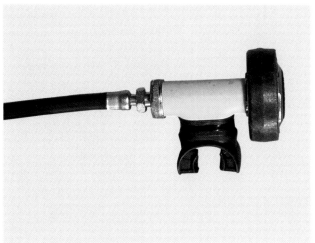

Above: The same type of second stage in yellow, for use as an octopus rig.

stage that collect condensation from exhaled breath and return it with the breathing gas to combat dry mouth. Regulators come with a soft silicone mouthpiece for comfort. Mouldable mouthpieces are available as accessories. These are usually immersed in hot water before the owner bites on them to mould them to fit his or her mouth.

ALTERNATE AIR
(OR OTHER BREATHING GAS) SOURCES

Alternate source of breathing gas second stages (also known as octopus rigs because there is yet another low-pressure hose) are either connected to the

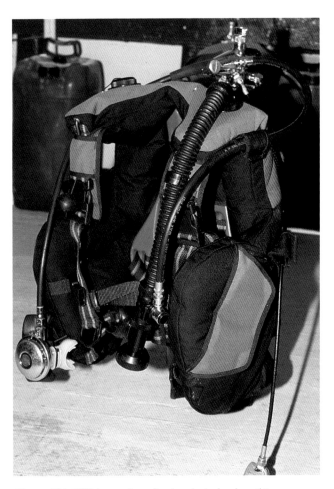

Above: This BCD has a direct-feed and a jacket-breathing mouthpiece, which can be breathed from in an emergency, though the octopus rig is easier to use.

regulator by their own low-pressure hose or to the direct feed for the BCD. In the latter instance, the hose will be so short that in a buddy-breathing situation the diver wearing the BCD should use the alternate source and the buddy should use the main second stage. By convention, separate alternate sources are yellow for easy identification by a low-on-breathing-gas buddy.

If not connected to the low-pressure hose of the BCD, the end containing the second stage should be attached to the owner's chest so that it can be easily found by the buddy and will not dangle in sediment, on the coral or snag. If it is attached with Velcro, the buddy will easily release it.

Another alternate source is a Pony Bottle – a small scuba cylinder, with its own regulator, strapped to the main cylinder. There are self-contained ascent bottles with built-in regulators such as Spare Air units, but they do not contain enough breathing gas to be really useful.

REGULATOR ACCESSORIES

Both ends of the flexible hoses are subject to stress where they are crimped to the fitting containing the connecting thread, but the worst strain occurs at the first stage end where the hose has the highest curve. Sleeves that protect the hoses from excessive bending can be fitted at these ends, but they can hide damage so they should be checked regularly. With some regulators, the curve is such that the hoses should be disconnected from the first stage before extended transport such as air travel. This requires the correct size of spanner for reassembly and the correct blanking plugs to be fitted before travelling.

REGULATOR MAINTENANCE

Ideally, you should wash the regulator with freshwater while it is still connected to the cylinder valve with the breathing gas pressure still turned on. Otherwise, disconnect the regulator from the cylinder, but leave it in position while opening the gas slightly, allowing a gentle gas flow to clear moisture from around the inlet of the first stage. Then securely fit the dust cap and keep the first stage higher than the second stage while rinsing it with fresh water. Do not press the purge button.

If you cannot wash the regulator for several dives, when the opportunity does occur, keep the first stage well above the second stage while immersing it in fresh water overnight. When storing regulators make sure there are no sharp bends in the hoses.

Regularly inspect the external filter of the first stage high-pressure inlet. A white or greenish colour shows that water has entered the first stage and might be inside a recently used cylinder. A brown or reddish filter indicates rust from inside a steel cylinder and a blackish or oily filter indicates a cylinder filled from a defective compressor or compressor with a defective filter system.

Replace damaged hoses. Have regulators serviced after six months of heavy use or one year of light use or whenever there is problem with its breathing output or visible damage.

When a regulator is fitted to a cylinder, point the glass of the pressure gauge away from people as you turn on the breathing gas, because the glass may blow out. Check that the cylinder is full by reading the pressure gauge and listen for a leaking O-ring. If the O-ring is leaking, replace it, otherwise turn off the breathing gas until you are about to dive.

Instrumentation and accessories

Some instruments emit audible bleeps or even 'talk,' but these can be very annoying to other divers. Check your instruments often.

Because of the effects of time and depth on divers, there is certain information that is required on every dive. This includes

- the maximum depth reached during the dive
- the current depth
- the actual time spent underwater (bottom time)
- the current gas pressure in the cylinder so that the diver will know roughly how much longer the breathing gas will last.

Divers must carry instruments that provide at least this information as well as a dive planner or decompression tables, or a diving computer, in case the planned bottom time or no-decompression time is exceeded. Ideally the diver should also have a waterproof compass in case the visibility underwater deteriorates.

Above: An analogue 300m (1000ft) true diving watch.

Above right: A submersible pressure gauge is used to show scuba cylinder pressure, the last 30–50 bar are often red.

Right: A Bourdon-type gauge. Pressure straightens the tube, moving the pointer.

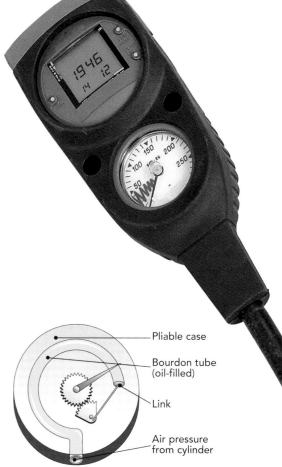

Pliable case

Bourdon tube (oil-filled)

Link

Air pressure from cylinder

SUBMERSIBLE PRESSURE GAUGES (CONTENTS GAUGES) AND CONSOLES

The only way that a diver can tell how much breathing gas is left in the scuba cylinder is with a submersible pressure gauge, also called a contents gauge and, technically, a manometer. These are connected to the high-pressure port of the first stage. If the connection is by a high-pressure hose, some divers fit a console to this gauge so that they can have most of their instruments – pressure gauge, compass and depth gauge or diving computer – in one place.

There are pros and cons to using a console. It is useful to have all the instrumentation in one place. However, one has to hold the console in one hand to read the instruments and the connecting hose needs controlling to prevent it dangling

on coral or snagging. Photographers already have their hands full so many prefer to have most instruments mounted on their wrists. An expensive computer fitted in a console is likely to go with checked baggage for flying, whereas a wrist-mounted one can be worn in the passenger cabin.

There are hose-less digital pressure gauges with a wireless transmitter at the first stage and a receiver at the diving computer or a separate gauge.

The most common mechanical pressure gauge is the oil-filled Bourdon tube type. This is a circular or spiral tube, filled with oil, sealed at one end and closed with a flexible diaphragm at the other. When the high-pressure hose is connected to the outside of the diaphragm, the pressure transmitted to the oil straightens out the tube. The far end of the tube connects, via levers and gears that

magnify the movement, to a pointer that moves across a pressure scale.

In digital gauges a pressure transducer is used to convert the pressure sensed to a voltage level. This is changed by an analogue-to-digital (A/D) converter to a digital signal that is readable by a microprocessor, which performs any mathematical and logic operations. The display can be a digital readout or a graphic.

DEPTH GAUGES

Depth gauges do not measure depth but pressure. They are usually calibrated for seawater at sea level, which means that they will not be accurate for freshwater or for diving at altitude. There are conversion tables for equivalent depths in freshwater and for altitude diving above 300m (1000ft). Some depth gauges are calibrated for freshwater and others can adjust automatically for freshwater and altitude.

There are two things to consider when buying one: whether the user can replace the battery and whether it would be better to buy a dive computer which contains a digital depth gauge.

Far Left: By attaching a console to the pressure gauge, the depth gauge and compass can be conveniently kept together.
Left: Knives are stored in a scabbard (sheath), which should have a positive lock to stop the knife falling out.

Most depth gauges function like Bourdon tube pressure gauges or by outside water pressure acting on a thin metal diaphragm in a sealed case. On descent a pointer moves up the scale while pushing a secondary pointer (zeroed before each dive) ahead of it. On ascent the main pointer moves back down the scale, but the secondary pointer remains where it is, showing the maximum depth reached.

Capillary depth gauges have mostly been superseded. They are made up of a small-diameter, clear plastic tube, wrapped around a circular dial, with the open end of the tube next to zero on the dial. The air in the tube is compressed when the surrounding water under pressure moves into it. While it is one of the most economical and accurate depth gauges, they are only accurate to 9m (30ft) and can clog with debris and air bubbles or salt crystals. Digital depth gauges are the most accurate.

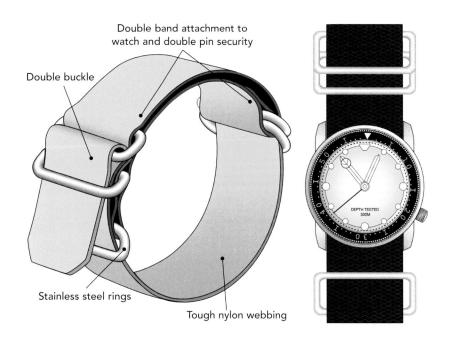

Double band attachment to watch and double pin security

Double buckle

Stainless steel rings

Tough nylon webbing

DEPTH TESTED
300M

Left: Long-lasting woven-nylon straps are available that pass through both watch retaining pins and have a double buckle. All strain is on the strap rather than the pins and if one pin or the buckle fails the watch is not lost.

Right: Analogue watches should have fluorescent hands and numerals and a one-way rotating ratcheted bezel. The bezel is aligned with the minute hand at the start of a dive so that the difference between this time and how far the minute hand has moved round the bezel when you next read it, is the elapsed time. The advantage of the uni-directional bezel is that if it catches on something and is moved, it can only move in the direction that increases the elapsed time, thus adding a safety factor if any decompression stops are required.

UNDERWATER WATCHES AND TIMERS

Dive computers (*see p82*) have largely superseded underwater watches and timers, but batteries can and do fail, so unless you dive with an extra computer for backup, you should also dive with a watch or timer.

The quoted water resistance of watches is only for a static position and does not allow for the extra pressure generated by movements such as swimming, so only watches quoted with a water resistance suitable for 200m (656ft) or more should be used for diving. Digital diving watches should have large numerals and a back light. The stopwatch function is started at the beginning of the dive to show elapsed time. Some digital watches include a thermometer. Activating buttons that are too small are difficult to operate with cold hands or when wearing gloves.

Neoprene rubber straps do not last long and some metal straps will not fit over an exposure suit. These straps are attached to the spring-loaded pins at either end of the watch so the loss of one of these pins or the opening of the buckle means the loss of the watch.

Underwater timers work like dive computers, they are usually activated when the timer descends below 1m (40 inches) and deactivated above that.

DIVING COMPUTERS

Diving computers combine the functions of a watch and depth gauge with various algorithms related to diving tables on the theoretical take-up of nitrogen by various body tissues, with built-in safety factors (*see below and p118*). The advantage of computers over tables is that they can monitor the dives and surface intervals continuously. Computers rely on having batteries in a good state of charge so divers should either enter the water with two computers or with a separate watch, depth gauge and diving tables as a back-up. Diving computers can be purchased with the display in metric or imperial units and some are adjustable for either. Those with small digits can be difficult to read.

Computers eliminate the need for calculations, especially when the diver performs more than two dives in a day. Most diving computers have a thermometer; some automatically compensate for altitude; give adjusted no-decompression times and depths; and automatically recalibrate the depth display for freshwater instead of seawater. Some computers can be adjusted for different breathing gas mixtures; some for the amount of conservatism required in the use of the algorithm; some try to allow for work-rates; and some can download logbook functions to a personal computer. Most diving computers warn the diver if he or she is ascending too fast; will calculate how long the diver should wait before flying; and have a dive planning simulator for further dives. Some will calculate decompression; and some will allow for recent thinking on making deeper stops on the ascent. However, computers are not infallible. They are based on theory, have different degrees of conservatism and at least one model has been found to base some of its calculations on an assumption that is incorrect. Divers using computers should still dive conservatively.

Top: Two different makes of computer (the left one has user-replaceable batteries) and room key on a wrist band.
Right: Batteries fail, so either dive with two computers or take a separate watch, depth guage and diving tables as back-up.

Above: This diver wears a compass permanently attached to his BCD so that he cannot forget it and enter the water without it.

Cutting instruments, knives and shears

Diving knives are multipurpose tools used for prying, digging, measuring, pounding, knocking against the main cylinder to attract other divers' attention and, most importantly, cutting ropes, ships' baggage nets, fishing nets, fishing lines and seaweed, all of which could entangle divers and are particularly dangerous underwater. If the main knife is used as a tool then the diver should also have a separate small knife that is only used for cutting.

Serrated blades are more effective for cutting ropes. Normal knife blades are not efficient for cutting discarded monofilament fishing nets or lines because they stretch.

Some knives have a small sharp groove for cutting monofilament line, but several tools have been specially designed for this. Many divers prefer cut-through-anything shears. There are designs that combine a diving knife with shears.

All knives are stored in a scabbard (sheath), which can be attached to a diver's limbs with flexible straps or placed in a built-in exposure suit pocket. Larger knives are normally attached to the outside of the leg, but for wreck diving or other situations where the knife could get snagged, are attached to the inside of the leg. Some divers attach a small knife to their arm in case they get too snarled up to be able to reach a knife attached to the leg.

DIVING COMPASSES

Diving compasses are identical to land compasses except for being waterproof. More expensive models are larger, easier to read and filled with liquid to help dampen down the oscillations of the needle or compass card (*see p109*).

Compasses are not required on most dives, but underwater visibility is rarely more than 30m (100ft) and sudden changes in conditions or currents can seriously reduce visibility. It is wise to have one permanently attached to your console or BCD.

Remember that large ferrous metal objects such as wrecks will affect the compass reading.

Above: A sturdy dive knife is essential for cutting ropes or fishing nets. Attach the scabbard (sheath) to the outside of your lower leg, where it can be easily reached.

Underwater lights and batteries

Underwater lights come in all shapes, sizes and powers. Those used to illuminate nooks, crannies and wrecks in daylight can be large and powerful, but those used on night dives should be low-power to avoid scaring marine creatures into hiding. Powerful lights use rechargeable Nickel-Cadmium (NiCd or NiCad) or Nickel Metal Hydride (NiMH) batteries. Low-power lights can also be powered by alkaline batteries.

The cadmium in NiCds is a highly toxic heavy metal. Batteries are environmentally unfriendly in general, but NiMH batteries do not contain toxic ingredients.

Underwater lights can have wide-angle or narrow beams or switch from one to the other. Their bulbs can be anything from standard, halogen and xenon to high intensity discharge (HID) that uses a high-voltage arc instead of a glowing filament to light-emitting diode (LED) technology. LEDs do not burn out, have impressive battery life and will not break if the light is dropped. They glow instead of emitting a beam and produce a cooler (bluer) light than halogen or xenon bulbs. It penetrates quite well.

Lights designed to illuminate video subjects will have light of the colour-temperature equivalent to that of daylight. Without the cooling effect of the water, powerful underwater lights can be damaged by overheating and should not be left switched on in air.

Dive lights require care. When changing the batteries, check the O-ring and gland for damage and carefully regrease them. Remove the batteries for long storage; weak batteries can leak or build up a pressure of hydrogen gas, which is explosive. If a light floods, it may be saved if the batteries are removed immediately and everything rinsed in fresh water. Remove the batteries for travelling as the light may overheat and melt if switched on accidentally.

Attention-gaining devices

A useful safety device in open water is the surface marker buoy (SMB), a highly visible surface float that sometimes incorporates a dive flag. SMBs are connected to the diver by a thin, strong line. This line is wound around a reel to avoid entanglement in excess line and it can be reeled out easily on descent and reeled in on ascent.

When diving in strong currents, choppy seas, poor visibility or swimming out from the shore, SMBs are good for safety. Where jet skis, water-skiers, pleasure and commercial boats ply the same area, it may be law to use them.

SMBs can be augmented with flashing strobe lights for night diving or in poor visibility. Chemical light sticks can be used, but

Top: The main function of SMBs is to let the surface boat cover know where the divers are at all times and provide it with a means of communicating with the divers by jerking it sharply.
Above: SMBs are attached to the diver by a thin, strong line.

some areas now ban them for environmental reasons.

Most SMBs are inflatable for easy transport. Only one diver of a buddy pair or group diving together, would display an SMB, since the lines are easily tangled if several are used. However, each individual diver should carry a delayed-deployment SMB, rolled up in a BCD pocket, in case of separation from the group or buddy. The tube types can also be used as lifting bags.

Above: *'Rescue sausages' are highly visible orange or yellow tubes about 1.5m (5ft) long, closed at the top end. It is either open at the base for inflation by the diver's regulator second stage or it has an oral inflation valve.*

The open-base type of rescue tube must be inflated underwater. The better open-base tubes have an internal baffle that stops them from accidentally deflating at the surface. Rescue sausages and collapsible flags can be raised above the swell when on the surface.

Most SMBs, and all the tube types, require a small sinker weight attached to their base to help them float in the upright position.

Every diver's worst nightmare is floating on the surface in heavy seas with their surface cover a long way off or completely out of sight. Apart from SMBs you can carry manual whistles, compressed breathing gas whistles that connect to the direct-feed, a heliograph, waterproof flares or dye markers that colour the water over a large enough area to be seen from a search aircraft. When diving in a country where an air

search is possible, there are waterproof emergency radio beacons similar to those used by yachtsmen. It is important that divers in this predicament remain together, tied together with a buddy line.

HELIOGRAPHS
Use old CDs for reflecting the sun's rays to attract the attention of the boat cover. Some divers stick two old CDs together so that both sides of the heliograph become reflective for ease of use.

POWER WHISTLES (HORNS)
These are much more effective than oral whistles at attracting the boat cover. To avoid damaging your hearing, they should be held clear of the ears and pointing away.

Even power whistles can be drowned out by loud music on the boat so insist that music be turned off while divers are in the water.

Above: *Power whistles, also called air horns, are whistles powered by low-pressure compressed breathing gas. They are fitted in line with the direct-feed hose where it feeds breathing gas into the BCD.*

PINGERS, BANGERS, KNOCKERS AND RATTLES

There are several devices that can be used for gaining the attention of other divers when underwater. For short distances the cheapest method is to tap the scuba cylinder with the handle of a diving knife or, more conveniently, use a pinger or rattle.

The diver pulls the bead of a pinger away and releases it to strike the scuba cylinder with a loud ping that can be heard clearly underwater.

Rattles are small stainless steel tubes containing ball bearings that rattle when the tubes are shaken.

Below: Pingers, also called bangers or knockers, are a bead of hard plastic threaded onto a loop of bungee cord which is slipped around the scuba cylinder.

Jon line (general utility and buddy line)

A jon line is a 2 or 4m (6½ft or 13ft) length of strong line, 25mm (1-inch) tape or bungee cord with any number of uses including that of a buddy-line. It is connected to the diver with a karabiner (snaplink) and the other end has a special spring clip that will securely lock round rope, anchor chain or shotlines with one hand operation.

If the current is strong while the divers are descending, they can loosely wrap their jon line around the anchor line or shotline to avoid being swept away. When ascending, a jon line enables divers to hang on an anchor line or shotline with hands-free attachment during safety or decompression stops. It is particularly useful where several divers are holding the same depth. Bungee cord takes up the shock and much of the movement while attached to an anchor line or shotline of a boat or buoy that is bouncing around in a swell.

You can also imitate a prusik knot with the end of the line. Wrap the end several times around the anchor line, pull it tight and knot it,

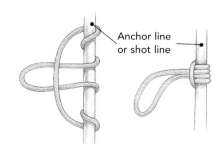

Above: Instead of using a clip on the anchor line you can use a short loop of line to form a mountaineer's prusik knot and clip to that. You can easily move this along the anchor line by hand to change your depth.

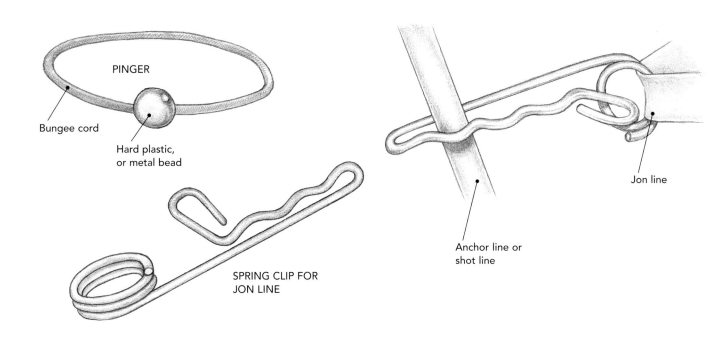

PINGER

Bungee cord

Hard plastic, or metal bead

SPRING CLIP FOR JON LINE

Anchor line or shot line

Jon line

then use a karabiner to clip the line to itself. Jon lines were named after the originator, Jon Hulbert.

LINE REELS

Enclosed reels minimize the line spilling over the edges, but if they jam underwater they are more difficult to clear. Open-face reels require more care when paying out the line, but if they jam underwater they are easier to clear.

DIVE SLATES

Regular buddy-pairs and photographers and their models will have a limited set of signals, some divers learn sign language and there are expensive instruments for voice communication, but most divers carry a plastic slate. This is a semimat white plastic board that is lightly roughened with sandpaper on both sides so that it can be written on with an ordinary lead pencil. There are other writing instruments and easily erased magnetic screens, but a plastic slate and pencil works best. The main use for a dive slate is to confer with another diver, but it can be used for note-taking, checklists, dive plans, navigational details or logbook information. Glow-in-the-dark slates are useful on night dives.

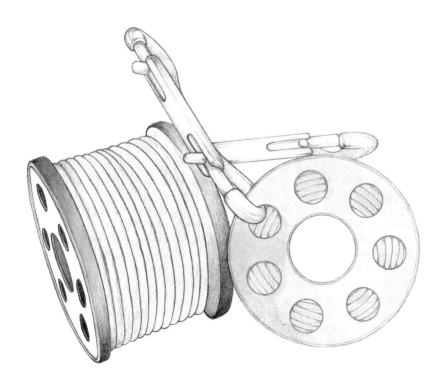

Above: Line reels are used to pay out line to a surface marker buoy or to set out a safety guideline when penetrating a wreck or caves.

Electronic shark repellent

Sharks have a sensory system called the Ampullae de Lorenzini – gel-filled canals connecting the surface of the snout to the nervous system – that are sensitive to the tiny electrical impulses generated by muscle movement in all animals. Predatory sharks home in on their prey by sight, smell and pressure waves, but when they get close, many close their eyes with a nictitating membrane (or in the case of Great Whites, roll their eyes backwards) and use their Ampullae de Lorenzini. This system is particularly useful when prey is buried in the sand. Other objects that produce electricity fool the system, which is why Great White Sharks mouth metal boats and propellers.

The Natal Sharks Board, a South African government agency created to protect divers, surfers and swimmers while preserving the shark population, researched electronic repellents to reduce shark attacks. Following a device patented in America in 1962, they found the pulsing electric field most disliked by the more dangerous sharks (the Great White, Tiger, Bull and Oceanic Whitetip) and incorporated it into a battery powered unit and marketed it in 1995 as the Shark POD (Protective Oceanic Device).

The battery pack and one electrode was strapped to the diver's scuba cylinder and another electrode attached to one of the diver's fins. The cable with the on/off switch is brought over the shoulder for accessibility. The elliptical electrical field created repels sharks at between 1m (3ft) and 7m (23ft) without affecting other creatures, though divers have felt shocks in metal fillings. The unit is not effective in freshwater because it will not conduct the electrical current, similarly, both electrodes must be in the water to complete the circuit for the system to work.

In January 2002 an Australian company SeaChange Technology Pty Ltd acquired an exclusive license to produce smaller, cheaper and more energy-efficient versions and marketed units under the name Shark Shield.

Dive flags

Flown on its own, the international 'A' Flag signifies that a vessel has divers in the water so other craft should keep clear and reduce speed. It is illegal to fly it when there are no divers in the water.

American recreational divers have produced their own diving flag. It does not have any legal international meaning and is often flown outside diving establishments and on vessels that do not have divers in the water. Some diving operators or shops add their own logo to this flag.

Diving compressors

For recreational diving we use high-pressure, low-volume compressors to fill scuba cylinders. Only non-toxic lubricants should be used and the air intake must be kept up-wind from possible contamination such as the exhaust of an internal combustion engine or wet paint.

To reach the very high pressures required by divers, the compressor has three or four stages; pumping to progressively higher pressures. After each stage the gas is cooled and filtered. Compressors have condensation-release systems to discharge any condensed water and filters that clean and dry the

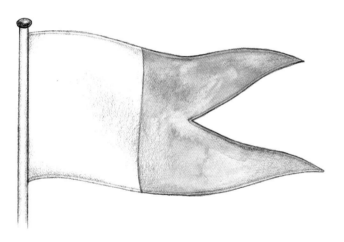

Above: The official flag that covers both professional and sport diving is the maritime International Code of Signals 'A' Flag, Alpha. Flown on its own, it signifies that a vessel has divers in the water and other craft should keep clear.

Above: The American diving flag has no international meaning. It is often flown on vessels even when they do not have divers in the water. Unlike the Code of Signals 'A' Flag, it is not illegal to do so.

Above: *Large compressors at fixed locations are driven by three-phase electric motors. The compressed air is stored in a reservoir system, known as an air storage bank, and decanted into scuba cylinders when required.*

Above: *Where compressors have to be mobile they are driven by an internal combustion engine and connected directly to the scuba cylinders. Petrol (gasoline) engines are lighter to move around, but diesel engines give less trouble in hot climates.*

gas. These must be changed regularly. When filling, scuba cylinders should be placed in a water bath to keep them cool.

Enriched Air Nitrox and DNAx

Blending oxygen with air requires high oxygen concentrations. These need equipment that is free of contamination (oxygen clean) to reduce the risk of explosion and fire. Air can now be denitrogenated through a semi-permeable membrane system and, because it never exceeds 40% oxygen, the equipment does not have to be fully oxygen clean.

Low-pressure air goes through a filter system to remove hydrocarbons and other contaminants. Then the air passes into a membrane canister that contains thousands of hair-like, hollow membrane fibres. The oxygen is more transferable than the nitrogen so it permeates across the membranes at a manageable rate. The proper gas ratio is adjusted with a needle valve and some of the nitrogen is dumped as waste gas. The denitrogenated gas is then fed to a standard compressor for directly filling scuba cylinders or storing the gas in a Nitrox bank to be decanted as required.

Equipment care

Any equipment that has moving parts can malfunction so it should be regularly inspected and well-maintained with routine servicing. Divers should be thoroughly trained in how their equipment functions and be able to cope with any equipment malfunction. (*For a list of tools and spares, see p182*).

All equipment will last longer and is less likely to malfunction if kept out of the sun and washed with freshwater after each use. Seawater contains a variety of salts and other minerals that can be corrosive and cause jamming or deterioration of equipment. Chlorine and mild acids added to swimming pool water to retard the growth of bacteria, fungus or algae, can also damage equipment. Direct sunlight can damage rubber or silicone products such as the face mask, fins, wet suit etc. Strong sunlight can also damage diving instruments such as computers, depth gauges and pressure gauges by overheating and distortion of O-ring seals. Diving equipment should not be left on the open deck of a dive boat or on a beach.

BASIC TRAINING

No reputable diving establishment will supply you with full scuba cylinders or allow you to dive without an instructor unless you have a certification card (C-card) from a recognized training agency. This C-card will normally be recognized by dive centres affiliated to other training agencies as long as you can produce evidence of regular and recent diving experience, usually in the form of an up-to-date diving logbook. If you have not dived for a while, you should take a refresher course. Training requires practice so that when problems occur, the diver will react correctly without having to think about it. You can enrol with a diving club for several months of weekly training sessions and enjoy the camaraderie of a club environment; or take an intensive, much shorter course with a diving school. The system you choose depends on your temperament, cash flow and time available.

Diving schools aim at imparting competence sufficient for diving in warm tropical waters. Diving in more demanding conditions will be taught on further courses. The advantage of diving schools is that classes will be small, in some cases one-to-one. Courses run by clubs take longer and their more advanced courses often include training that diving schools consider to be specialist courses.

Which training agency?

Nowadays there is little difference in the quality of training by recognised training agencies (*see p11*). Training agencies and instructors will vary the order in which they teach subjects, this book only contains the basics. Lectures will be given on the science, physiology and first aid that relate to diving, and dive planning.

A short swimming test will inform the instructor that you are comfortable and confident in the water. This is followed by a similar test using snorkel equipment and then lectures on the basics of diving equipment and diving.

Basic scuba equipment

Students must first become familiar with the basic scuba equipment and learn how to check everything before use.

Full scuba cylinders have a dust cap or strip of sticky tape over the valve outlet to signify that they have been filled. Remove this and open the cylinder valve briefly to clear water or dust from the outlet. Check the valve-to-regulator O-ring for nicks and wipe a wet finger around it to remove any salt crystals or hairs; this will help it to form a good seal. Remove the dust cap from the regulator first stage and slip its connector over the valve's outlet. Make sure that it is the right way up and the correct size for the recess in the cylinder valve. Do up the yoke-connector (A-clamp) or DIN screw fitting hand-tight.

Point the pressure gauge away from anyone in case the glass blows out and open the valve slightly while listening for the sound of leaking air. If you can hear a leak you may not have fitted the regulator to the valve correctly so close off the valve and try fitting the regulator again. If you can still hear a leak then either you require a new scuba cylinder-to-regulator O-ring, or the fitting on the regulator is the wrong size for the recess machined into the scuba cylinder valve. Inform your instructor and the correct fittings will be sorted out for you.

Now turn the valve fully open until you feel resistance and close it off by a quarter of a turn. At this stage, check the pressure gauge to make sure that the scuba cylinder is full.

The vast majority of divers still use normal air as their breathing gas and therefore this air is also used for inflating their BCDs and, if worn, dry suit. However, where divers use other breathing gases such as Nitrox, Heliox or Trimix, in most instances this will also be used for inflating their BCDs and, if worn, dry suit. For the sake of brevity, we have often used the word 'air' when in fact 'breathing gas' would be a more accurate term.

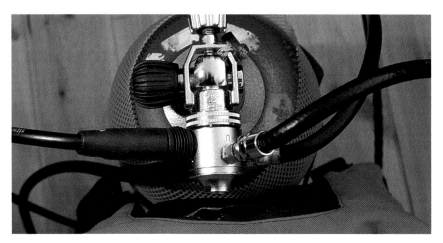

Above: *The correct way to fit a regulator first stage to a scuba cylinder valve using a yoke-connector (A-clamp).*

Now place the second stage mouthpiece into your mouth and get used to breathing through it. Second stages vary in the size and angle of their mouthpieces so you may have to try several before you find one that is comfortable. This should be taken into account when you purchase your own regulator. Breathe through the second stage while looking at the pressure gauge: if the needle swings drastically then something is wrong, either the cylinder valve is not fully open or the regulator requires servicing. In either case the equipment must not be used until the fault has been remedied.

Once you have confirmed that you have a full scuba cylinder, it is time to close the valve, remove the regulator first stage and fit the BCD. First close the valve and then release the air pressure by pressing the purge button at the centre front of the second stage, you will then be able to undo the regulator to scuba cylinder valve yoke or DIN screw connector and remove the regulator.

Above: Inspect the cylinder-to-regulator O-ring for cuts, hairs and salt. Wipe it with a wet finger for a better seal.

Above: Turn the valve on to blow away any dust.

Above: If you use one, fit the BCD emergency cylinder to the scuba cylinder and fill it up slowly by opening both valves.

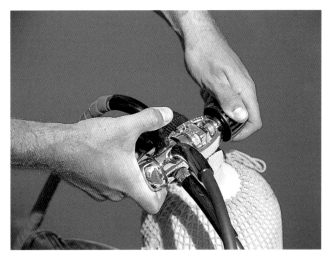

Above: Fit the regulator first stage yoke-connector (A-clamp) or DIN fitting to the cylinder and do it up.

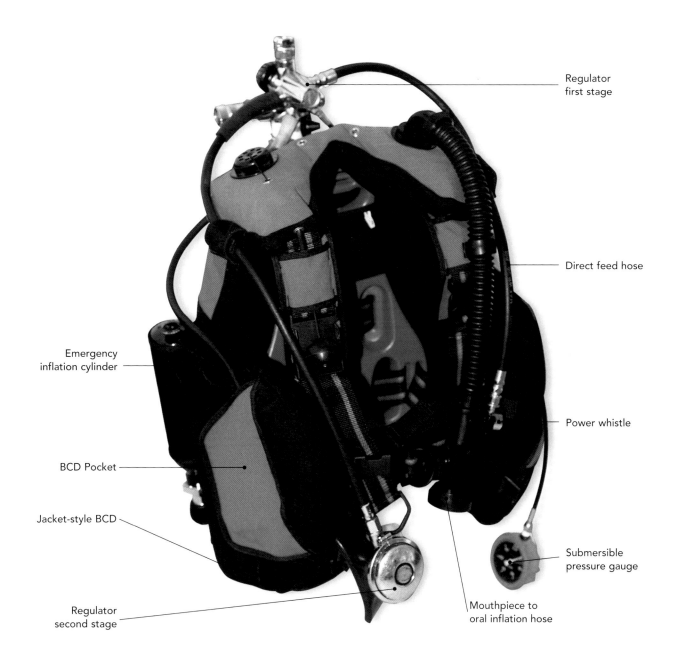

Regulator
first stage

Direct feed hose

Emergency
inflation cylinder

Power whistle

BCD Pocket

Submersible
pressure gauge

Jacket-style BCD

Regulator
second stage

Mouthpiece to
oral inflation hose

Filling the BCD emergency cylinder

If your BCD has a refillable emergency cylinder, you should fill it before fitting the regulator. Ensure that the main scuba cylinder is at full working pressure, remove the emergency cylinder from your BCD by undoing its yoke-connector and connect it to the scuba cylinder valve. Fully open the valve of the emergency cylinder and then slowly open the valve of the scuba cylinder. When the sound of air flowing between the two cylinders ceases, close both valves. The valve on the emergency cylinder has a purge button on a spring. You must depress this button to purge the air remaining between

Above: BCD, regulator and accessories fitted to a scuba cylinder, with the BCD's emergency cylinder shown fitted in the left of the picture.

the valves before you can disconnect the emergency cylinder. Refit the emergency cylinder to the BCD and briefly open the valve to make sure that the BCD inflates correctly.

Fitting the BCD and regulator to the scuba cylinder

BCDs have straps on a cam-action buckle (called cam-bands) that will fit around cylinders of various diameters. They are usually made of webbing that may stretch when wet, so soak them in water before fitting them around a cylinder. They should be slipped over the cylinder with the BCD backpack facing the outlet of the cylinder valve and far enough down so that the valve is just higher than the top of the BCD backpack. Do not undo these straps completely because they are threaded through a cam-action buckle in such a way that they can not come loose by mistake. Once in position, pull the straps as tight as possible and force the cam over on itself until it locks into position.

Refit the regulator first stage so that the low-pressure hose for the primary second stage (the one through which you intend to breathe, not the octopus rig), passes over whichever shoulder would put the second stage the correct way up in your mouth. Connect any low-pressure direct feed hose to the BCD and press the inflation valve to make sure that it is working.

Fit all hoses into their retaining clips or Velcro-covered tabs and, with a buddy holding the weight of the equipment, slip into the shoulder straps of the BCD. Make sure that nothing is trapped beneath them and adjust the straps for comfort. Lean forward and tighten the waist strap. Bend backwards and check that the regulator first stage does not hit your neck or head. If it does, it is too high. Loosening the shoulder straps of the BCD will lower the regulator first stage, but if they

Top: A cam-band with the cam-action buckle in the open position.

Centre: This scuba cylinder is protected by a plastic mesh sleeve. The cam-band has the cam-action locked closed over it.

are too loose it can strike your head when you jump into the water – so you will need to lower the scuba cylinder in the BCD cam-band/s.

Point the pressure gauge away from anyone, in case the glass blows out, and open the scuba cylinder on/off valve. Fit the primary second stage into your mouth and try breathing through it. If the hose to the primary second stage is too long or too short, the mouthpiece will either push or pull at your mouth. This can be adjusted by rotating the scuba cylinder slightly within the BCD cam-band until the mouthpiece fits comfortably. Fit the weight belt and enter the water.

Above: *A diver showing excellent buoyancy control over Acropora corals near Râs Muhammad while using a single bladder Buoyancy Compensator Device.*

BCD AS LIFE JACKET

A BCD can make it difficult to achieve a face-up position at the surface. The height of the scuba cylinder where it is attached to the backpack of the BCD affects the diver's angle of flotation. Adjusting this height may be a compromise between achieving face-up flotation and being too high, when the regulator first stage will strike the back of the diver's neck when leaping into the water. Divers can fit some of their weights directly to the scuba cylinder. In an emergency at the surface you may have to move weights around to the rear of your body to achieve face-up flotation or jettison them altogether to float higher in the water.

The cylinder, BCD and weights can be donned in the water. Fit the BCD and regulator to the cylinder, turn on the valve and make sure that everything is functioning correctly. Inflate the BCD and float it in the water. Get into the water and don the whole unit. Get someone to hand you the weight belt, taking care not to drop it in open water. Deflate the BCD.

Pool training

You are now ready to try breathing underwater. Do not wear your fins. Fit the primary second stage mouthpiece into your mouth, fit your mask and get into the shallow end of the swimming pool.

Next you must learn correct weighting. Wear all the equipment you expect to use in the pool, and ensure that you can quickly release the weight belt if you have a problem. Begin by fitting one small weight to the belt, put the belt on and do it up. Bend forward in the water and let your legs float up behind you. One weight is unlikely to be enough, so you will have to do this several times, adding a weight each time until your body slowly sinks down to the bottom. You have now found the correct weight to wear in freshwater when dressed as you are. You will require more weight in saltwater or if wearing an exposure suit. Having done this, practise how to release the weight belt with one hand in an emergency.

CLEARING THE SECOND-STAGE MOUTHPIECE

This is best practised by kneeling on the bottom in shallow water so that you can stand up with your head clear of the water if you encounter problems.

While in your mouth the regulator second stage will not allow water to leak in unless the exhaust valve is damaged or has collected

Above: *The first step in dive training is learning to breathe underwater using scuba equipment. With the instructor standing by, hold onto the ladder or side of the pool bend over and submerge your head. This does not feel natural. At first there will be a tendency to hold your breath and you will be conscious of each breath sounding surprisingly loud, but you will slowly relax.*

grit that prevents it from sealing. However, if you remove the mouthpiece, the second stage downstream of its valve will fill with water. It is cleared by breathing out through the regulator before you breathe in. If your second stage has a top and bottom, you must fit it into your mouth the right way up, with the exhaust valve at the bottom. If you have insufficient breath left to clear the second stage, you can clear it by holding it clear of your mouth and pressing the purge button. The mouthpiece itself must remain at the lowest point of the second stage to ensure that the air inside the second stage keeps the water out. The easiest way to do this is by holding the second stage above your head with the mouthpiece pointing downwards while you press the purge button and tilt your head back so that you can refit the mouthpiece into your mouth while it continues to be the lowest point of the second stage. Once the mouthpiece is back in your mouth you should breathe out before you breathe in.

CLEARING THE MASK

All masks will leak at some time. Also, another diver can accidentally knock it off your face. If the mask is still in place, there are two possibilities. If the mask is fitted with a purge valve, you can clear most of the water by snorting out through your nose into the mask. However, purge valves cannot be relied on and often collect grit to become the cause of the leak. More effective is to tilt the head back, press one hand gently against the top of the mask and snort out strongly through the nose. This will displace the water through the bottom of the mask.

To practise for a situation where your mask is knocked off, remove it completely, make sure that it is

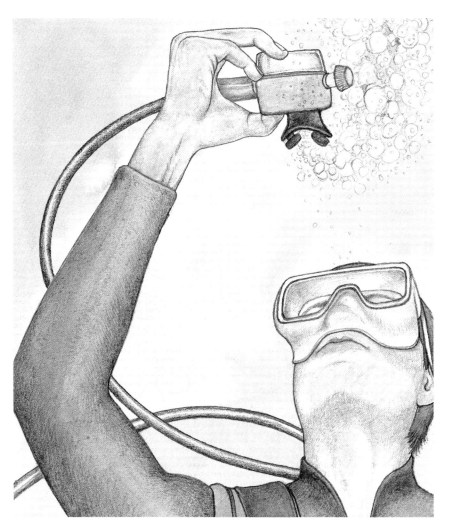

Above: Clear the second stage of water by holding the mouthpiece above your head and pressing the purge button.

MISTING FACE MASKS

Face masks mist over due to the temperature difference between the diver's face and the water. There are many remedies for this ranging from proprietary demisters to toothpaste and the diver's own spittle, but the cheapest effective remedy is washing-up liquid. Whatever demisting agent you use, rub a couple of drops over the inside of the glass and leave it there until you are about to enter the water, then flush it out of the mask with water and put the mask on. Freshwater will work just as well as seawater for washing out the demisting agent.

Above: To fit the mask, hold the strap away from the mask and ensure the mask is the correct way up.

Above: Clear hair from the forehead if necessary and fit the mask over your face. Then pull the strap over the back of your head.

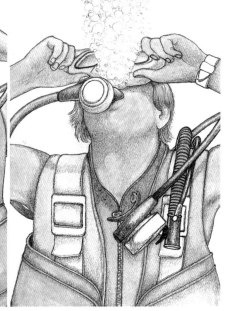

Above: Tilt the head back, press the top edge of the mask and snort out through the nose to force water out of the mask.

the right way up, hold the strap in one hand and the mask in the other. Clear hair from the forehead if necessary and fit the mask over your face. Pull the strap over the back of your head, tilt your head back, press the top edge of the mask and snort into it to clear out the water. This should be practised in progressively deeper water.

You might ask what happens if you have a camera in one hand. I place either the lanyard over the crook of one arm or bend the strobe arm and put that over the crook of one arm to free the hand.

SHARING THE AIR (BUDDY BREATHING)

Before you can leave the safety of shallow water you must practise sharing air. If you keep a constant check on your pressure gauge and begin your ascent when the scuba cylinder is about one-quarter full, you should never run low on air. However, you can have an unforeseen problem such as a burst O-ring between the scuba cylinder valve and the regulator first stage, a sudden leak in the high-pressure hose or having to swim against a strong current.

Most divers have an octopus rig or an alternate air supply attached to their BCD direct feed. This is the easiest way to share air as each has the equivalent of a second stage.

Signal that you are out of air, then take your buddy's alternate air supply, make sure it is the right way up and that the mouthpiece remains pointing downwards. Purge the unit of water, keep the mouthpiece pointing downwards, place it into your mouth and breathe out before you breathe in. When sharing air, buddies should hold onto each other's shoulder straps and ascend slowly. It can happen that someone does not have an alternate air supply, so you must train for this; first on land and then in shallow water.

Signal that you are out of air, approach your buddy face to face and take a firm hold of each other's BCD shoulder straps. The diver who still has air (the donor) takes two breaths and then puts the second stage close to the recipient's mouth with the mouthpiece pointing down. The recipient takes the second stage, keeps the mouthpiece pointing down, purges it, puts it in the mouth, breathes out and then takes two breaths before handing it back to the donor. This cycle should be repeated. In this kind of emergency both divers would be ascending slowly, so the diver who is not actually breathing through the mouthpiece, should exhale gently to stimulate the release of expanding air while ascending.

Once you are comfortable with this exercise you can repeat it while swimming horizontally.

In a real life situation the diver who is out of air is likely to be stressed and may not behave rationally. If you do not have a highly visible octopus, the distressed diver may grab for the second stage in your mouth. Be prepared for this, always have your own alternate air supply and be prepared to use it yourself if your buddy grabs your primary second stage.

Below: *Buddy breathing, where two divers share a single air supply, is made easier by using an alternate air supply (octopus rig), but divers must also be prepared to share the second stage of one air supply.*

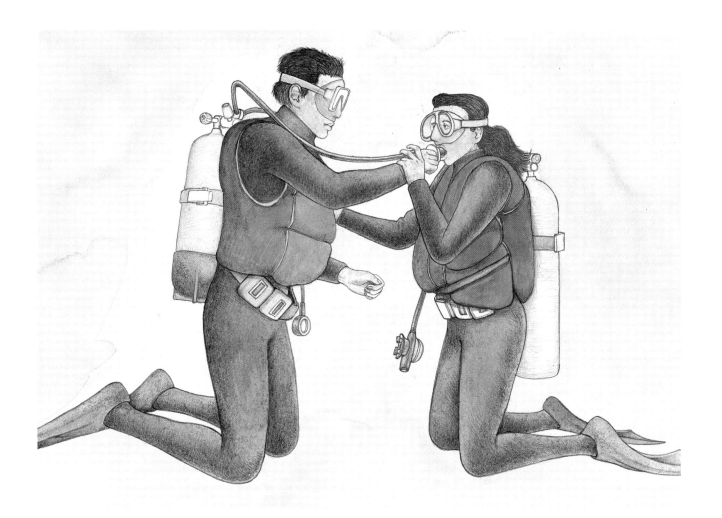

Hand signals

Hand signals are not standardized, so if you dive with someone who has trained with a different agency, you should compare hand signals before you dive. It is easy to say 'decide on which hand signals to use before a dive' but in situations of stress divers are likely to revert to those they have been trained with, so it is better to be able to recognize each other's hand signals.

ok?/ok

ok?/ok

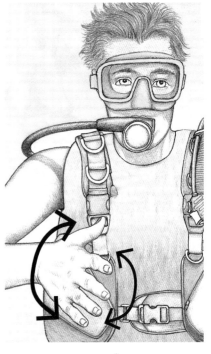

not ok

come here

stop/hold it/stay there

go down/going down

which direction?

go that way

you lead, I'll follow

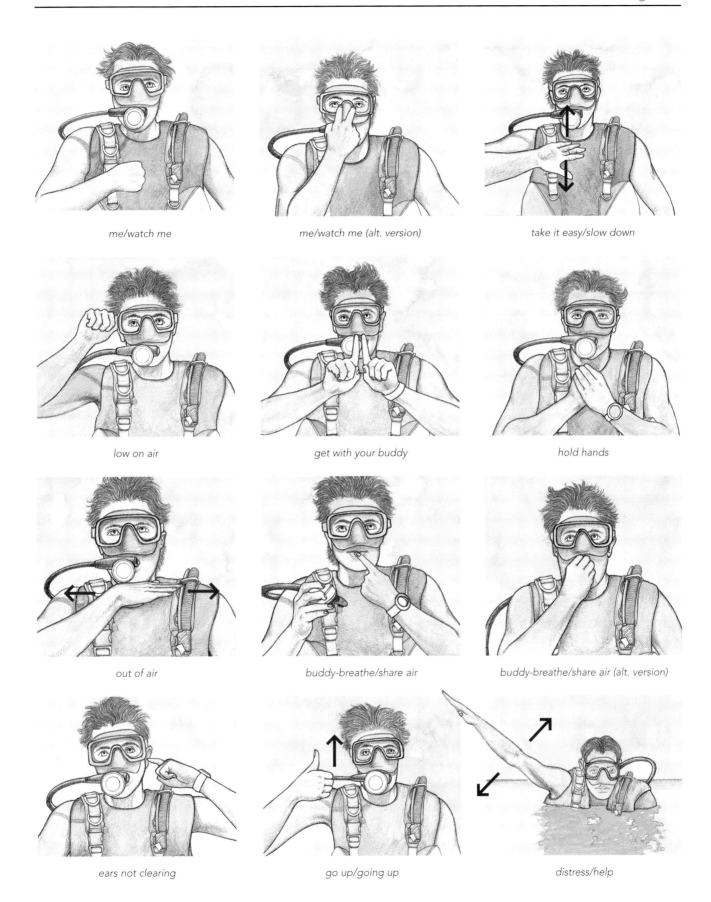

me/watch me

me/watch me (alt. version)

take it easy/slow down

low on air

get with your buddy

hold hands

out of air

buddy-breathe/share air

buddy-breathe/share air (alt. version)

ears not clearing

go up/going up

distress/help

Training in deeper water

Swim to the deep end of the pool, signal to your instructor that you are about to descend and expel any excess air from your BCD. There are two methods of descent from the surface: feet first or head first. With either method it is important to be correctly weighted. If you have too much weight you will have a rapid and possibly unsafe descent, could experience problems with your ears, sinuses and mask squeeze and, if over a coral reef, could crash into live coral and kill it. If you have too little weight you may have to make several tiring attempts to get below the surface.

Descents should be slow and controlled and you should keep an eye on your buddy so that you can keep together without colliding.

If you suffer from equalization problems or are carrying anything, it is easiest to descend feet first. If you are correctly weighted, breathing out hard will be enough to initiate your descent. If you have no equalization problems you can make a surface dive. This is the same as that performed by experienced snorkellers and is often referred to as a duck-dive or pike-dive.

Ascents should be slower than your smallest bubbles. Get into the habit of breathing out as you ascend and checking above you to ensure that you are not likely to bump into anything or anyone on the surface. Once back on the surface, look around you, inflate your BCD if necessary and give the okay signal to your instructor.

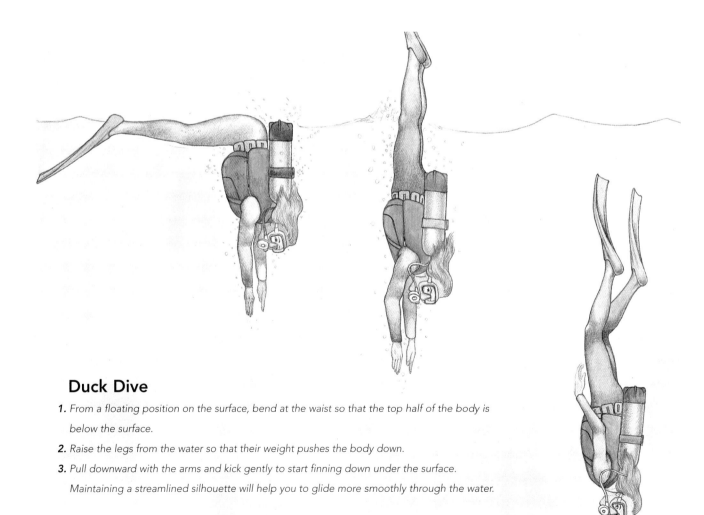

Duck Dive

1. *From a floating position on the surface, bend at the waist so that the top half of the body is below the surface.*
2. *Raise the legs from the water so that their weight pushes the body down.*
3. *Pull downward with the arms and kick gently to start finning down under the surface. Maintaining a streamlined silhouette will help you to glide more smoothly through the water.*

Mobility and buoyancy

In order to be comfortably mobile underwater you should be neutrally buoyant. If you are too buoyant you will tend to float upwards, while if you are not buoyant enough you will tend to sink. Only if you are neutrally buoyant will you be able to maintain your position. You require sufficient weight to leave the surface without floundering, but too much will make you sink too quickly.

Your overall buoyancy is also affected by the equipment you carry. Underwater lights and cameras can act as weights, but large housings may be buoyant and require their own weights.

On descent you will lose buoyancy as items compress. This effect is greatest near the surface. Small changes in buoyancy can be compensated for by your breathing. A large breath will expand your chest and make you more buoyant. A forced exhalation or shallow breathing will contract your chest and make you less buoyant.

As you dive deeper you will have to feed some gas into your BCD to compensate for loss of buoyancy. On ascent you will need to dump (vent off) gas from your BCD to compensate for increasing buoyancy. You will also need to dump gas from your BCD to compensate for the increasing buoyancy of the cylinder as the air is used up. To feed gas into your BCD, either press a button on the direct feed

---

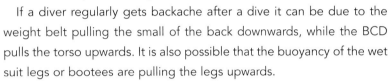

HOW TO WEAR WEIGHTS

Weights should be worn evenly on the weight belt, a mirror image of each other on both sides of the body and positioned as far forward as is comfortable without interfering with the quick-release buckle. Nothing is more uncomfortable than a lopsided weight belt or weights catching between the cylinder and your back.

If a diver regularly gets backache after a dive it can be due to the weight belt pulling the small of the back downwards, while the BCD pulls the torso upwards. It is also possible that the buoyancy of the wet suit legs or bootees are pulling the legs upwards.

- Check that you are not carrying more weight than you need.
- Try wearing an athlete's neoprene back support.
- When wearing a thin wet suit make sure that the bootees are not manufactured from thicker neoprene, which would cause the lower legs to be more buoyant than the upper legs.
- Try wearing ankle weights. These will keep the legs in a lower position, removing some of the strain on the back.
- Try using a weight harness or BCD with an integrated weight system.

---

from your regulator or, if you have one, by briefly opening the valve on the small emergency cylinder that you filled from the main scuba cylinder before the dive.

It is also possible to add breathing gas to the BCD orally while underwater. Unclip the BCD's large corrugated tube, breathe in from your regulator and remove the second stage mouthpiece from your mouth. Place the mouthpiece attached to the BCD's corrugated tube into your mouth, exhale briefly to clear it of water, press the BCD purge button and exhale. You must release the BCD purge button before taking your mouth away or gas will escape from the BCD and some water will flow in. You must also clear the regulator's second stage mouthpiece of water before you breathe from it again. You may have to repeat this cycle several times to achieve the desired buoyancy so the easiest method is to use the direct feed if you have one.

Familiarization exercises can help you overcome feelings of disorientation, improve confidence and teach you to control small changes in buoyancy automatically with your breathing.

1. Forward roll – From a standing position, take a deep breath to increase your buoyancy and, as your body rises, roll forward, pulling water towards you with your hands and arms to draw your body round. When back in a standing position, breathe out to reduce your buoyancy.

2. Backward roll – As above but perform the roll in reverse: push the water away from you with your hands and arms to drive your body around.

3. Horizontal roll – Lie clear of the bottom and twist your body in a barrel roll. You can use your hands, one pushing the water and the other pulling the water to help you perform the roll.

4. Maintaining neutral buoyancy – Position yourself clear of the bottom and relax. Observe how breathing deeply causes your body to rise and exhaling deeply causes you to sink. Regulate your breathing until you can maintain your body at a constant depth. An aid to this exercise is to suspend hoops at different depths and then to practise swimming through them without touching the sides of the hoop.

REMOVE AND REPLACE BCD, SCUBA CYLINDER AND REGULATOR

Kneel on the bottom, keep the primary second stage in your mouth, undo the BCD waist strap or cummerbund, loosen the shoulder straps and slip out of the BCD. Pull BCD and cylinder to your front and lay it on the bottom of the pool. Your buoyancy will not be affected if you keep your weight belt on. Take in a medium breath, turn the air off, remove the primary second stage from your mouth, place it carefully on the scuba

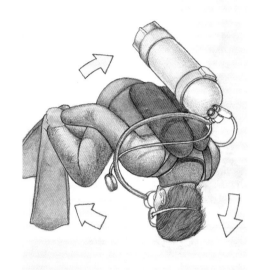

Above: By performing roll exercises, divers can get used to the disorientation produced by not having much gravity.

Above: Maintaining buoyancy – You can control your buoyancy with your breathing so that when you are neutrally buoyant, you will be able to maintain your position at the desired depth.

Above: To inflate the BCD orally, inhale from your regulator, then exhale into the mouthpiece attached to the oral inflation tube. Repeat this until the BCD is inflated.

cylinder and give an okay signal to your instructor. Now reverse the process, turn the air on, hold the second stage so that its mouth-piece is pointing downwards and briefly press the purge button to clear it of water. Tilt your head back, keep the mouthpiece point-ing down while you place it in your mouth, then breathe out into the mouthpiece before breathing in. Now put your arms through the BCD's shoulder straps and lift it over your head so that it slips on. Do up the waist strap or cummer-bund, making sure that it does not interfere with the quick-release buckle of your weight belt and give your instructor the okay sign.

Ditch and retrieve

Once you are confident you can try 'ditch and retrieve'. Take off the BCD, scuba cylinder, mask and regulator first stage. Remove your weight belt, but hold onto it while you take a deep breath. Turn off the air then remove the primary second stage from your mouth, lay it on the scuba cylinder, carefully drop the weight belt and swim to the surface. While treading water, look down and locate the weight belt, your first target, because without it you will be too buoyant. Take a medium breath, dive to the weight belt and lay it over one knee. Locate the scuba cylinder valve, turn on the air, hold the sec-ond stage so that its mouthpiece is pointing downwards and briefly

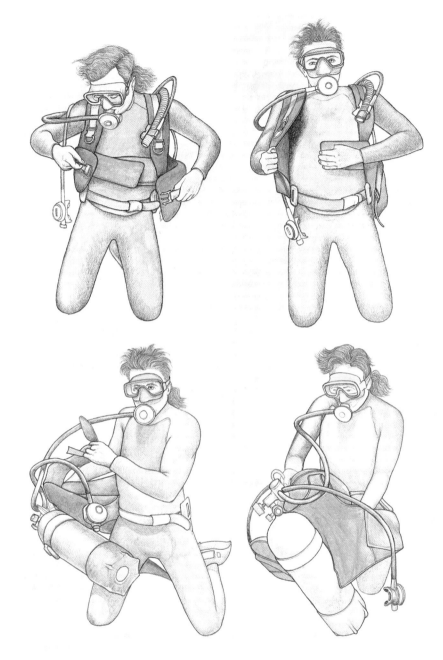

press the purge button to clear it of water. Keep the mouthpiece pointing down, fit it in your mouth and breathe out before breathing in. You can now take your time locating the fuzzy dark object that is your mask. Refit your mask, clear it of water and put on the BCD.

Above: *Ditching a BCD and cylinder.*
1. Loosen the straps.
2. & 3. Remove the arms in turn from the shoulder straps, undo the waist belt and/or cummerbund and take off the BCD.
4. Lay the BCD and cylinder in front of you on the bottom of the pool.

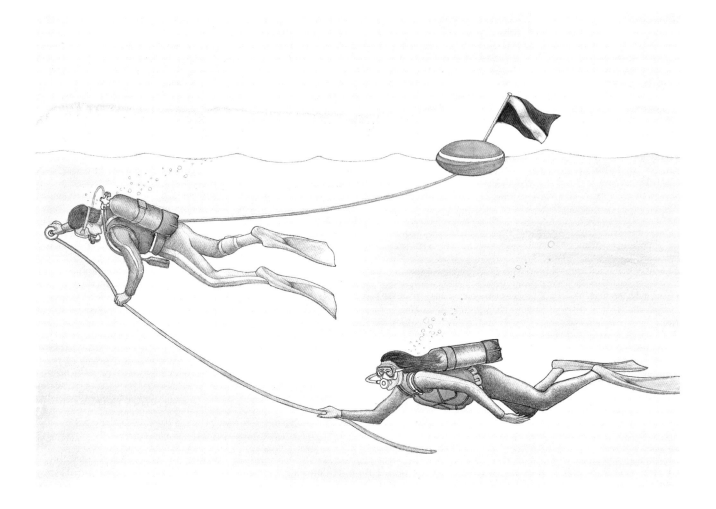

The buddy system

For safety, divers dive in pairs. Buddies can provide reminders and may see things that the other has missed. They double check each other's equipment and keep constant watch on each other to be quick to notice if the other requires assistance.

Before entering the water a buddy pair will help each other kit up and check on each other that:

- both feel well
- both understand the hand signals to be used
- the air supply is fully turned on
- the scuba cylinders are full by checking the pressure gauge
- the direct feeds are fitted correctly to the BCD and, if worn, the dry suit
- the BCD harness and weights system are not fouling any other equipment
- each knows how to inflate or deflate the other's BCD and, if wearing one, dry suit
- both know how to release the integrated weight system, if worn by one
- each buddy has the necessary

Above: When using a surface marker buoy and/or buddy line, it should be held in your hand, for safety reasons, and not tied to any equipment.

instrumentation – either a diving computer or a watch, depth gauge, and dive planner or decompression tables
- each diver has a mask, fins, snorkel, diving knife and compass and that they are fitted correctly
- there are no dangling straps or trapped hoses.

When diving as a buddy pair:

- Both divers should understand the action to be taken if they are separated.
- Once in the water they should check each other's equipment for damage; give each other and any boat cover the okay signal; each give the descent signal; and make sure that the other is ready by giving the okay signal; then descend together.
- Keep close together and if one has problems with equalizing ears or sinuses, stop and wait until both are ready and able to continue descending.
- If one diver is deploying a surface marker buoy, the other should be on the opposite side of the buoy, to avoid becoming entangled.
- If one diver wants to change direction, this should be conveyed to the other and agreement on the new direction should be signalled.
- When the dive is over (or one diver has reached a prearranged gas pressure), give each other the ascent signal and keep together while slowly ascending.
- If visibility is poor, use a short length of line to help keep together. Do not tie this buddy line to any part of your equipment – this can be dangerous in an emergency.
- If buddies become separated they should search for each other, but if they cannot find each other within one minute, both should abandon the dive, ascend slowly and reunite on the surface.

Below: A group of divers in training stand in the safety of shallow water so that buddy pairs can check through each other's equipment.

Preparing for open water diving

In open water there are surface hazards such as boats, jet skis and windsurfers, and choppy water. Divers should learn the following procedures for ascent:

- Give the ascend signal and make sure that your buddy understands by returning it.
- Look up and fin gently towards the surface.
- Keep an eye on each other so that you can keep together.
- Ascend slower than your smallest bubbles and make sure that you breathe out.
- Rotate your body to get an all-round view.
- Vent your BCD as necessary, while you ascend.
- Watch out for surface craft as you approach the surface.
- Hold one arm above your head as protection from unseen surface craft.
- Once on the surface, check in all directions for approaching surface craft.
- Inflate your BCD.
- Give the okay signal to your buddy and boat or shore cover.
- Swim to shore or the boat or, if you are on a drift dive, wait for the boat to pick you up.

Right: *When ascending, rotate your body to check it is clear in all directions. Raise one arm above your head as you near the surface for protection from boats and other surface craft.*

If you have been low on air or out of air when ascending, the small amount of air left in your scuba cylinder may have expanded enough to give you a few breaths when near the surface, but it is unlikely to give enough air to inflate the BCD. Some BCDs have a one-off-use carbon dioxide (CO_2) cartridge for surface inflation, while others have a small emergency cylinder fitted to the BCD that is filled from the scuba cylinder before each dive. You can also inflate a BCD orally (*see p103*).

For your first open water dive the instructor will give you a dive plan. This is a briefing on what to expect during the dive, how deep you plan to go and for how long, any tests that are to be carried out and any backup plans to use if things do not go as planned. If there is a current you begin by swimming into it so that it will bring you back to your starting point when you decide to return.

Underwater navigation

You cannot see far enough to navigate underwater. You can use natural features for reference – rock or coral outcrops, Gorgonian Sea Fans, which grow at right angles to the prevailing current, or sand ripples, which normally run parallel to the shoreline. But your best friend on a featureless bottom is a waterproof compass.

Compasses have a lubber line – a centre line that marks the fore and aft of the compass, a needle or card that indicates magnetic north and a rotating bezel or index marks that can be turned to line up with the north pointing needle.

The compass itself is divided into 360 degrees that follow in a

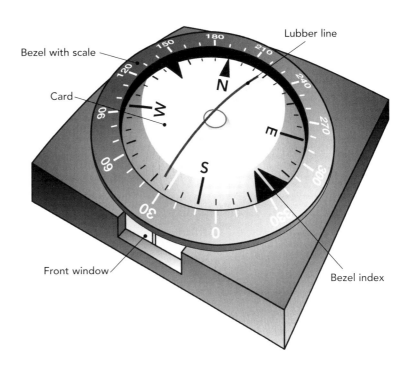

Bezel with scale

Lubber line

Card

Front window

Bezel index

Top: Gorgonian Sea Fans always grow at right angles to the prevailing current.

Above: *On an indirect reading compass (shown) degrees are marked clockwise on the rotating bezel. On a direct reading compass they are marked counter-clockwise on the compass housing.*

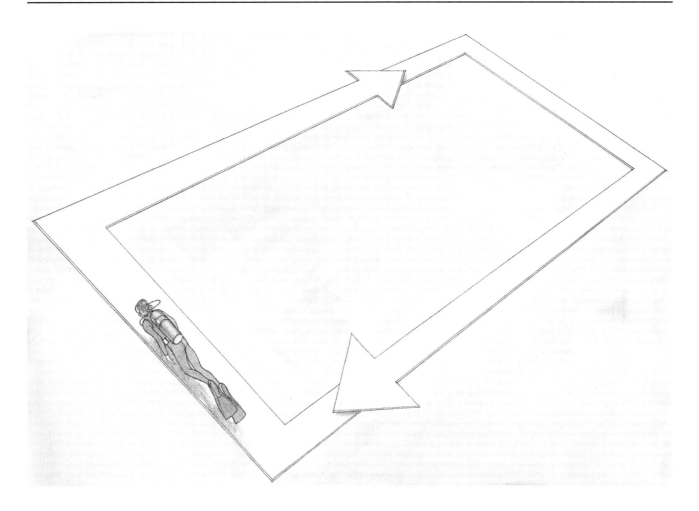

clockwise direction from 0° (north), through 90° (east), 180° (south), 270° (west) and then back to north again at 360° or 0°.

The lubber line indicates the proposed direction of travel and you must keep your body in line with it. The magnetic needle is affected by steel scuba cylinders, dive knives, watches, some depth gauges, electronic instruments, cameras and strobes (flashguns). Hold the compass at a maximum distance in front of and in line with your body by using both hands.

An important part of diving is being able to find your way back to

your starting point. As a last resort you can surface and swim back to your point of entry or, if boat diving, try to catch the attention of the boat crew and have it come to you, but there are several problems with this approach. A big swell will make it difficult for the boat crew to see you and make it difficult to swim. Even in calm water, swimming on the surface is more strenuous than swimming underwater and progress will also be hindered by surface currents and wind.

It is tempting to surface, take a sighting and compass bearing and descend to swim towards it. It is not

Above: Divers following a rectangular course make three right-angle (90°) turns and must remember to travel the same distance or length of time on each of the parallel sides.

a good idea to do this more than once, since this type of 'bounce' or 'saw-tooth' diving can lead to DCS. It is the equivalent of surfacing and then beginning another dive without taking a surface interval. Some diving computers will 'cry foul', close down and cease giving information until a suitable surface interval has passed.

DIVE PATTERNS

Triangular dive patterns involve two turns. Set out along a compass bearing for a fixed time or fixed number of fin strokes and at that point turn right through 120°, add 120° to the first compass bearing and follow the new bearing for the same time or number of fin strokes. Turn right through 120°, add another 120° to the compass bearing and follow this new bearing back to the starting point.

Rectangular patterns are slightly more complicated since there are three right angle (90°) turns and you should travel along parallel sides of the rectangle for the same time or number of fin strokes.

There are three ways to practise your use of a compass. The distances involved underwater are too small to require corrections for the difference between true north and magnetic north, but you will have to correct for currents. To estimate how far you have travelled along a particular bearing, count fin strokes. You can use your watch to time yourself, but this gets complicated if you try to make allowances for time spent resting. The figures for bearings, fin strokes and time can become complicated; you can also be distracted by something interesting, so write everything down on an underwater slate.

Begin with a simple out-and-back route, pick a time or area where there is no current, swim out along a bearing and try to maintain a straight course. As you progress, take note of distinctive features on the seabed such as a coral head, Gorgonian Sea Fan, or a shipwreck. A steel shipwreck will affect your compass, so disregard it until you are clear of the wreck. When you feel that you have gone far enough, turn around through 180°, add 180° to the bearing that you followed out to get your reciprocal bearing to follow on the way back. Check that you pass the same distinctive features.

Triangular or square compass courses are more interesting because they constantly cover new terrain.

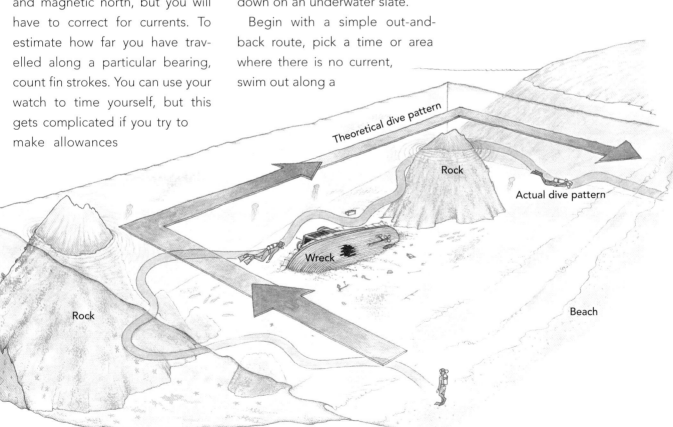

Theoretical dive pattern

Rock

Actual dive pattern

Wreck

Rock

Beach

PLANNING

All dives should be planned. The leader of the dive will give a detailed briefing that covers the expected time in the water, what the tides and currents are doing, what you can expect to see on the dive, what depth you should expect to dive to and how long you can dive before ascending.

Plan the dive and dive the plan

Determine the best time to dive. In most regions the water is calmer in the morning than in the afternoon when the wind increases, but the state of the tide may be more important. Dawn and dusk are good times for fish action and the animals encountered on night dives will vary with how long it has been dark.

Divers should also take into account the season, weather, the weather forecast, their own health and fitness, their normal rate of breathing gas consumption, the depths and times of their last few dives and the surface intervals between those dives and the dive they are about to perform. They must also think about the dives that they plan to do next. If the conditions are not good, you could change your plans and dive at a more sheltered site or you may have to abort diving for that day.

If you are not diving with a diving operator, make sure that your plans are known to someone who

Above: Detailed dive briefings should inform the divers of the current, depth and time of the dive, and what divers can expect to see.

is not participating in the dive and agree on how long that person should wait before informing the authorities if you do not return by a certain time.

However, dives can be over organized, especially at warm-water destinations where many dive operators have to worry about the safety of divers who only dive occasionally. These divers are often herded into groups and expected to follow the dive master around on a very short, shallow, easy dive, pose for the obligatory video and be out of the water in less time than experienced divers would consider suitable.

A warm diver has a faster blood circulation and therefore more nitrogen is exchanged between the blood and the tissues, which increases the chance of suffering DCS. It is safer to be cold and inactive during a dive, although only photographers subject themselves to that. Still, it makes sense to not rush about and overheat.

Dive planners and decompression tables

It takes time for the body to absorb and release nitrogen. It is possible to dive and return to the surface before the body absorbs enough nitrogen to cause any problems. Back on the surface, excess nitrogen will continue to be released by the body. However, if divers perform another dive too soon after the first, they will start the later dive with excess nitrogen in their tissues (residual nitrogen). Workers on fish-farms have developed DCS after performing several dives to 9m (30ft) without taking long enough surface intervals between dives.

The rate of nitrogen absorption and release are not uniform for all body tissues or even for the same

types of tissue located in different organs. The solubility of nitrogen differs between tissues such as bone, cartilage, fat, muscle and tendon. The rate of blood flow (perfusion) also varies with the

type of tissue, from none (cornea) to high (nerve and brain tissue). Perfusion is lower for muscles at rest. To account for the various types of tissue, and the range in perfusion, designers of tables

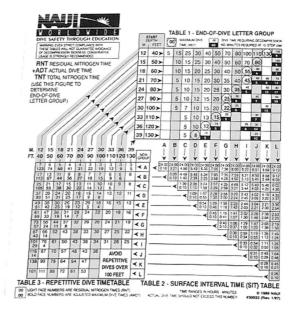

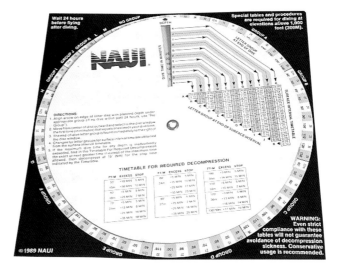

This page and opposite: Each dive training agency produces its own set of tables or planners. Some of these are just printed tables, while others are more complicated, with various graduated sliding or revolving scales that mate up like the scales of a slide rule.

theorized a set of compartments, each with its own 'half-time'. These are not actual anatomical compartments or even types of tissue.

Research led to established time limits (no-stop times) for any given depth to minimize the risk of DCS. These limits assume that the diver then makes a direct ascent (a square-profile or square-wave dive), at a sensible rate, since the ascent itself is decompression. These time limits (and maximum depths for recreational diving on normal air) differ between countries and training agencies, who print their own dive planners and recompression tables. They all have the same basic functions, but vary in their degree of conservatism. None will eliminate the risk of DCS as each person is different.

If these time limits are exceeded, some tables will suggest the depth and duration of staged decompression stops (pauses required on the ascent) to enable the release of enough nitrogen for safety. Dive planners and decompression tables give the fastest rates of ascent and the shortest time required on the surface for outgassing nitrogen before diving again (the surface interval). They enable divers to calculate how the interval affects the next dive because of the estimated amount of nitrogen remaining in the body tissues (residual nitrogen) from the previous dive.

Dive planners and decompression tables require that divers record the dive time (time elapsed since leaving the surface), the maximum depth reached, the current depth and the time spent at any decompression stop. Back on the surface, if more dives are planned within the next 16 hours, divers need to time the surface interval and use the dive planner or decompression tables to work out a surface code. This estimates the residual nitrogen in the body.

Surface codes are often represented by a letter group. Divers will accumulate more nitrogen on the next dive, which must be added to the residual nitrogen. By combining the details of the dive with the surface interval, divers can work out which part of the table to use for the next dive, and an appropriate time and depth for that dive. If times or depths fall between figures on the tables, the largest figure should be used.

When using tables for multi-level dives, you should go to the deepest level first, then progressively ascend. Special tables are available for diving at altitude and also for diving on Enriched Air Nitrox.

Sawtooth diving

Sawtooth diving (ascending and descending several times) probably increases the risk of DCS because of micro-bubble formation at depth. While ascending micro-bubbles begin to release nitrogen harmlessly. However, if the diver descends again, more nitrogen will enter the tissues and on re-ascent will flow into the existing bubbles, enlarging them.

Repetitive dives

After surface intervals greater than 16 hours, there is no excess nitrogen remaining in the tissues and the next dive is treated as if it were the first. If you are making repetitive dives over several days you should take a complete day off after four days.

Decompression dives

These are not recommended for recreational divers and some American recreational dive planners do not allow for them, but European dive tables do. There may be times when, for whatever reason, divers exceed the no-stop time limit at a given depth. If this happens they must make stops on the ascent for long enough to let excess nitrogen diffuse out (staged decompression stops). Recommended depths and times differ between agencies.

If only one stop is required, it is usually at a depth of 3–6m (10–20ft). If the divers have been deeper or exceeded the no-stop time for longer, they will have to make additional stops at greater depths and then a longer one at 3–6m (10–20ft).

The final dive, late in the day (such as a night dive) should be lilmited to 6m (20ft), since this is not considered to increase your nitrogen loading.

Finishing a dive

All dives, whether decompression or not, are best finished with a three or five-minute precautionary stop at 3–6m (10–20ft). In rough conditions or a swell, it is easier to hold a stop at 5m (16ft), which allows some leeway if the swell causes you to ascend a little.

Reduced Gradient Bubble Model theory

Recommended by NAUI, and incorporated into some diving computer algorithms, the Reduced Gradient Bubble Model (RGBM) theory says that on any dive greater than 12m (40ft), a one-minute stop at half of the maximum depth before continuing the ascent to the shallow decompression or safety stops may help to prevent DCS. This minute can be deducted from the shallowest decompression stop.

The reason for this 'rule of halves' is that Doppler ultrasound detectors have shown that microbubbles are formed even during non-decompression dives. The theory is that micronuclei that can 'seed' the bubbles, causing them to coagulate and grow larger, are created all the time. Once inside a bubble, a gas molecule is isolated from the circulation and tends to remain where it is. It has to diffuse back into the tissue before the circulation can transport it back to the lungs. If bubbles form at depth, they will not dissolve quickly while decompressing in the shallows. By reducing the chance of the build-up of micro-bubbles, less time is required when decompressing in shallow water. Bubbles will leave the body faster if small bubbles are kept small by the pressure of a deep stop, which gives the bubbles the chance to collapse as the gas is squeezed back out of the bubble and redissolved. With less obstruction, the blood flows faster, transporting the redissolved gas to the lungs where it is exhaled.

This theory assumes a square-profile dive, those who work their way slowly up a coral reef into the shallows have always been using this approach.

Altitude and flying after diving

Most calculations are based on ascending to sea level. If you are diving at altitude (in an inland lake), you need tables or computers designed for the purpose. Altitude diving is considered to be any elevation above 300m (1000ft) but below 3000m (10 000ft). Above that range you require a different set of tables.

If you fly before most of the extra nitrogen has been released, the reduced pressure in aircraft cabins could cause large bubbles to form.

Current medical opinion suggests divers wait 24 hours before flying or 48 hours after dives requiring decompression stops.

Above: *Divers working their way slowly up a reef or wall decompress gradually as they ascend. This diver is shown approaching a red sponge (Cliona vastifica).*

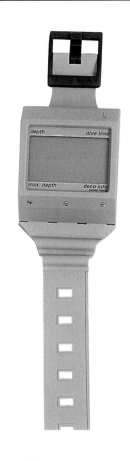

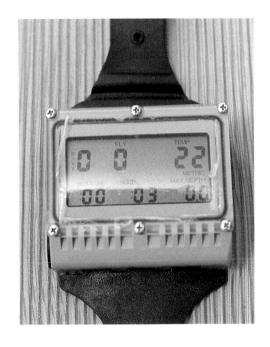

Above: *Diving computers come in various styles and calculate with different algorithms. Some have owner-replaceable batteries and different levels of conservatism. Those with small numerals can be difficult to read by older divers.*

Diving computers

Except for backup use, dive tables have become as rare as horse-collar BCDs. Divers without a computer are losing out on bottom time. Computers give more latitude than the tables, which assume that divers spend all their time at maximum depth, whereas dives are usually multilevel. Computers also allow for the different rates of nitrogen absorption and release theorized for different body tissues at different depths. You can also scroll through the possibilities for a profile for your next dive. They eliminate errors and save time on calculations.

Some diving computers can recognize the salinity of the water while others are calibrated either for seawater or freshwater. They include the information supplied by most other instruments, except the compass. Some computers are integrated with the breathing gas supply – either connected to the first stage high-pressure port through the high-pressure hose or by a transducer and wireless (hoseless) transmitter. This enables a rough estimate of the breathing gas remaining.

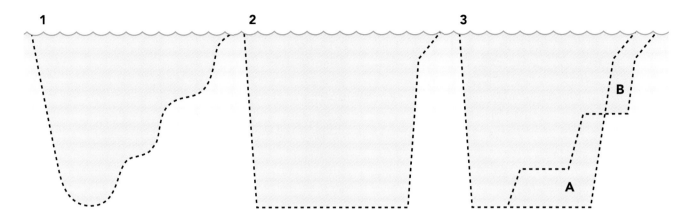

1: *This is a common profile of a dive.*

2: *Decompression tables would treat this dive as a 'square-profile' dive, i.e. they would treat the dive as if all the bottom time was spent at maximum depth. This system either reduces the amount of possible diving time or calculates more time to be spent on decompression than is necessary.*

3: *This illustration shows how a modern multilevel diving computer treats this dive. Each time you ascend to a shallower depth you are no longer absorbing nitrogen at the same rate as you did at the maximum depth. Area A represents the nitrogen absorption for a 'square-profile' dive as in Fig. 2 (which did not actually occur). Area B represents the extra dive time available at a shallower depth because less nitrogen was actually absorbed at maximum depth.*

Diving computers measure time and depth and relate these either to decompression tables or 'tissue models' for the rate at which nitrogen might be absorbed or released. From these, different manufacturers use different mathematical models (algorithms) to calculate decompression or no-decompression times. Different algorithms have different degrees of safety. Probably the greatest advantage of a diving computer is that if the diver deviates from the planned dive, the computer will adjust for the new dive profile.

However, diving computers are not infallible. They are calculated on algorithms based on research with fit young men. Some diving computers make allowances for cold water and higher-than-normal rates of exercise. They do not allow for people who are overweight, unfit or over 50, although the rate of conservatism can be adjusted on some computers.

Some computers are designed to stop supplying information if you go into decompression. These are best avoided because they become unusable when you most need them – when you have made a mistake! Full-function decompression-stop diving computers supply information on the depths and times of the stage decompression (pauses during ascent) necessary if you have exceeded the limits of no-stop diving.

Battery failure is common, so either dive with two computers or carry decompression tables, a watch and a depth gauge as backup. Computers either switch themselves on in humid climates or their batteries discharge more quickly in hot countries. If you travel to areas where support is non-existent it is worth buying a unit with owner-replaceable batteries and carrying spare batteries in your spares box.

Most diving computers will allow you to scroll through recent data to recall information for your logbook, but some can interface with a personal computer. You can then upload your previous dive profiles as a method of maintaining your logbook. This information is also indispensable for doctors if you suffer decompression sickness. Some of the functions of the diving computer can be altered manually.

HINTS FOR COMPUTER-ASSISTED DIVING

- Buy a computer with displays that are large enough for you to read easily and simple to understand when you have mild nitrogen narcosis or are stressed – this is not the time to be trying to understand ambiguous figures, graphics or icons.

- The clear self-adhesive masking tape used when spray-painting vehicles can be stuck over the display – it is tough, waterproof and easily replaced.

- Read the owner's manual – each model has its own operation and method of display. Learn your computer's features.

- Do not exceed the ascent rate specified by the computer manufacturer.

- A computer that switches itself on in one metre (40 inches) of water will eliminate any chance of you forgetting to switch it on.

- Buy a computer that emits an audible warning whenever you violate the rules of diving. However, if it is mounted on your wrist do not wave your arms about or the unit will assume that you are ascending too fast and react with audible warnings.

- Underwater photographers usually have their hands full with photographic equipment, which makes it difficult to pick up and read computers that are fitted into consoles – a wrist-mounted unit will be more convenient.

- A back-light feature is useful in dim light when wreck, night or cave diving.

- Never share your computer with another diver – diving depths often vary in a buddy pair.

- Manufacturers use different algorithms – if your buddy's computer quotes different times, use those given by your own. Computers take into account your total nitrogen loading over many dives and surface intervals, but not all dives may have been made with the same buddy.

- Keep surface intervals to a minimum of one hour.

- Do not dive to the computer's limits. The chances of developing decompression sickness increase with depth, frequency of diving and the longer the diver spends at depth. Other contributing factors include poor circulation, exertion, dehydration, cold, drugs (including alcohol and caffeine) and poor physical fitness. Avoid sawtooth diving and always make a precautionary shallow safety stop.

- If your computer and your back-up fails, abort the dive to minimize any further exposure to nitrogen. Try to pair up with someone who entered the water before you did and use that diver's instruments to regulate your ascent and decompression or safety stops. If you cannot find anyone else, ascend very slowly. If you are diving from a boat, ascend the anchor line hand-over-hand. When you can see the surface, stop at the depth of a reasonable safety stop. Stay at this depth for at least 5 minutes, preferably 10. Measure the minutes by counting seconds. At this depth even a small amount of breathing gas will last for a long while – and you are just one kick away from the surface if you do use it up. Do not dive again for 24 hours.

Above: *A wrist-mounted unit is more convenient for photographers and others who have their hands full with equipment.*

Understanding the sea and dive planning

WEATHER

Some regions are known for consistently bad tropical cyclones or monsoons at certain times of year and resorts shut down for that period. Regions where this is an occasional problem stay open, but offer cheaper rates during the bad weather season.

Although not of tropical cyclone strength, bad weather can occur anywhere at any time. During inclement weather diving can be quite pleasant once you descend below the swell. The problem is getting out of the water into the boat in a heavy swell and getting the boat to and from the dive site.

TIDES

Tidal streams are a horizontal movement of water, which usually flows in one direction for a known period of time and then returns along roughly the same path for a period of time. The two periods may not be the same. Understanding tides will help you pick the best time to dive according to your preferences. Neap tides and slack water offer easy diving for wreck diving or photography. Spring tides and full flow offer a greater chance of encounters with pelagic species such as sharks and sailfish.

Tides are caused by the combined effects of the centrifugal force of the spinning earth and gravitational attraction of the moon and, to a lesser extent, the sun. Despite its size, the sun is so far away that its effect on the tides is only about half that of the moon.

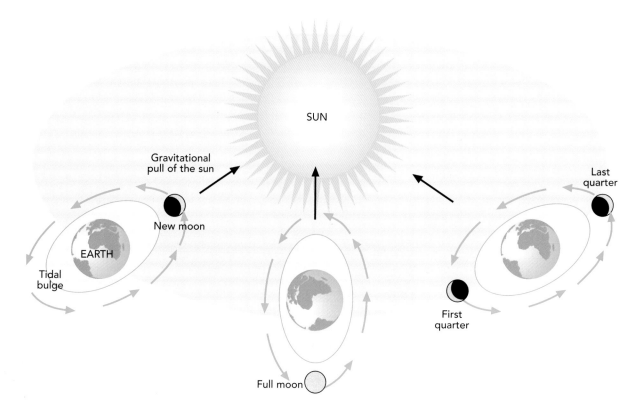

*1: **New moon** – with the sun and moon aligned, their combined gravitational pull creates the highest spring tides (maximum difference between high and low water).*

*2: **Full moon** – although the sun and moon are in line, their gravitational pull is in opposition. However, this also results in spring tides.*

*3: **First and last quarters** – the sun and moon are not aligned; this produces neap tides – those with least variation between high and low tides.*

One tide cycle runs from high water to low water and back to high water. This usually takes 12 hours (semidiurnal). In some regions one tide may be so much stronger than the other that the tide cycle appears to take 24 hours (diurnal), depending on whether the sun or the moon is dominant. Some regions experience a mixture of diurnal and semidiurnal tides. The normal tidal day is 24 hours and 50 minutes (the rotation of the earth on its axis relative to the movement of the moon about the earth). Some islands and reefs appear to have four tides per day if the flow along one side is longer than along the other.

Spring tides, those with maximum range (and strength), occur twice a month near a new or full moon. Equinoctial spring tides, which have even greater range, occur near the equinoxes. Neap tides, those with minimum range (and least strength), occur twice a month around the first and last quarter of the moon. The words 'spring' (an outflow of water) and 'neap' (scanty) come from Old English.

Ebb tides flow off a reef or land and can contain sediment that reduces visibility. Flood tides flow onto a reef or land and, if they flow over a hard substrate, the visibility will be good. When the tide is in full flow the current will be strong and will be even stronger if the water has travelled over a large expanse of open ocean without intervening land or shallow reefs to slow it down. Currents are usually strongest half way between high and low water. Either side of low or high tide, when tides are reversing direction, there will be a short period of slack water (especially at low tide) where the current is either light or non-existent. However, along open coasts the turn of the tide may occur at half-tide. Local tide tables enable you to calculate flood and ebb tides and fast or slack water.

Wind and barometric pressure affect the height of tides, increasing or opposing the movement of tidal water. The shape of the shoreline also has an effect – where stretches of water are enclosed by a shoreline with a funnel shape, tides are amplified as the funnel narrows. The upper parts of Nova Scotia's Bay of Fundy have the world's highest tidal range, 16m (52ft).

THE SEA STATE

Sea state is the result of weather conditions. The friction between the wind and the water slows the wind and converts the energy into waves. The waves formed travel in roughly the same direction as the wind that formed them, but the water itself makes little progress.

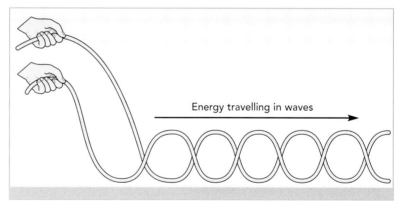

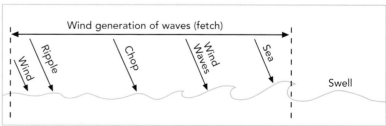

Top: Waves can be compared to a stretched-out rope that is given a vertical flick at one end – a wave travels along the rope, but the rope itself does not move forward.

Above: Some common wave terms. The sea state is the result of weather conditions. Fetch is the distance over which a swell has been built up by the wind.

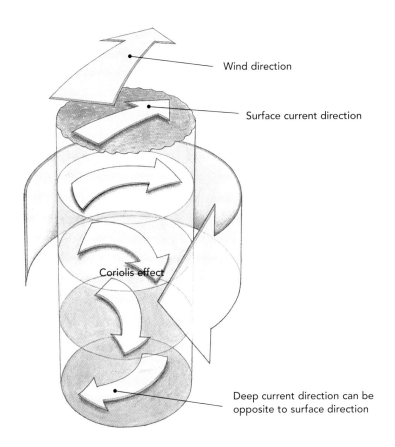

Wind direction

Surface current direction

Coriolis effect

Deep current direction can be opposite to surface direction

Above: *The wind does not push a current straight ahead. The water moves at an angle of 45° to the wind direction (45° to the left in the southern hemisphere and 45° to the right in the northern hemisphere). This is known as Ekman Transport or the Ekman Spiral if it includes the water column, and is a result of the Earth's rotation (Coriolis force).*

The wind produces the waves, but swells may be caused by a weather system far across the ocean. There may be swell present even if the wind is calm.

When waves enter shallow water, contact with the seabed interrupts their circular motion,

Below: *The water within a wave moves with a circular motion that diminishes with depth.*

causing them to flatten out and become a subsurface back-and-forth motion called surge. Friction with the seabed causes the water there to move more slowly than water at the surface. Wave height increases as the depth decreases. When water depth is roughly the same as wave height, the wave tumbles forward and 'breaks'. Waves breaking offshore indicate the presence of shallow water in the area where they are breaking.

WAVE TERMS

Wave crest – top of a wave.

Wave trough – bottom of a wave.

Wave length – horizontal distance between two adjacent crests.

Wave height – vertical distance between the trough and crest of one wave form.

Sea waves – waves formed due to the direct action of local winds.

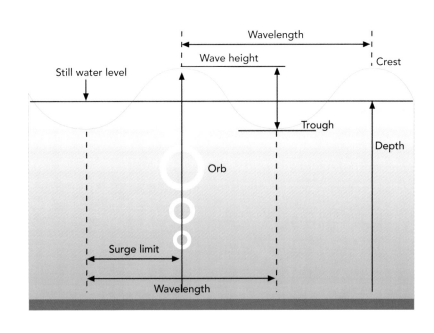

Still water level – level that the water surface would assume if it were not affected by waves (flat calm).

Wave period – time interval between the passing of two successive troughs (or crests).

Wave train – a long series of waves.

Chop – short-crested waves that follow the onset of a moderate breeze, and break readily at the crest.

Fetch (in terms of wave growth) – the distance on the ocean over which the wind has blown at a constant velocity.

Knot – a unit of speed equal to one nautical mile per hour (about 51cm or 20 in per second).

Surf – waves as they reach the area between the shore and the area where breakers start to occur.

CURRENTS

Ocean currents are horizontal and vertical circulation systems produced by the earth's rotation, gravity, wind friction, and variations in water density due to temperature and salinity. Some local currents, upwellings and downwellings are caused by wind and temperature fluctuations, the El Niño-Southern Oscillation Phenomenon (ENSO) or horizontal currents striking a reef wall. More consistent current patterns in the world's oceans affect climate, conditions for diving and which migratory species can be found at what time in a normal year.

Where ocean currents and tides do not cause local currents, they are mainly caused by differences in water temperature or the wind. Where the sun's heat falls on a shallow reef, currents may be non-existent in the early morning, but get progressively stronger until mid-afternoon. Sometimes the current on the surface flows in a different direction to the current deeper down.

Charts and pilots

Maritime charts are the sailor's equivalent of maps. Sailors use them in conjunction with a *Pilot*, a guidebook that lists important details about the area and any recent updates. Charts contain a lot of information for divers, from prominent features through direction and distance, to the timing and direction of tides.

MERIDIANS OF LONGITUDE

Meridians of longitude are drawn vertically around the world, intersecting at the geographical north and south poles. There are 360 lines, separated by one-degree intervals. Each degree is divided into 60 minutes and each minute is further divided into 60 seconds.

Longitude gives us an angular distance up to 180° east or west of the Greenwich meridian.

Longitude is shown at the top and bottom of charts.

Below: By international agreement the meridian of longitude running through Greenwich in London, is the base line, 0°. The distance between meridians of longitude get progressively smaller towards the poles, so they should not be used to measure distances.

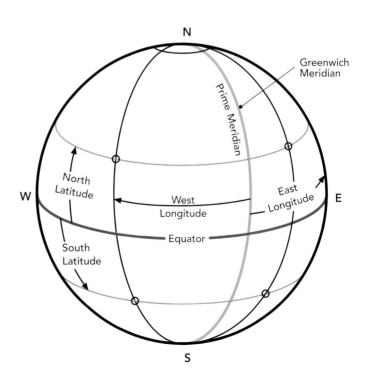

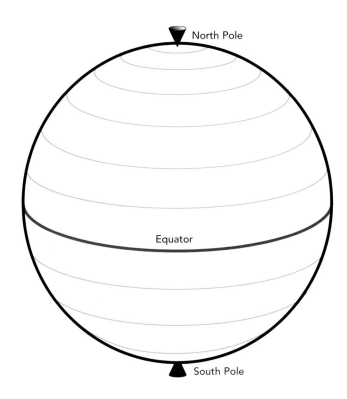

Above: Each minute in the latitude scale is one nautical mile (1.852 kilometres or 1.15 statute miles) so parallels of latitude are used for measurements.

Navigation on the surface

When shore diving, the site is usually easy to find from the entry point. However, finding an offshore site is not that easy unless you have a Global Positioning System receiver. If you are within sight of the shore, most divers still rely on transits (marks). Compass bearings are taken on two or more lines

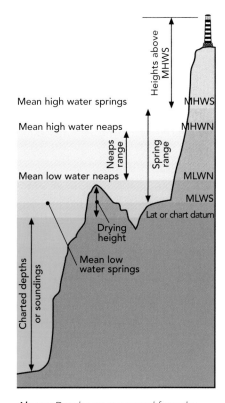

Above: Depths are measured from the chart datum (low water of the lowest likely tide). Heights (of lighthouses, for example) are measured from above Mean High Water of a Spring Tide (MHWS). The height of a lighthouse depends on its importance to shipping – allowing for the curvature of the earth, the higher the light, the further it will be visible.

PARALLELS OF LATITUDE

Parallels of latitude are drawn parallel to the equator, which is known as 0°. The north pole is 90°N and the south pole 90°S. Degrees are divided into minutes and minutes into seconds. Parallels of latitude state how far we are north or south of the equator and are shown at either side of charts.

Minutes are shown as a single quotation mark (') and seconds are shown as a double quotation mark ("). For example, Sharm el Sheik is 27°15'N 34°17'E

Charts contain at least one compass rose, a circle graduated at 1° intervals from 0° to 360° and give the variation between magnetic north (shown by your compass needle) and geographic north (used as a basis for the chart). This is only correct for the year in which the chart was printed, but annual variations are given.

In areas of high tidal range it is important for divers to know the depths, so that they can combine these with local tide tables and plan the best time to dive a particular site. Tide tables give the predicted times of high and low water for every day of the year at standard ports. You may have to add a correction to this for the area in which you are diving.

of sight, where each line of sight itself lines up with easily visible and fixed features, such as lighthouses, tall buildings, church steeples or a natural feature.

Where these lines of sight intersect is the position of the site. The wider the angle between the alignment of the bearings, the more accurate the result.

Global Positioning Systems (GPS)

Finding a dive site that does not have any obvious features above water is easy with a Global Positioning System (GPS) receiver. It will get you close enough to a wreck to pin-point it with an echo sounder (a device that determines changes in the depth of the seabed by emitting a high-frequency sound and timing how long it takes to echo back).

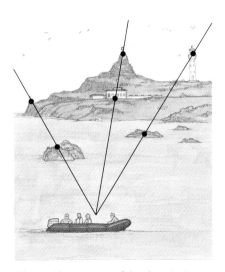

Above: *The position of the dive site is where the bearings of lines of sight to obvious fixed features intersect.*

The US Military have placed 24 NAVSTAR satellites plus four spare ones in orbit 20,000km (12,400 miles) above the earth, with each one transmitting its precise position and correct time. When first made available for civilian use, the signals were less precise than the military ones. However, in May 2000, President Bill Clinton decreed that the United States would stop the intentional degradation of the GPS signals available to the public.

GPS receivers must have a direct line of sight to satellites, the signals will pass through clouds, glass and plastic, but not through solid objects such as buildings, mountains or heavy tree cover. A receiver must be locked on to the signals from at least three satellites to calculate a two-dimensional latitude and longitude position. If receiving signals from four or more satellites, the receiver can determine the user's 3D position (latitude, longitude and altitude). A GPS unit can calculate other information such as speed, bearing, track, trip distance, distance to destination, even sunrise and sunset time.

Fixes from four or more satellites are preferable because the four fixes will enclose a volume of space, rather than converging on a single point. This is mainly due to a less accurate quartz clock in the GPS receiver, so it re-calculates the fixes until they converge on a

Above: *GPS receivers have revolutionized the task of finding dive sites that are beyond the sight of land.*

single point, then corrects its own clock setting. By correcting for internal clock errors and the time it has taken to receive each signal, a GPS receiver can compute its own latitude and longitude down to within 5m (16ft). In times of conflict the American military can move some of the satellites to gain more accuracy in the theatre of conflict, or turn them off altogether, so a European system is planned.

Anything that relies on batteries or electronics can go wrong. You must be able to navigate accurately by traditional methods, especially in remote areas.

Current Global Positioning Systems only work for depths up to 1m (40 inches) under the surface of the water and are of no use for underwater navigation.

TYPES OF DIVING

One of the attractions of diving is its variety. Depending on your fitness you can take a gentle swim or a high-voltage drift dive in a strong current. Some divers prefer clear, warm water while others are happy with limited visibility or cold water. It may require several dives to cover a large wreck. Most training agencies offer speciality courses.

Above: Diving in the warm, clear water of the tropics, surrounded by colourful marine life. The main danger with such clear water is that you are likely to dive deep without realizing it.

Above: Many of the more popular diving holiday destinations are in areas where tides and currents are minimal and sea conditions usually calm.

Temperate versus tropical waters

Many divers do most of their diving in temperate waters where shipwrecks are the most popular sites. The marine life can be just as interesting as in tropical waters, but the visibility and surface conditions may not always be that good.

Diving in the tropics is more relaxing. Wear thin exposure suits against creatures that sting, but the best chance of ruining your holiday comes from sunburn or insect bites when not diving.

Shore diving

Shore diving is cheaper than day-boat diving, but seldom as good. There may be long swims across fringing reefs and photographers get grit on their equipment. Shore and day-boat diving are preferred by those with poor sea legs.

Above: Shore diving is cheaper than day-boat diving, but seldom as good. It is preferred by people with poor sea legs or non-diving partners.

Above: One method of entering the water from a beach is to fit the fins to your feet and shuffle backwards until you are deep enough to turn around and swim.

DIVING FROM A BEACH

There are two ways of entering the water from a beach. Either fit the fins to your feet and shuffle backwards into the water until it is deep enough to turn around and swim, or walk in, carrying your fins until the water is deep enough for swimming and then fit them while your buddy supports you. Where possible, shuffle your feet, this will help you to detect holes and rocks and push bottom-dwelling animals safely out of the way. If there is surf, fit your fins first. In light surf it will be easier to shuffle backwards into the water. If the surf is heavy, shuffle sideways into the waves, pause as a wave strikes you and move again when it has passed.

DIVING FROM AWKWARD ROCKS

Climbing over slippery rocks in full diving equipment can be difficult and you must have knowledge of the local tides. Low water could result in a large drop into the water and be too high for divers to climb out at the end of the dive.

Wear hard-soled bootees and make several journeys to the water's edge, each time carrying as

Above: Sit on the water's edge and use your hands to lower yourself into the water slowly. Only leap in if the water is clear and obviously deep.

little equipment as possible. Leave one hand free to steady yourself on each trip. Put on your fins, sit at the water's edge and use your hands to lower yourself into the water. Time your entry so that you hit the water at the top of a swell or wave, then fin out hard to allow the backwash to carry you away from the rocks. When exiting, time it so that you use the highest point of a wave or swell to lift you onto the rocks. If you fail, wait for the next wave. Avoid using channels or gullies, as these will have a stronger surge.

ENTRY FROM A JETTY

There are two ways of entering the water from a jetty: a long stride or a forward roll. For the long stride entry, you should first inflate the BCD slightly, ensure that your buddy is also ready to enter the water and that the water is clear of other divers or obstructions. Hold the mask and regulator's primary second stage in place with one hand so that neither are dislodged when they hit the water. Use your other hand to push down the BCD waist strap so that the scuba cylinder cannot bounce up and strike

1: Hold the mask and primary second stage regulator with one hand and push down on the BCD strap with the other.

2: Take a long stride out from the jetty, making sure your cylinder is clear and will not catch on the edge of the jetty.

3: Keep your hands in position until you float back to the surface, then locate your buddy and move clear of the area.

1: A forward roll entry is suitable for heights of up to 1m (3ft).

2: Fold your body forward so that your back hits the water first.

3: Keep your head and legs tucked in as you enter the water.

your neck when the scuba cylinder hits the water. You can then take a long stride outwards so that the scuba cylinder will be well clear of the jetty. For an entry height up to 2m (6½ft) above the water, keep one leg extended forward and the other leg extended backward until you hit the water.

For an entry height above that, bring your legs together before you hit the water to avoid discomfort on impact.

There are likely to be other divers wanting to enter the water so join your buddy and swim clear of the entry point.

For an entry height up to 1m (3ft) you can use a forward roll entry. Since you do not have to hold onto your diving equipment, your hands are free to carry other equipment.

However, fragile equipment and cameras should either be lowered into the water on a cord first, or handed down to the diver by someone else.

Exiting the water would always be up steps or a ladder and the water would normally be calm enough for you to remove your fins before climbing out.

Boat diving

The most important thing with all boat diving is for the person in charge to have some way of monitoring that all the divers are accounted for before the boat can move anywhere.

Above: All divers must be accounted for at all times when diving from a boat. This is particularly important when leaving the site after a dive or snorkel.

1. Hold your mask and regulator primary second stage in place and push down on your BCD waist strap.

2. Make sure your fins will not catch on anything in the bottom of the boat, then roll backward into the water.

3. Keep holding onto your mask, regulator and BCD until you float back to the surface.

ENTRY FROM AN INFLATABLE OR OTHER SMALL BOAT

In small boats there is rarely room to move around. Kit up with all equipment except fins and mask before boarding. Keep your mask around your neck to protect it.

Pairs of divers sitting on opposite sides of the boat should enter the water simultaneously to avoid rocking the boat. Usually the coxswain (helmsman) will check that the water is clear and then give the order to enter.

Fit your mask and put the regulator's primary second stage into your mouth. Check that your scuba cylinder is turned on, that the water behind you is clear and that your fins will not catch on anything on the floor of the boat. Hold your mask and regulator primary second stage in place with one hand and, when the coxswain gives the order, roll backwards with your legs together. Join your buddy and swim clear of the boat to give others clear water for entry.

Above: Small boats and inflatables are usually crowded; divers should board almost fully kitted up, sit down and put on their fins.

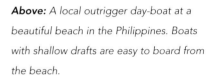

Unless the boat is moored, surfacing divers have little chance of reaching it if the wind is blowing it away from them. The coxswain should motor the boat upwind of the divers, disengage the engine from the propeller and let the boat drift downwind to the divers. Hold onto the boat with one hand and with the other release the weight belt and pass it into the boat unless your weights are integrated with your BCD. Undo your BCD waist strap, slacken or disconnect one of the shoulder straps, take the second stage mouthpiece out of your mouth and slip your free arm out of the BCD. The BCD,

Above: A local outrigger day-boat at a beautiful beach in the Philippines. Boats with shallow drafts are easy to board from the beach.

regulator and scuba cylinder can then either be taken by someone in the boat or clipped to lines attached to the boat for retrieval once you are on board. Keep your fins and mask on. Clasp the boat's gunwale or lifelines with both hands. Pull up with your arms and kick your fins at the same time. This will propel you far enough over the top of the gunwale or pontoon to get your body into the boat. Take off your mask and fins, collect and tidy up your equipment and move to one end of the boat to leave room for others to board.

If you have a back problem, the scuba cylinder and weights can be donned in the water (*see p95*).

Above: The live-aboard boat S/Y Poolster hangs off from Bluff Point below the solar-powered navigation light at Sha'b 'Ali, North Egypt.

Above: With fixed moorings, small day boats can be moored over the dive site without anchor damage.

Above: You can enter the water from a day boat or live-aboard with a long stride as you would off a jetty.

If anchored or moored in a strong current, there should be a floating 'granny line' running the length of the boat from mooring line or anchor line to the stern platform or hang-bar. A 'trail line' (also called a tag line) clear of the ladder, should trail backwards from the boat. Divers can hang onto these while waiting for their buddies and pull along the granny line to the descent line. These lines are also needed at the end of the dive so that some divers can hang onto them while waiting for the ladder to become clear and then pull themselves to the boat against the current.

Exiting the water would always be up steps or a ladder, either on the side of the boat or onto a rear platform. When the sea is calm you would remove your fins and hand them up to someone in the boat before climbing the ladder. If the sea is rough you would be better

DAY-BOAT DIVING

Day boats leave for near-shore sites once or twice a day. Night dives are an optional extra. There may be lots of equipment to be carried to the beach or jetty. There is room to move around on a day boat. It will carry at least two cylinders per diver plus a few spares to cover leaks and emergencies. Divers change their BCDs and regulators to a full cylinder after the first dive.

Above: On day boats scuba cylinders are stowed in special racks so divers can leave kitting up until they are 15 minutes from the dive site.

Above: Centre-spine ladders are easier to climb while wearing fins.

off keeping your fins on, because if a wave throws you back into the water, it will be difficult to swim without fins while wearing a BCD and scuba cylinder.

Climbing a rocking ladder in full equipment is difficult so it is worth practising in calm conditions.

DIVING FROM A LIVE-ABOARD BOAT

With live-aboard diving there is less carrying of heavy equipment, no swimming over fringing reefs, biting insects are left behind when you leave port and sailing overnight maximizes the diving time on remote offshore sites. There are fewer restrictions on night dives and divers get three to five dives each day instead of heading back to shore after two. Photographers do not risk sand damage to O-rings and have more time to sort out cameras

Above: Entry from a live-aboard is the same as from a jetty, either using a long stride or by rolling forward.

Above left: Several day boats moored at a near-shore dive site.

Left: With day boats there may be lots of equipment to carry to and from the accommodation and the beach or jetty.

and charge batteries between dives. On the minus side, everybody may not get on well; narrow boats and boats that ride high in the water will roll in the slightest chop; some people cannot sleep on a moving boat; and really bad seas can be frightening.

Live-aboard boats seem expensive, but you get more dives for your money and food is included.

Although live-aboard boats often offer five dives per day, it would be better to do fewer, quality dives, rather than five, some of which may be mediocre. Tides and currents can affect visibility or make the dive uncomfortable (see tides p120 and currents p123 and repetitive dives p115).

Most divers do not like there to be more than eight people in the water at the same time.

Make sure that the boat has a foolproof diver check-in and check-out system. Boats have left divers in the water and sailed off.

Top: Live-aboard boats that are wide and low in the water will be more stable in rough weather.

Centre: Some motorized live-aboard boats have a sail aft (usually a lugsail) that acts as a stabilizer when set while the boat is under way.

Right: Large live-aboard boats should either have two tenders serving separate dive sites, or have a rota system whereby only half their clients are in the water while the other half are resting.

At the dive site you may be close enough to leap in as you would off a jetty, but it is more likely that you would be taken there in an inflatable or small tender.

SILENT ENTRY

Sometimes divers may wish to approach a creature without scaring it into flight. From a large boat you should climb down the ladder, but from a smaller boat you should turn onto your stomach and lower yourself gently into the water.

DIVING FROM A KAYAK

Diving from polyethylene sit-on-top kayaks is ecologically friendly and they are easy to transport. They reduce long surface swims and, with practice, make it easier to get through surf.

Wear your bootees, wet or dry suit, though once through the surf and in calm water you can roll down the top half. Pre-assemble the scuba cylinder, BCD and regulator and store it as central

and low as possible. If you can get it into a hatch, place it cylinder down and inflate the BCD to hold it in position. Keep the weight belt central and make sure that everything is tethered and tied down tight. You require lots of bungee cord and tethers with snap links at both ends or with a loop at one end. Everything must be tethered to the kayak when not tethered to you. You will also need an anchor, dry bag, water bottles, dive flag, sun hat and sunscreen.

Pull the loaded kayak to the water's edge, watch the surf and, at the beginning of a lull, pull the kayak out into knee-deep water, jump on and paddle like hell directly into the waves.

When you are ready to dive, put your fins on first and take them off last. Straddling the kayak with fins in the water gives stability and if you fall off fins are necessary for getting back onboard.

It is possible to use the over-the-head manoeuvre to don the scuba cylinder, BCD and regulator unit while on the kayak, but most divers would inflate the BCD, float the unit in the water and then don it. Keep it tethered to the kayak until

you have it fully on your person. Make sure that all hatches are firmly closed and that the paddle is secured to the kayak. Then either tow it, or leave the kayak tied to a mooring, or take an anchor down with you and place it safely. On a drift dive in current it would be better to tow the kayak.

Getting back on board is the difficult bit. Most divers remove their weight belt, place it in the kayak and tether it. Add air to the BCD, take it off and tether it. Keep your fins on, float on the surface at 90° to the kayak, with your hands on top of it. Kick hard and lunge forward while pulling the kayak underneath you until your stomach is onboard and your upper body is lying across the centre of the kayak. Roll onto your bottom, then pivot to a sitting position and swing your feet onboard. Place everything back on board, tethered and tied down. This is rather like learning to windsurf, only practice will make you proficient.

Left: For diving from a kayak, the polyethylene sit-on type is used. It requires practice to get back on board in the water.

Above: *A wall is near vertical and may be overhanging or undercut, while drop-offs are steep slopes of 60–85°.*

Reef diving, drop-offs and walls

Reefs may have several distinct profiles. The top of the reef is likely to be a coral garden with smaller species of fish and crustaceans. Slopes or drop-offs have larger gorgonias and larger fish in shoals. Walls also have larger pelagic species, especially when over deep water.

Inshore fringing reefs tend to have poor visibility (*see p31*), but are good study areas because they harbour immature species.

Where offshore reefs have lagoons, these are convenient for safe anchorage, muck diving and snorkelling, but most divers would find better diving outside the reef. Channels into lagoons are good places to dive when the current is running as the nutrients carried attract small fish and these in turn attract larger predators. It is usually safer to dive on an incoming tide because, when the current is flowing out, the divers may be difficult for the chase boat crew to see in a large expanse of sea. Where one side of a reef is longer or more contorted than the other side, the current on the longer or more contorted side is slowed down more than that on the other side. When the currents from both sides meet again at points on the lee end of the reef they are travelling at different speeds and produce whirlpools and upwellings full of nutrients that

Above: Leaf Scorpionfish are found in several colours. They lie on the reef, rocking around in the current like leaves, waiting for unsuspecting prey.

attract large shoals of fish. In turn these fish attract sharks and other predators. If you can find shelter from the current, these are great places to dive.

Where a tide travels unimpeded across a large expanse of sea and strikes a reef wall there are likely to be strong upwellings and downwellings.

Submerged reefs in open water require a knowledgeable skipper or GPS to find them. Descend quickly to the lee of the reef to find shelter from the current before you get swept off. These reefs usually have top diving and pelagics.

Muck diving

First coined by Bob Halstead in Papua New Guinea, muck diving is usually over a silty or sandy bottom, but it can also be over coral rubble. Concentrated observation will locate small and often colourful or weird creatures camouflaged against their environment. Divers soon found these strange creatures in Indonesia's Lembeh Strait, Borneo's Mabul, Kapalai and Lankayan and in the Philippines' Anilao, Boracay, Puerto Galera and Malapascua. Often the visibility was just so good that no one had looked for such small creatures.

These creatures do not move far and usually have specific habitats so most divers may need local dive guides to help locate them. Many are so small that it is worth carrying an underwater magnifying glass (*see p31*).

Drift diving

Drift diving can vary from pleasantly drifting along a wall to being swept along walls and gullies with the probability of encountering large pelagic species. The main problems are those of good chase-boat cover and becoming separated from diving buddies. Divers not actually using surface marker buoys should carry a delayed deployment surface marker buoy or better still, a high visibility rescue tube or collapsible flag, which can be raised above the swell to be more visible to the boat cover (*see p84*).

The chase-boat crew should follow the surface marker buoy or divers' bubbles and be alert. It is bad practice to have music blaring so loud that the crew cannot hear divers' whistles when they surface. Power whistles are best for attracting the boat cover and an old compact disk (CD) can be used as a heliograph to reflect the sun and attract attention.

Buddies, and preferably the whole group, should enter the water together to avoid getting separated on the surface, and try to keep together underwater. If divers do get separated from their boat cover, it is wise to use a buddy-line, inflate the BCDs and conserve air. It is usually best to retain weight belts unless buoyancy is a problem, but in some circumstances it may be better to jettison the scuba cylinders.

If you want to fin ashore and are wearing a normal BCD, rather than wings, it may be less tiring to fin on your back. The buddy-line should be untied before trying to swim through surf or breakers.

Diving in strong currents with reef hooks

When diving in strong currents, collisions with the environment are rare. The water-flow usually sweeps around the object, taking the divers with it. A surface marker buoy (SMB) lets the surface boat cover know where the divers are (see p84). Only one diver of a buddy pair or group diving together should display an SMB, but each diver should carry a delayed deployment SMB.

In strong currents, conditions are unpredictable. While divers are rewarded with big animal encounters, dealing with the currents often takes precedence. One must react quickly, decreasing buoyancy when caught in a strong upwelling, or increasing it when caught in a strong downwelling. Sometimes you can escape a strong upwelling by swimming away from the reef, and a strong downwelling by

Top Centre: Reef hooks are only used in certain areas when strong currents are running and divers must pause to watch the action.

swimming towards the reef, but the best thing is to swim to one side. Downwelling currents do not normally affect a wide area and, contrary to sensational reports, most strong downwelling currents occur at walls and dissipate before reaching extreme depths. However, if you feel that your life is in danger, this is one situation where you may have to 'climb' sideways along the reef. Remember that whatever countermeasures have been taken in an up- or downwelling, they must immediately be reversed to re-establish neutral buoyancy when divers are no

longer in that particular current. Keep an eye on the bubbles of the divers ahead – if they begin ascending very fast, descending or moving in circles, then they are in an upwelling, downwelling or washing machine-type current that you can either avoid or plan for.

Extremely strong currents only occur for brief periods at certain times of the month (see tides p120) and are only felt when hanging on to a reef, not when drifting with the current. Some currents may be so strong that divers can be swept off the reef. Some divers overcome this by using a reef hook, a

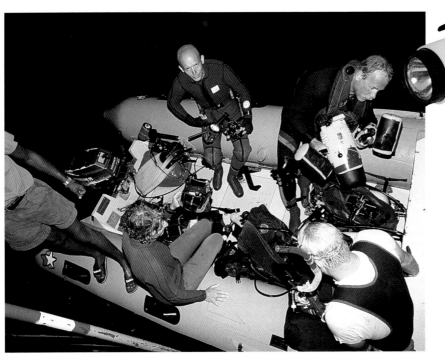

Above: Underwater lights come in many variations, so choose one to suit your needs, and always carry a spare.
Left: Departing for a night dive on the wreck of the Umbria in the Red Sea, off Sudan.

shark-fishing or decorator's S-hook filed blunt. The hook is attached to one end of a short, strong line that has a karabiner (carbine hook or snaplink) attached to the other end. This is hooked into a patch of dead coral on the reef and the karabiner is clipped to the diver's BCD. Some air is then added to the BCD to keep the diver clear of the reef.

Face into the current or it will feel as though the mask and regulator are about to be ripped from your face. Once attached in this way, you can relax, catch your breath, let your heartbeat return to normal, check instruments and watch the fish action. Of course reef hooks will damage the coral, but less so than by a diver scrabbling around on the reef attempting to stay on it.

Night diving

Predators are most active at dusk and dawn because they can rise unseen from the dark to take prey made visible against the lighter sky. At first, night diving can be fraught with anxiety as visibility is reduced to the narrow beam of your light, shadows move around ominously and noises seem to be amplified. However, you soon relax. Many fish hide in crevices or under the sand at night, but some fish and many invertebrates prefer to feed at night.

Most of the interesting creatures are out between 19:00 and 21:00 hrs but for the rarer creatures and parrotfish in their cocoons you should dive after 22:00 hrs.

Avoid diving on a full stomach. When planning a night dive, choose a shallow area with little

wave and current action and easily recognizable features for navigation. Dive the area during the day to familiarize yourself with the topography. When setting out at night, mark your designated point of exit with a light. The easiest night dives are along reef edges.

Above: Divers must dive after 22:00 hrs if they wish to find parrotfish sleeping in their protective mucous cocoons.

Above: Light up the hand that is making the signal, but point your light downward to avoid blinding your buddy or other divers.

replaces all the nitrogen) or Trimix (where helium replaces some of the nitrogen). The proportions of each gas in the mix are changed according to the requirements of the particular dive plan to reduce nitrogen narcosis and oxygen toxicity but, being a lighter element, helium introduces other problems as it is absorbed more easily. Diving in this way requires considerable planning over breathing gas mixtures, decompression gases and schedules (*see p150*).

Divers can swim out along the face at one depth and return along it at a shallower depth. If there is a current, then set out against it and return with it.

Powerful lights will scare the animals. Carry a spare light as a backup (*see p84*). Spend some time with your lights switched off. When your eyes are accustomed to the dark, wave your arms about and you will notice phosphorescent plankton and, in caves, you may spot the bioluminescence of flashlightfish. Some corals will fluoresce when a light shines on them.

Avoid blinding other divers with your light. If you wish to catch their attention, point your light at the seabed and move it in a circular motion. Then make the required hand signal but light it up with your light pointing downwards.

Deep diving on normal air

Recreational diving limits on normal air vary with the training agency and the country. So for some deep diving starts at 30m (100ft), for others at 40m (130ft), and for others at 50m (165ft).

Deep dives require careful planning. Full scuba cylinders should be fitted with regulators and hung at the depths of any planned decompression stops. Backup divers should be kitted-up on the boat. These backup divers should not have dived so that they do not have any nitrogen already in their tissues if they are called upon to help the divers in the water.

Diving beyond 50m (165ft) on compressed air is hazardous. Commercial and Technical recreational divers make deep diving safer by using mixed gases: Heliox (where helium

Above: A diver peering into the captain's bathroom on the Umbria *wreck, Sudanese Red Sea.*

Above: Diving along the well-lit gangway of the Umbria is relatively easy, but deeper penetration should be treated as diving in enclosed environments.

Diving in enclosed overhead environments

When diving in enclosed overhead environments, divers cannot easily reach the surface in the event of equipment failure. It is strongly recommended that divers take a course of instruction before penetrating large wrecks, caves or diving under ice.

WRECK DIVING

Wreck diving is one of the most popular forms of diving, but wrecks can be sharp, break up or be snagged with fishing lines, fishing nets and baggage nets. Any level of diver can enjoy diving around a wreck, but penetrating large wrecks is advanced diving similar to cave diving.

Plan dives to coincide with slack water and wear gloves for protection from sharp metal. Carry a sharp knife and a suitable monofilament line cutter or shears for cutting fishing line and nets. Most divers strap their diving knife to one of their legs, but in this position it can be dislodged by the lifeline or tangled up in fishing lines or nets. Have a separate, smaller knife attached to one arm or inside a BCD pocket.

If there is a current, divers must quickly descend the shotline to get into the lee of the wreck. In bad visibility divers may have to use a further guideline from the bottom of the shotline. The first pair of divers onto the wreck should tie off the shotline and the

---

RESTRICTIONS ON DIVING ON MARITIME WAR GRAVES

There is a small minority of divers who cannot resist disturbing wrecks or the temptation to remove brass and other artefacts. Diving on deep wrecks has been facilitated by the introduction of technical diving for recreational divers and this has worried people connected with those who lost their lives in this century's maritime military conflicts and disasters. In an effort to give greater protection to maritime war graves and military wrecks against trophy hunting, 16 wrecks have been designated as Controlled Sites – where no diving is allowed without a special permit.

final pair to ascend should release it. Take extra care on wooden wrecks, which may collapse.

Serious penetration requires redundant equipment: large single scuba cylinders with two completely separate regulators on an H- or Y-valve, or twin scuba cylinders connected by a manifold with a centre isolation valve and two separate regulators, one on each scuba cylinder valve (*see p64*). Wrecks are sharp places so a dual system of buoyancy is recommended, either a dry suit plus a BCD or a dual-bladder wing-type BCD. A spare low-volume mask can be carried in a pocket.

Have a good dive-light and carry at least one other powered by disposable alkaline batteries as backup. A narrow beam will minimize backscatter from particulate matter. Some wreck divers fit small lights to hard helmets to leave their hands free, but in very bad visibility, the light can reflect straight back into the eyes. As you descend, twist-on lights may switch on as the increased pressure squeezes their casings, so check these often throughout the dive. Make sure that all equipment is streamlined against the body with bungee cord where necessary, to prevent snagging.

Exhaust bubbles, fins, hands and the diver's wake disturb sediment so the visibility can quickly become zero. Tie off a guideline outside the wreck before penetration, feed it out as you go and tie back doors or hatches so that they cannot close in a change of current. Lines should have some tension, but not so much that they could be severed by sharp edges. When wrecks are specifically sunk for divers they are environmentally cleaned and all doors and hatches are removed. Use the rule of thirds on breathing gas supply – turn around when one-third of the breathing gas is used up, leaving one-third for finding the way out and back to the surface and one-third for emergencies.

Above: *Gunter's Cathedral, Coron, Philippines. Stirring up the sediment or a sudden change of current can quickly reduce visibility in a cavern or cave to zero.*

Minimize the amount of silt stirred up by bending your knees 90° to keep them away from the bottom. Move the fins from the knees or the ankles (flutter kick) or a frog kick. For moving through hatchways or narrow passageways, pull with the fingers and glide, but watch for sharp edges.

CAVERN AND CAVE DIVING

The type of cave diving that is taught on most cave diving speciality courses teaches how to plan the dive, how to carry scuba cylinders mounted at the diver's side and how to treble up on all equipment in case of failure. Most importantly, you learn how to lay a guideline and attach direction indicators to it so that you can find your way back out of cave passages in zero visibility. This type of cave diving is well within the realm of most divers.

There is another type of cave diving, done by divers who are cavers first and dive as a way to extend their range of cave exploration. Modern cave penetration of this type can consist of multi-day expeditions with long periods underwater, breathing mixed gases and surfacing only after long and complicated decompression schedules. Only extremely experienced divers should attempt this type of cave diving.

Cavern diving is always within sight of daylight, but cave diving is beyond any source of daylight and requires laying a safety guideline and separate backup sources of light and breathing gases. The safety guideline should be taut, have reliable tie-off points and should not have to be crossed over because it must be easily followed in zero visibility by letting it run through the fingers. Most important is the rule of thirds: divers turn around when a third of their breathing gas is used up leaving a third for finding their way out and a third for emergencies.

Sediment is easily disturbed, so divers must learn to make gentle, shallow fin-strokes as under wreck penetration above.

Above: *Cave diving demands exceptional planning and trebling of equipment. Novices must never enter caves unaccompanied.*

DIVING UNDER ICE

Ice diving requires specialized equipment and thorough preparation – even the best equipment can fail. The temperature of the water cannot drop below -1.8°C (28.7°F) or it would be frozen solid, the real problems are caused by the air temperatures, which can be several tens of degrees colder, especially with wind-chill. Nowadays all ice divers wear dry suits with several layers of undergarments, gloves and a hood that covers as much of the face as possible. The resulting bulk requires considerable weight to neutralize the diver's buoyancy. In extreme conditions even metal weight belt buckles fail. Full-face masks mean that, if the regulator fails, the diver cannot easily access the backup.

For redundancy the divers should each have two completely separate regulators, either on separate scuba cylinders or on a single cylinder with a V-manifold. The scuba cylinders should be filled with air that is as dry as possible and they and the regulators stored out of the wind in a dry place until the divers enter the water. The regulator first stages should be environmentally sealed against the ingress of water and not be breathed through until the first and second stages are both submerged to avoid condensation freezing the regulator.

Ice diving can either take place in a lead (a crack in the ice) or in a

hole cut through the ice. Ice movement can cause a lead to close, trapping the divers beneath thick ice. Where a hole is cut, a triangular shape will enable two divers to get in and out of the water simultaneously by using the sides of the hole at separate corners for leverage. Ideally there

Top: *When diving under ice, all divers should be attached to a tether line manned from above the ice.*
Above: *Diving under ice is a surreal experience, but divers must take care not to get the tether line tangled up.*

Above: Because of the bulk of warm undergarments, a lot of weight is required when diving under ice.

Diving under ice is a surreal experience: the ice forms amazing shapes and at high latitudes the animals exhibit gigantism, growing extremely slowly, but living to an old age, becoming much larger in the process.

Freshwater diving

Freshwater is less buoyant, more likely to carry parasites that may lead to an infection and there are no charts for most freshwater sites. Some freshwater sites are at a high enough altitude to require

Above: A diver climbing down to Cayangan Lake, which is fed by a hot spring. All equipment has to be carried.

should be shelter beside or over the hole where divers can kit up and keep out of the wind. In its simplest form this would be a windbreak, but where possible it should be a vehicle, trailer or tent. Small items of equipment are easily lost in snow so place them on a groundsheet or in a vehicle. Hot drinks and food should be available before and after the dive.

The divers should each be attached to a line strong enough to haul them back to the surface. Each line should be tied off to an immovable object and attended by someone whose sole job is to tender that line, feeling for an agreed series of signals from the diver.

Erratic pulls, unreadable pulls or no response, all signal an emergency so the diver should be pulled up. The surface crew have to remove ice continually to keep the hole from freezing over. The ice may be continually cracking open so they would also have to watch out for this. If there are Polar Bears, they need to be armed.

The divers below should never lose sight of the hole. Usually there is bright light, but in lakes or during plankton blooms there may not be, in which case a scuba cylinder fitted with a regulator and a flashing light should be lowered. At sea the tides still operate so that the ice is constantly moving.

the use of special dive tables and corrections to the measured depths. Heavy rain can reduce freshwater visibility to zero and could lead to rapidly rising water levels and flash floods. In some areas lakes or rivers are fed by hot springs. Be careful – they can get very hot!

Diving in lakes is relatively easy, but diving in rivers can be difficult if they are fast flowing. In general the current will be slower near the riverbank due to the friction of the water against the bank. Before entering a river you must consider where you can exit. One way to move along the river bottom against the current is to use hooks for purchase on the bottom so that you can pull yourself along.

Freshwater and brackish-water sites, particularly lakes, quarries, dams, canals and slow-flowing rivers, are likely to carry infections such as Weil's disease (Leptospirosis) and, where it is endemic, Bilharzia (Schistosomiasis).

Above: Scrambling over rocks to dive in Cayangan Lake.
Left: Divers check their equipment before descending into the hot water of Cayangan Lake, Coron, Philippines.

EXTENDED RANGE
(Technical Diving)

Extended range or technical diving uses a variety of breathing gas mixtures other than normal air to reduce the problems associated with nitrogen and oxygen under pressure. All divers require detailed training before these breathing gases can be used.

Enriched Air Nitrox

Any mixture of nitrogen and oxygen is Nitrox, but to divers it means air enriched with oxygen. In 1989 American Nitrox Divers International (ANDI) copyrighted the term SafeAir for a mixture of air enriched to between 22 and 50% oxygen.

By increasing the percentage of oxygen, and thus decreasing the percentage of nitrogen, divers will absorb less nitrogen during a dive and have less to eliminate during the ascent. EANx 32 contains 32% of oxygen and 68% of nitrogen. (EANx stands for Enriched Air Nitrox, with the number denoting the percentage of oxygen). National Oceanographic and Atmospheric Administration (NOAA) Nitrox I has 32% of oxygen and NOAA Nitrox II has 36% of oxygen.

When diving on Nitrox you can calculate dive plans from Nitrox tables, which will give you longer no-decompression stop times at the maximum depth. Alternatively, you can calculate dive plans from air tables, which will give an extra safety factor. If you go into decompression, this will be shorter if calculated from Nitrox tables, but have a greater safety factor if calculated from air tables. Many divers feel less fatigued after diving on Enriched Air Nitrox, though there is no scientific proof of this,

Above: Divers kitting up to use Nitrox. At this stage they should always analyze the oxygen content of the mix before using it in the water.

and many experience a lower rate of breathing gas consumption.

Another use of Nitrox is that divers who have been deep (whether breathing air or other gas mixtures) can shorten their decompression times at shallow depths by changing to a mixture containing 50–80% oxygen. This enables faster elimination of excess nitrogen if using air, or helium if using mixed gas. The diver usually has a small scuba cylinder (pony bottle) of high-concentration Nitrox fitted with its own regulator from which to breathe at shallow depth. Sometimes a cylinder of high-concentration Nitrox, fitted with its own regulator, is hung at a shallow decompression depth on the anchor line or shotline.

However, due to the risk of oxygen toxicity, depths are limited by the percentage of oxygen in the Nitrox mix – the partial pressure of oxygen should not exceed 1.4ata (see p23). The higher the percentage of oxygen, the shallower the maximum depth.

There may be circumstances when a diver has to go deeper than the risk of oxygen toxicity allows on the Nitrox mixture used.

If the diver has a separate small cylinder of normal air fitted with its own regulator, it is possible to switch and breathe from this cylinder for a brief, deeper foray and switch back to Nitrox afterwards.

The recommended oxygen tolerance units (OTUs) should not be exceeded, particularly on repetitive dives, because oxygen breathed at higher than normal partial pressures over long periods affects the central nervous system.

High concentrations of oxygen cause combustion on contact with oils and greases, so cylinders and valves that have contact with pure oxygen during blending must be kept scrupulously oxygen clean. Standard regulators should be suitable for Nitrox mixtures of up to 40% oxygen. For higher concentrations you should replace regulator O-rings with ones that do not require lubrication.

Breathing gases for deep diving

The two limiting factors for deep diving are oxygen toxicity and nitrogen narcosis. Oxygen toxicity is the most critical, as no adaptation or tolerance can be built up. Once oxygen exceeds a partial pressure (ppO_2) of 1.6ata, the diver is in an uncharted zone with unpredictable consequences. Nitrogen acts as a narcotic, and a tolerance or adaptation to nitrogen narcosis can be built up, but at some stage, all divers will be overwhelmed and eventually lose consciousness.

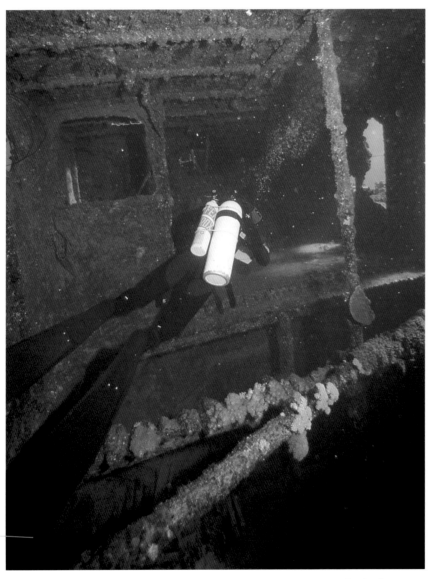

Above: Diver carrying a smaller cylinder of Nitrox for decompression attached to his main scuba cylinder. Tienstin *wreck, Abu Galawa, Egypt.*

Heliox and Trimix

The most common breathing gases for deep diving are Trimix and Heliox. Trimix is a mixture of helium, oxygen and nitrogen made up by mixing helium with air (also known as Heliair) or by mixing helium with pure oxygen and air. This makes it possible to reduce the nitrogen level (to reduce nitrogen narcosis at depth) and reduce the percentage of oxygen to below 21% (to avoid oxygen toxicity). However, the helium conducts heat away from the body more quickly than nitrogen during respiration and, because the helium is a smaller molecule, more of it is absorbed, more quickly, by the tissues and this has to be eliminated during decompression. For some profiles this requires slower ascents and deeper decompression stops to avoid the helium outgassing too quickly.

Heliox is a mixture of helium and oxygen. Without any nitrogen present, narcosis is kept to a minimum, but decompression times are extended.

At depths beyond 120m (400ft) on Heliox and 180m (600ft) on Trimix the diver can suffer High Pressure Nervous (also called Neurological) Syndrome (HPNS). For diving at these depths the National Oceanographic and Atmospheric Administration (NOAA) advises adding 10% of nitrogen to the breathing mix and using very slow descent rates – 30cm (1ft) per minute beyond 120m (400ft) on

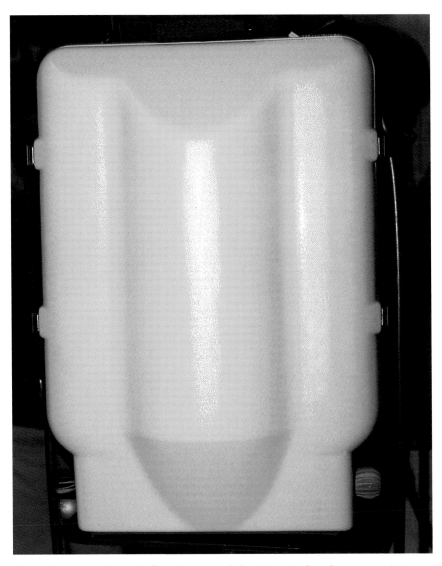

Above: *The Inspiration is the first CE-approved closed circuit rebreathing system. It is approved to 50m (165ft) with air as the diluent gas (40m;130ft recommended) and 100m (330ft) with Heliox. CE is the European standardization mark, Conformité Européene.*

Heliox and 180m (600ft) on Trimix. This is not really an option for recreational divers.

As divers go deeper they must reduce the oxygen content of their breathing gas – there is almost an optimum mix for each depth. As they descend, divers use one or more 'travel-mixes' with progressively smaller percentages of oxygen and then switch to a 'bottom-mix' with an even lower oxygen content. However, bottom-mixes have too low an oxygen content to sustain life at shallower depths. During ascent divers switch back to the travel-mixes. Shallow decompression stops will be shorter if divers switch to mixes high in oxygen.

Those diving deep using Heliox or Trimix have several clearly-marked cylinders of different gas mixtures and must be able to identify the correct regulator, attached to the correct cylinder, for each phase of the dive. Ideally they should be able to distinguish each regulator by touch as well as sight in case they are caught in zero visibility or lose their mask. This has led to the development of modern rebreathers, in which the breathing gas mixture can be modified as the depth varies.

Rebreathers

The acronym SCUBA stands for Self-Contained Underwater Breathing Apparatus. When using an open-circuit system, we waste most of the oxygen we breathe by exhaling into the water.

Some companies have modernized closed or semiclosed circuit scuba equipment for recreational use. Termed rebreathers, the carbon dioxide in the diver's exhaled gases is chemically removed by passing it through a 'scrubber' of Soda-Lime, the commercial

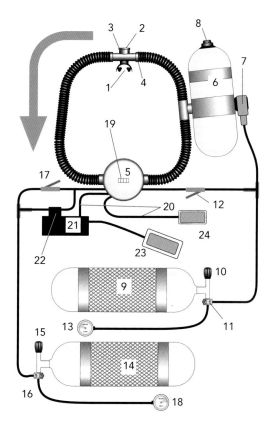

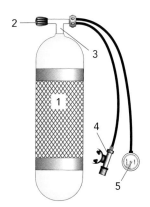

OPEN-CIRCUIT SCUBA
1 Gas supply cylinder
2 On/off valve
3 Regulator First-stage
4 Regulator Second-stage
5 Pressure gauge

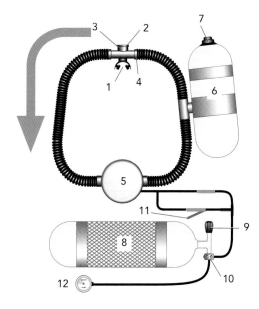

SEMICLOSED REBREATHER
1 Mouthpiece
2 Mouthpiece shutoff
3 Downstream check-valve
4 Upstream check-valve
5 CO_2 absorbent canister
6 Counterlung
7 Overpressure release-valve
8 Supply gas supply cylinder
9 Supply gas on/off valve
10 Supply gas regulator
11 Manual supply gas bypass
12 Supply gas pressure gauge

CLOSED-CIRCUIT REBREATHER
1 Mouthpiece
2 Mouthpiece shutoff
3 Downstream check-valve
4 Upstream check-valve
5 CO_2 absorbent canister
6 Counterlung
7 Diluent addition valve
8 Overpressure release-valve
9 Diluent supply cylinder
10 Diluent on/off valve
11 Diluent regulator
12 Manual diluent bypass
13 Diluent pressure gauge
14 Oxygen supply cylinder
15 Oxygen on/off valve
16 Oxygen regulator
17 Manual oxygen bypass
18 Oxygen pressure gauge
19 Oxygen sensors
20 Oxygen sensor cable
21 Main electronics
22 Oxygen solenoid valve
23 Primary display
24 Secondary display

product is a mixture of calcium and sodium hydroxides. Some oxygen is added to the gases so cleaned and that mixture is breathed again, hence the name rebreather. The inhaled breathing gas is warm and moist because the chemical reaction involved in the absorption of carbon dioxide is exothermic, generating warmth and moisture. The closed-circuit system does not dump any gas into the water until the diver ascends. The semiclosed circuit system only dumps a small portion of each breath. In this way divers get long diving times out of a relatively small amount of breathing gas. Rebreathers can be based on Nitrox or, for deeper diving, Trimix or Heliox.

Rebreathers must be meticulously prepared and checked. They require considerable maintenance and a constant eye must be kept on gauges. A very experienced rebreather user, who was a Nobel prize-winning scientist, died as a result of a simple mistake.

THE ADVANTAGES OF USING A REBREATHER INCLUDE

- Gas efficiency, which is useful with expensive gases, especially helium.
- Less chance of dislodging silt in enclosed overhead environments.
- Quieter operation, so that the diver can get closer to some skittish marine life.

DISADVANTAGES

- Cost – rebreathers are generally more expensive to purchase.
- Rebreathers are complex to operate, require additional training, strict discipline to detail and have more components that can and do go wrong. The warm, moist hoses and counterlung are a perfect environment for the growth of bacteria so they should be stripped down and cleaned after each day of use.
- Most manufacturers refuse to sell rebreathers to anyone who has not passed a training course in their use.

Above: A diver prepares to use a rebreather at a BS-AC 'Try-a-Rebreather' session.

Above: The Dräger Dolphin Rebreather, a recreational Nitrox semiclosed rebreather, is easier to use than closed-circuit ones.

Above: Under the futuristic cover of Ambient Pressure (Buddy) Inspiration closed-circuit rebreather.

DIVING WITH A PURPOSE

Diving is an adventure and many continue with speciality courses, including technical diving. There is the possibility of working around the world (very poorly paid) as an instructor and eventually running a diving operation. Some divers study diving history or archaeology, research and search for shipwrecks, explore caves or have an interest in marine biology and helping marine charities. Others dive as part of their profession. Whatever their interest, many divers will want to photograph or video underwater. Police forensic diving is an occupation that requires dedication. Military diving may involve exciting forays into real or simulated enemy territory, but it will often be boring with searches under ships or marine installations. Some divers become involved in commercial diving or treasure hunting, but often these are not the glamorous, well-paid jobs that they are made out to be and are beyond the scope of this book.

Marine biology

Our understanding of underwater life is mostly worked out by marine biologists.

Many organizations offer divers the chance to be paying guests and learn about the underwater environment in exotic locations. These divers then act as the marine scientists' eyes. These organizations often take the first step in gathering enough information to enable third world countries to set up marine protected areas or marine parks.

Many scientific surveys are happy to be informed of particular animal sightings and environmental changes and several local governments, training agencies and charities organize the clean-up of rubbish from beaches and shallow water.

Archaeological diving

Archaeological diving is usually restricted to academics, but many historical sites that were once on land, and ancient wrecks, have been found by amateur divers.

Archaeological sites have been charted, excavated with precision and artefacts recovered for museums by divers guided via a video connection to archaeologists. Many wreck sites are still in busy shipping lanes and others have problems with tides.

Underwater archaeology is not restricted to the sea – ancient sites are found in lakes, rivers, springs and wells. Less ancient, but equally interesting, artefacts are found near bridges and waterside drinking establishments.

Underwater still photography

Underwater still photography requires some technical competence. The new digital cameras are more forgiving in that you can discard failures without having to pay for them.

You cannot change films or prime lenses in this environment so you need to have a clear idea of what you wish to photograph before you take the plunge. Another possibility is to have a

Top: *Exploring wrecks is of great interest to most divers, but few are in such clear water as the* Umbria *off Port Sudan.*
Above: *Several organizations make use of amateur divers to act as photographers and surveyors for scientists.*

SEMIPROFESSIONAL DIVING

The authorities in many first world countries have laws that cover semiprofessional diving. In these countries, if you do any diving for monetary reward, including instructing, photography, filming and even supporting film crews, you will have to pass further courses and more detailed medical examinations under the local health and safety rules. These courses and medicals are not difficult, but they cost money so you must calculate the cost against the possible gain.

Above: A housed camera set up for macro photography; the larger flashgun is set to give twice as much power as the smaller one, which is set to fill in some of the shadows.

and others. Although they have been discontinued, there are still plenty of these cameras around.

WATERPROOF HOUSINGS

Technical advances of land cameras are the main reason for the demise of the Nikonos. Land cameras are used underwater in metal or Plexiglas waterproof housings. Metal housings are strong, reliable, work well at depth and will last a long time if properly maintained. They are heavy to carry, especially when travelling by air, but have buoyancy in water. Their higher cost is justified if one is using an expensive camera that deserves the extra protection.

Plexiglas housings are cheaper, but more fragile and require careful handling, above and below the water. Some models compress at depth, making the control rods miss the camera controls. These control rods can be adjusted to work at depths, but then do not function properly near the surface. Most underwater photographs are taken near the surface, so this is not serious. These housings are lightweight to carry on land, but often too buoyant in the water where you have to attach extra weights.

Underwater cameras, housings, flashguns and cables have O-ring seals to keep the water out, these and their mating surfaces or grooves must be kept scrupulously clean. O-rings should be lightly greased with special grease (usually silicone) to prevent flooding.

zoom lens on a housed camera. If the water is calm you can carry one camera for wide-angle and another for close-up or macro. In strong currents a non-reflex camera will be smaller and easier to handle.

There are several waterproof film and digital non-reflex cameras, that do not need waterproof housings, but if you want the best lenses at this level you need a Nikonos V. More magazine covers have been shot with this camera and its 15mm lens than all other cameras put together. It has a Through-The-Lens (TTL) automatic exposure system and dedicated flashguns (strobes) made by Nikon

Housings without controls, which are designed for auto-everything cameras, require fast films for reasonable shutter speeds and lens apertures in low light.

When balancing flash with daylight, cameras with faster flash synchronization speeds, $\frac{1}{125}$ or $\frac{1}{250}$ of a second, give sharper results by avoiding the double images associated with fast-moving fish.

Masks hold your eyes away from the viewfinder, so buy the smallest volume mask you can wear. Cameras with optical action finders or eyepiece magnifiers are useful in housings, but this is not so important with autofocus systems.

Good buoyancy control is essential. Do not touch coral or wear fins over sandy bottoms, they will stir up sand. Photographers do not swim around much, so wear a wet suit for warmth.

Light refraction through your mask and through the camera lens causes objects to appear one third closer and larger than in air. Reflex focusing or visually estimated distances remain correct, but if you measure distances by ruler, these must be reduced by one third when setting the lens focus if it is inscribed in 'in-air' distances.

If you are using a waterproof housing with a flat port, (window), in front of the lens, refraction increases the focal length of the lens and decreases its sharpness, due to the individual colours of light being refracted at different angles and speeds (chromatic

Above: A diver with a Nikonos camera set up with a single flashgun. Note that he is kneeling on dead sand so that he does not touch the coral.

aberration). This is most pronounced with wide-angle lenses, which should be corrected by using a convex dome port. Dome ports require lenses to be able to focus on a virtual image at around 30cm (1ft) so you may have to fit supplementary positive dioptre lenses to some camera lenses.

LIGHTING, FILTERS AND FLASHGUNS

When the sun is at a low angle, or in choppy seas, much of the light fails to enter the water. To take advantage of the maximum light available it is best to photograph two hours either side of the sun's highest point. Sunlight can give

spectacular effects underwater, especially in silhouette shots, but generally you should keep the sun behind you and on your subject.

Water acts as a cyan (blue/green) filter, cutting back red, so colour film will have a blue/green cast. For available-light photography, different filters are sold to correct this in either temperate or tropical waters, but they reduce the already limited light available. Flash will put back the colour and increase apparent sharpness.

Modern flashguns (strobes) have TTL automatic exposure systems. Underwater, large flashguns have good wide-angle performance usable up to 1.5m (5ft). Smaller

flashguns have a narrow angle and only work up to 1m (40 inches), diffusers widen the angle covered, but you lose at least one F-stop in output. Most land flashguns are more advanced than underwater flashguns and can be housed for underwater use (*see Flash with digital cameras p160*).

Flashguns used on or near the camera will light up suspended matter in the water like white stars in a black sky (back scatter). The closer these particles are to the camera, the larger they will appear. Keep the flash as far as possible above and to one side of the camera. Two narrow-angle flashguns, one on each side of the camera,

Above: *A diver being taught how to use a Nikonos camera set up with a single flashgun for close-up photography. Note that they are kneeling on dead sand.*

each pointing slightly outward, but with their light overlapping in the centre, often produce a better result than a single wide-angle flashgun. However, the result will be a little flat instead of giving the modelling light that distinguishes features by showing shadows.

When photographing divers, the eyes in the mask must be lit and in focus. Flashguns with a colour temperature of 4500 Kelvin will give more accurate skin tones and colour by replacing some of the red that the water has filtered out.

In a multiple flash set-up the prime flashgun will meter by TTL if available and, unless it has TTL-Slave, any other unit will give its preprogrammed output so this should be set low to achieve modelling light. TTL-Slave flashguns should have a lower output than the main flash for the same reason.

Although objects appear closer to your eye and the camera lens underwater, the flash must strike the subject directly to illuminate it. Narrow-angle flashguns must therefore be aimed behind the apparent subject, to hit the real subject. Built-in aiming/focusing lights, or a torch strapped to the flash will aid this problem and focusing during night photography. Built-in aiming/focusing lights are best powered by separate batteries or the main flash battery will not last for a complete dive.

DIVER AND WRECK PHOTOGRAPHY

Diver and wreck photography are the most difficult. Even with apparently clear water and wide-angle lenses there will be back scatter and flash is essential to light a diver's mask.

NIGHT PHOTOGRAPHY

Focusing quickly in dim light is difficult and many subjects disappear when lit up, so pre-set the controls. Many creatures only appear at night and some fish are half asleep, making them more approachable.

PHOTOGRAPHING FISH

The scales of fish reflect light in ways that vary with the angle. Silver fish reflect more light than coloured fish and black fish almost none at all. Therefore you should bracket exposures – with automatic flashguns simply alter the film speed setting on the camera.

Some fish are strongly territorial. Surgeonfish, triggerfish and sharks will make mock attacks on a perceived invader and these situations can make strong pictures if you are brave enough to hold your ground. Manta Rays are curious and will keep coming back if you react quietly and do not chase after them. Remember that if an eye is in the picture it must be lit and sharp, it is acceptable for the rest of the

Above: *A diver set up for photographing in strong currents.*

animal to be slightly blurred. Angelfish and butterflyfish swim off when you first enter their territory, but if you remain quietly in the same place they usually return.

DIGITAL CAMERAS AND THEIR USE UNDERWATER

Digital cameras appear to work out cheaper because they eliminate the cost of film and processing. When using low-resolution images, you can get a lot more shots onto a memory card than on a film. You can discard failures and keep on photographing a subject until you get it right – so long as it does not move. Where available, storing images in RAW enables the correction of the white balance, and therefore colour balance, when back on land.

Electronics give more problems in a saltwater environment, you have to carry a portable computer or several memory cards to download the images and if used professionally (heavily), the camera's service life is only about three years, so the saving in film costs is soon negated.

FLASH WITH DIGITAL CAMERAS

Many but not all digital cameras are not compatible with normal TTL flashguns as they cannot read the flash reflected off film. This is addressed with either a light sensor on the camera body to judge proper exposure or with special flashguns for different digital cameras. Many of these send out several pre-flashes and read their intensity when reflected back from the subject (DTTL). You can still use manual flash, shoot the picture, review the picture, make adjustments and shoot the picture again, but this takes time and the subject may have moved. You can delete shots that were not correctly exposed.

There are answers to TTL flash problems for underwater photography. One is to house a land flashgun that is dedicated to your digital camera, the problem with this method is that the land flashguns will not cover the field of view of very wide-angle lenses though they are fine for close shots. Also, independent manufacturers of wide-angle underwater flashguns now have models that feature special electronic circuitry for use with the newest digital cameras, yet they are still compatible with the popular film cameras used underwater including the Nikonos. A third solution is that the Fuji S2 Pro digital camera will work with all standard Nikonos-compatible underwater flashguns. Due to this and the fact that it is based on the Nikon F80/N80 camera body and utilizes Nikkor lenses, this camera has become popular for use in a waterproof housing.

Underwater videography

Video is much easier and the fact that the subject moves often covers mistakes. Most underwater videographers just set the camera on automatic, place it in a waterproof housing and go. Macro subjects may require extra lighting but other shots can be taken with available light and, if necessary, improved electronically afterwards. Back scatter is much less of a problem and the results can be played back on site and shot again if necessary, or the tape or disc can be wiped clean and used again.

With the correct connecting lead, most cameras can play back their video content on normal television sets and these are available

---

TIPS

- Point and shoot does not work. Get closer than arm's length and make sure the subject fills more than half the frame. Wide-angle close-up shots have impact.

- Limit people shots to head and shoulders unless you have very wide-angle lenses; for smaller creatures use macro lenses, close-up kits or extension tubes with framers.

- Where possible do not aim the camera downwards, always aim it horizontally or, better still, upwards, otherwise the background in the picture will be dark.

on live-aboard boats as well as at land resorts.

More expensive cameras have more controls and professional cameras have three chips – three CCD or CMOS sensors – each receiving the image through a coloured filter: red, green and blue.

When purchasing a waterproof housing you have to choose between electronic controls and manual controls. Electronic controls can be easier to operate and with fewer holes in the housing there is less chance of leakage. Some divers prefer manual controls because if something does go wrong with electronic controls when you are stranded on a live-aboard boat at sea, the whole housing can become unusable.

Most videographers are quite happy with videoing what they see for their own pleasure. There are underwater colour-correction filters for use without lights but if you want more professional results you will require proper lights. You must work out a story line and follow it, keep the camera steady, use the zoom sparingly, build sequences and keep each shot short unless the subject is particularly interesting. Ideally, for most subjects you would begin with a wide-angle shot to set the scene, then take a medium shot and then move in for a close shot. When visibility is poor, video macro subjects. When videoing a night scene, your normal lights will make the scene look as though it was

Above: Two Subal waterproof aluminium housings. The one on the left is set up for extreme wide-angle photography and the other for close-up, or macro, photography.

shot during the day unless you have lights that can be dimmed.

If you are going to show your results to an audience, good editing is very important. This can include cropping, dissolves, mixing, graphics and superimposing, altering the speed of movement and using a shot in reverse. The actual act of editing will make it obvious what improvements can be made the next time you shoot.

Most video cameras have dedicated battery packs so carry at least one spare and keep it charged.

  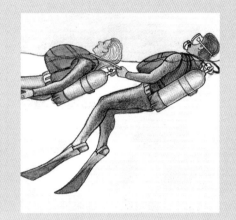

SAFETY AND FIRST AID

Always dive conservatively. If there is a recompression (hyperbaric) chamber in the area, ensure that you know how to contact the authorities that control its use or the evacuation procedures to reach it. Do not assume that the nearest recompression chamber is the most suitable, check out local information first.

  With correct training, scuba diving is a safe sport. There are many physiological situations that could affect a diver and some are covered in chapter 3. A recognized course in first aid should be a part of basic training. If there is more than one casualty, treat non-breathing casualties first and then breathing but unconscious casualties.

Basic rescue techniques

An unconscious diver is often easier to deal with. A conscious casualty in panic can endanger the rescuer, even result in a second casualty. In this circumstance, monitor the situation from a safe distance until the casualty calms down or becomes sufficiently incapacitated to pose no further threat.

The rescuer should face the casualty in order to be within easy reach of the controls for both divers' BCD inflation and dump valves, weight belt and, if worn, dry suit inflation and dump valves.

Take hold of the casualty in such a way that positive contact can be maintained. The casualty's BCD (and dry suit if worn), should be kept more buoyant than that of the rescuer so that if contact is lost the casualty would rise to the surface. (It is better for the casualty to rise to the surface in an uncontrolled manner than not at all). When inflating the casualty's BCD, the direct feed is easier to use because operating the small emergency cylinder will require two hands.

Make sure that you do not ascend faster than the smallest bubbles. If the ascent rate becomes too fast you will have to vent some breathing gas from your own and the casualty's BCD and, if worn, dry suit. If both of you have dry suits with wrist-mounted dump valves you will have to raise each of the arms with these valves. However, you may be holding the casualty's left arm with your right arm or vice versa and one of you may not have a dump valve on the arm concerned (by raising all four arms you risk losing contact). Instead, raise your arm which has a dump valve, but dump air from the casualty's dry suit by inserting a finger beneath the wrist seal of the casualty's raised arm.

You can vent breathing gas from both BCDs through their dump valves, but it may be easier to dump breathing gas from the casualty's BCD through the large corrugated oral-inflation tube by raising the tube and pressing its purge button.

The casualty may not have enough breathing gas left to achieve buoyancy with the BCD or dry suit. In that case try to lift the casualty by inflating your BCD. If that fails, ditch the casualty's weight belt and try again.

Above: When making an emergency ascent, divers wearing dry suits must raise the arm with the valve to dump air.

As you ascend make sure that you breathe out and push the casualty's stomach to make him or her breathe out too.

Once on the surface, inflate the casualty's BCD enough to give buoyancy, but not so much that you cannot give Expired Air Resuscitation (EAR), also known as mouth-to-mouth, mouth-to-nose and exhaled air resuscitation, if necessary. Do not inflate a dry suit if worn.

If the casualty has to be towed, the rescuer and the casualty should be on their backs. If faced with a long

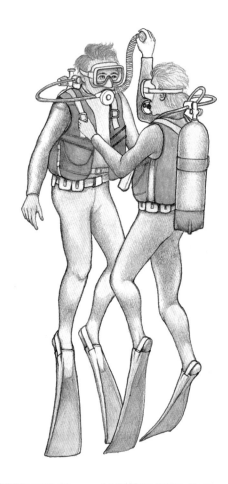

tow then the rescuer should ditch the casualty's weight belt and scuba cylinder. However, the rescuer's weight belt should stay on, as it will keep the legs lower in the water and make finning more efficient.

A conscious casualty should be towed from behind, with the rescuer holding onto part of the casualty's equipment, such as a BCD shoulder strap. An unconscious casualty will require a clear airway, so tow him or her by gripping the point of the chin to keep the head back. In a rough sea you will also have to place your other hand under the neck for support.

For other serious conditions related to diving refer to chapter 3, pages 34–45, but remember that some common ailments, including muscle strain, influenza, dengue fever and malaria, can give symptoms that mimic diving problems. However, it is best to treat such symptoms as diving related until specialist medical examination proves otherwise. Write down what you think has happened, the symptoms and the casualty's dive profile if you know it. If the diving computer permits downloading of the dive profile to a personal computer, leave it with the casualty. Pin this information in a conspicuous place for the attention of the medical facility.

Rough-and-ready non-specialist tests for decompression illness (DCI)

Check for confusion, convulsions, itchy skin, pain in any large joint, numbness, paralysis, pins-and-needles sensation, weakness and problems with vision and balance.

- Does the diver know who he or she is; where he or she is; what the time is?
- Can the diver see and count a number of fingers held up 50cm (20 in) in front of his or her face and

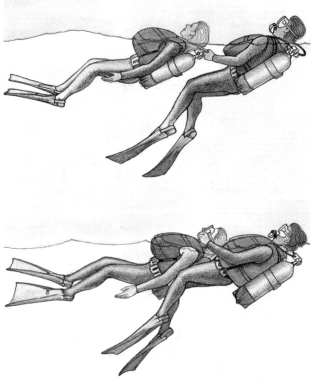

Above Left: Dumping air from the casualty's BCD through the oral inflation tube.

*Left: A conscious casualty can be towed by gripping a convenient part of his equipment, while an unconscious casualty (**bottom**) needs an adequate neck extension during the tow. This will require two hands.*

follow your hand with the eyes as you move it from side to side and up and down. Be sure that both eyes follow in each direction and look for any rapid oscillation or jerky movement of the eyeballs.

- Ask the diver to smile and check that both sides of the face bear the same expression.
- Run the back of a finger across each side of his or her forehead, cheeks and chin and confirm the diver can feel it.
- Check that the diver can hear a whisper with eyes closed.
- Ask the diver to shrug the shoulders and check that both sides move equally.
- Ask the diver to swallow, check that the Adam's apple moves up and then down.

- Ask the diver to stick out his or her tongue in the centre of the mouth – deviation to either side indicates a problem.
- Check that there is equal muscle strength on both sides of the body by asking the diver to resist as you pull and push each arm and leg away from and back towards the body.
- Check that the diver's body can feel a finger stroked lightly across the shoulders, down the back, chest, abdomen and each arm – upper and lower, inside and out, and the same on each leg.
- On firm ground (not on a boat), establish if the diver can walk a straight line and stand upright with the feet together, arms outstretched and the eyes closed?

Condensed first-aid kit

First-Aid manual

Pencil and notebook

Tweezers and scissors

6 large standard sterile dressings

1 large Elastoplast fabric dressing strip

2 triangular bandages

3 medium-size safety pins

1 pack sterile cotton wool

2 crepe bandages, each 50mm (2in) wide

eye drops

antiseptic fluid/cream

1 bottle vinegar

Antihistamine cream

Sachets of rehydration salts

Seasickness tablets

Decongestants (Sudafed)

Painkillers (Aspirin or Ibuprofen)

Anti-diarrhoea (Imodium)

Anti-aids pack (syringes/needles/drip needle)

Oxygen administration

The administration of pure oxygen is now recommended for most incidents of possible DCI, so all divers should take a course in this. Exposure to 100% oxygen at surface pressure over a prolonged period (8–12 hours) can lead to pulmonary toxicity in healthy adults. Symptoms include substernal pain and coughing. Paradoxically, the lungs may become less able to supply the body with normal levels of oxygen due to damage to the gas exchanging lining of the air sacs within the lungs.

BUDDY CHECKS

By keeping an eye on each other, you can ensure that a diver in trouble gets help quickly. Things to look out for include:

- Stress caused by swimming against a current
- Anxiety
- Rapid breathing
- A diver signalling that he or she is having problems breathing
- Erratic and uncoordinated movements (convulsions)
- Problems with buoyancy control
- Failure to respond to signals
- Wide, staring eyes
- Vigorously treading water
- Inactivity

DANGEROUS UNDERWATER ORGANISMS AND POLLUTANTS

The brochures are full of alluring pictures, young ladies in the latest swimsuits on empty palm-fringed beaches. The reality, however, can be different. A holiday can be ruined by sunburn and insect bites, although of most concern to divers are problems caused by underwater organisms and pollutants, most commonly coral cuts, fire coral stings and swimmer's ear.

Above left: *Crown of Thorns Sea Star (Starfish)*
Above centre: *Stonefish covered in algae.*
Above right: *Yellowtail Surgeonfish, showing scalpel at the base of the tail.*

If you do not wish to wear a wet suit, wear a thin lycra bodysuit or even an old pair of trousers and a T-shirt. These will protect you against cuts, scrapes, fire coral and jellyfish when diving, and sunburn when snorkelling. They will not protect you against the tiny stinging plankton found in open water that can even get under a wet suit, but antihistamine cream (after drying the skin) will take care of that.

Sun

The tropical sun reflects off white sand beaches and the water, so cover the skin as much as possible, use a sunscreen with maximum sun protection factor and keep to the shade when possible. Snorkellers should be especially careful about the back of the neck and the back of the knees. Above water it is important to protect the eyes with sunglasses that have lenses of optical quality.

Insects

Caribbean beaches are notorious for biting insects, but many other destinations have biting ants and mosquitoes. Take the correct malarial prophylactics where necessary, a good insect repellent, antihistamine cream for the bites and sleep in a mosquito net in bad areas. The mosquitoes that carry malaria bite after dusk, so cover up well then. The mosquitoes that carry dengue fever bite during the day. As yet there is no prophylactic or cure for dengue fever and it

has now spread to many diving destinations. The curse of insect bites is a good reason for choosing a live-aboard boat.

Swimmer's Ear

Swimmer's ear mostly affects those who snorkel a lot. Various preventive drops are available, including 5% acetic acid in isopropyl alcohol and aluminium acetate/acetic acid solution. The main symptom is extreme pain. Sometimes the cause is a fungus, for which Multifungin ear drops can be used. Other treatments are Otosporin (Polymixin B/Neomycin) and Polymixin B/Gentimycin, but the best course is prevention.

After every dive or snorkelling session, wash out the ears with freshwater, dry them thoroughly

and then add preventive drops to each ear. There are several proprietary mixtures (one of which is called Swimmer's Ear). Do not poke anything solid like cotton buds into the ears.

Harbours

Diving in or near harbours brings extra problems from pollution, raw sewage, oil and chemical burns from sewers, yachts, ships and port discharge. Diesel fuel on the surface of seawater burns sensitive skin and causes the foam neoprene of exposure suits to deteriorate. Wash yourself after each dive and wash all the equipment used while diving with freshwater at the end of each day. A course of antibiotic against gut infection might be required.

Above: As with other members of the Scorpionfish family, Lionfish have poisonous spines, which can cause intense pain and swelling if touched (see p170).

Fish that bite

Large fish can sever arteries or veins. A rescuer can often stop the bleeding from severed blood vessels by firmly pressing any material handy directly onto the wound. However, in the water, this is difficult, especially while helping a victim ashore or to a boat. In these cases, where bleeding could be fatal, a tourniquet can be used. Once ashore or in the boat, control bleeding by pressing directly on the wound, then remove any tourniquets. Stabilize the patient with blood or plasma transfusions before evacuating to an emergency facility.

Basic wound care is the same whether you have had an accident on land or been bitten by a fish. However, marine wounds have a higher risk of infection as the mouths and skins of marine animals harbour bacteria. Some wounds are further complicated by toxins, the flesh of natural prey and broken teeth. Wounds should be thoroughly cleaned, bleeding controlled and strong antiseptic added, many wounds will require treatment with an antibiotic. All ocean wounds, even small ones, carry a risk of tetanus (lockjaw), a deadly bacterial infection. Update your tetanus vaccination every five years.

Remove superficial flaps of skin, they create moist, dark areas that can harbour and promote bacterial growth. Do not remove deep flaps of skin or tissue, suture or tape them back into place.

Above: In general sharks are unlikely to attack divers, but they should always be treated with respect. The decomposition products of dead fish (even when several days old), are much more attractive to sharks than blood.

Any wound will take much longer to heal if the diver continues to get into the water. This is not a problem for someone on a two-week diving holiday, but it is a problem for dive guides who are expected to be in the water at least six days a week.

SHARKS

Where attacks have occurred they are usually connected with speared or hooked fish, lobsters rattling when picked up, or certain types of vibration such as that produced by a helicopter. People are more at risk when splashing on the surface than when diving. The main exceptions are the Great White Shark, the Tiger Shark and occasionally the Bull Shark. The Great White Shark can mistake a human for normal prey – sea lion and seal. Most Great White attacks occur off the coasts of California, South Africa and southern Australia. (*See Electronic Shark Repellent p87*).

BARRACUDA

Barracuda are usually seen in large shoals of several hundred fish up to 80cm (31 in) long. Lone individuals of twice this size have attacked divers, usually in poor visibility. It is likely that the barracuda mistook the sun's reflection on a knife or camera lens for a similar glint on its normal prey – small fish.

Treat victims by thoroughly cleansing the wounds and using antiseptic or antibiotic cream. Bad bites will also need anti-tetanus and antibiotic treatment.

MORAY EELS

Usually bites are the result of placing hands into holes to collect shells or lobsters or to remove anchors. Moray eels often refuse to let go so tearing flesh as you pull away exacerbates the wound. The wounds are notorious for tendon and nerve damage. They require thorough cleansing, usually need stitching and usually go septic so take antibiotics and anti-tetanus.

TRIGGERFISH

Large triggerfish, when guarding eggs in nests in the sand, are particularly aggressive and attack divers who get too close. Clean the wound and treat with antiseptic cream.

Venomous sea creatures

Many venomous sea creatures are bottom dwellers (benthic), hiding among coral, resting or burrowing into sand. If you must move along the sea bottom, which is not ecological, do so by shuffling along to push such creatures out of the way; this minimizes the chance of stepping directly onto sharp venomous spines, many of which will pierce fins. It is wise not to swim too close to the bottom, your equipment can damage coral and if you scare a stingray buried in the sand it could react with its barbed tail.

Above: *Moray eels are probably responsible for more bites on divers than all other marine animals put together.*

Right: *The teeth of large triggerfish are strong enough to bite through fins and draw blood on an ankle through a wet suit.*

BLUE-RINGED OCTOPUSES

With a beak that can penetrate a wetsuit, Blue-ringed Octopuses are small, beautiful creatures but definitely do not touch. The bite is painless, but it injects a paralysing neuromuscular venom stronger than any found in land animals. Residing in rock pools, crevices and coral rubble, the rings of the Blue-ringed Octopus only 'glow' electric blue when provoked. This is when it is most dangerous.

The venom is produced by symbiotic bacteria in the octopus's salivary glands. These bacteria are transferred from the mother to the young – even the eggs already contain enough venom to be dangerous. The venom is a cocktail of several poisons including the neurotoxin tetrodotoxin, which shuts down electrical signalling in nerves by binding to the pores of sodium channel proteins in nerve cell membranes. Nerve conduction is blocked and neuromuscular paralysis is usually followed by death. Despite fixed, dilated pupils and paralysis, the senses of the victims are often intact, aware of their surroundings, but unable to respond. If cardiopulmonary resuscitation (CPR) and Expired Air Rescuscitation (mouth-to-mouth) are applied until the poison has worked its way out of the victim's system (6–12 hours), recovery is possible. These animals should only be handled with forceps.

Above: The Tasselled Scorpionfish's method of camouflage is to adopt the background colour, but got it wrong this time! At night they are usually red and therefore easier to spot against coral if directly lit up with a light. Stonefish and scorpionfish do not move much. They are so well camouflaged that it is easy to put a hand on them unwittingly.

STONEFISH/SCORPIONFISH (INCLUDES LIONFISH AND TURKEYFISH)

Stonefish are the most feared, best camouflaged and most dangerous of the scorpionfish family. Stonefish have venom in the spines of the dorsal fin, which is raised when the fish is agitated. The venom in some species is as toxic as that of Cobras and can kill a child or a highly allergic adult. However, most healthy adults only suffer extreme pain. True Stonefish remain immobile in a horizontal position for so long that, depending on the habitat, they allow algae to grow on their body for further camouflage or sand may cover it. They are generally green, red-brown, grey or sandy coloured and are usually only seen if they move. Flatter than scorpionfish, their eyes usually face almost straight up and the mouth is hardly discernible for the camouflage.

The less toxic and more easily seen Scorpionfish have a more upright body shape and their eyes face sideways rather than upward, the mouth is usually obvious. They lie all over reefs in any position depending on the shape of the substrata. They do not rely on additional camouflage but change their body colour to match the substrate. The most common colour is dark red, but they can change through red and red-brown to white. Juveniles are usually hidden in nooks and crannies in the coral during the day.

Above: Spotfin Lionfish against a background of mixed corals. They pack a heavy sting in their beautiful spines. Lionfish are more of a problem on night dives when they often follow divers' lights. They are slow moving, unless swallowing prey, and hang around on reefs and wrecks.

The spines of the beautiful Lionfish/Turkeyfish pack a heavy sting, causing intense pain and swelling. Antivenins often exist, but require specialist medical supervision, do not work for all species and need refrigerated storage. It is rare that these are available when required.

Most of the venoms are high molecular weight proteins, which are broken down by heat. Clean the wound, apply a broad ligature or pressure bandage between the limb and the body. Immerse the limb in hot water at 50°C (120°F) for 30 minutes to 2 hours, until the pain stops. The cooling water from an outboard motor has been used, when no other supply of hot water was available. Several injections of local anaesthetic, around the wound site will ease the pain if they are available. The young or weak may need cardiac or respiratory resuscitation.

More at risk than divers are fishermen clearing their nets, line fishermen, lobster and shell collectors, who find it most productive to work at night. Many of them can vouch that this treatment works. The venoms can still be active in dead fish for 48 hours.

STINGRAYS

Stingrays can be the largest of the venomous fish and vary in size, from a few centimetres to several metres. The tail of the stingray carries at least one barb or spine that can be up to 37cm (14½ inches) long on top of the tail. Each barb is covered by a film of venom and mucus. These barbs point backwards, but can be used in any direction.

The venom contains toxic proteins. The effects of the venom may just be severe pain at the site

Above: Bluespotted Ribbontail Ray. Rays thrash out when trodden on, swum over closely or caught.

of injury. However, the larger stingrays have barbs long enough to penetrate a diver's guts or heart with more serious consequences, including death. For smaller stingrays, clean the wound and remove any barbs. Give the hot water treatment as for Stonefish, local anaesthetic if available, and follow up with antibiotic and anti-tetanus. Where larger barbs have penetrated the body seek urgent medical attention.

Rabbitfish also have venomous spines and **Long-jawed Squir-relfish** have a large opercular spine (situated on the gill covering), but neither are normally dangerous.

CONE SHELLS

Live cone shells should never be handled without gloves, preferably you should not be collecting them at all. The animal has a mobile, tube-like organ, which shoots a poison dart. The victim has initial numbness followed by local muscular paralysis, which may extend to respiratory paralysis and heart failure. Apply a broad ligature or pressure bandage between the wound and the body. Respiratory (EAR) and cardiac (CPR) resuscitation may be necessary.

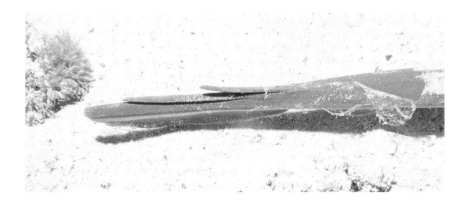

Left: Stingray tail showing two stinging spines. Although they point backward, they can be used in any direction.

Above: Poisonous sea urchin. Many urchin spines will pierce gloves.

Above: Spiky Sea Urchin, photographed at night. They occurr in the Indo Pacific.

SEA SNAKES

Although sea snakes are more venomous than land snakes they are not aggressive, unless provoked, and their short fangs will rarely penetrate a wet suit. Muscular paralysis may ascend up the limbs to the trunk and cause difficulty with breathing. If the injury is on a limb apply a broad ligature or pressure bandage between the body and the injury. Wash the wound and if necessary give CPR and EAR. Antivenin should only be given under medical supervision.

SEA URCHINS

The spines of sea urchins can be poisonous. They puncture the skin and break off, leaving painful wounds that often turn septic. For bad cases give the hot water treatment, which also softens the spines, making it easier for the body to reject them. Septic wounds will require antibiotics.

CROWN-OF-THORNS STARFISH

Crown-of-Thorns starfish have spines which pierce gloves and break off under the skin, causing pain and sometimes nausea lasting several days. Thirty minutes of hot water treatment helps the pain. Infections from these wounds are rare. If you cannot remove broken spines, or develop hives, breathing difficulty, numbness or weakness, get medical help. The symptoms usually disappear after spines are removed.

Above: Stinging hydroids often go unnoticed on wrecks, old anchor ropes and chains until you put your hands on them.

STINGING HYDROIDS

Stinging nematocysts are fired into your skin, giving quite a kick. They are not serious, but very painful and can cause large blisters on sensitive skin. Bathe the affected part in vinegar and apply antihistamine cream.

BRISTLE (FIRE) WORMS

Bristle (Fire) Worms have tufted bristles along the sides of their bodies that easily penetrate a diver's skin and cause a burning sensation. The bristles are easily removed with sticky tape, then wash the area with vinegar and apply antihistamine cream. No substance is guaranteed to relieve the pain and itching caused by these worms. Hives, a feeling of overall illness, or breathing difficulty could be signs of an allergic reaction, so seek medical help.

FIRE CORAL

Many people react violently from the slightest brush with fire coral. I have seen blisters 15 cm (5½ inches) across. Treatment is the same as for stinging hydroids.

JELLYFISH

Some of the more painful stings are from jellyfish in temperate waters. Stings can be treated with vinegar and antihistamine cream. This includes most of the jellyfish found in Australian waters, but there are more dangerous ones:

• Box Jellyfish also known as Stinger or Sea Wasp (*Chironex fleckeri*)

The Box Jellyfish of northern Australia is possibly the most venomous creature known to man. It has caused twice as many fatalities as sharks in these waters. It is difficult to see in murky water because it is transparent, but it can be 30cm (12 in) or more across the bell. It has a box shape with four corners, from which up to 15 thick, flat tentacles may hang. These tentacles may contract to a few centimetres or extend to 3m (10ft) or more in length. Its occurrence is

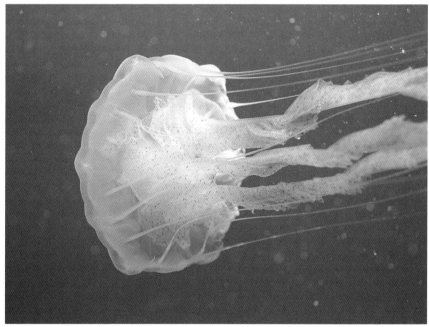

seasonal and it invades shallow water beaches in calmer weather along the north Queensland coast past Great Keppel Island. Stings have occurred in every month of the year except July, but fatal stings have only been registered from September to May.

Top: Fire coral, Millepora species, are not true corals, but members of the class Hydrozoa, so are more closely related to the stinging hydroids.
Above: Scyphozoan jellyfish of the class Scyhpozoa. Apart from those in lakes, most jellyfish sting, though few are dangerous.

Although there are other box jellyfish whose sting is not as dangerous, Chironex was thought, until recently, to occur in Australian waters only. It has now been seen in nearby areas of the Indo-West-Pacific Ocean.

The tentacles of the box jellyfish adhere to the skin, discharging nematocysts causing skin lesions and excruciating pain. Immediately flood the area with household vinegar to keep undischarged nematocysts from firing. This does not relieve pain, but prevents additional stings. Do not touch the tentacles, scrape them off with a knife or stick. For pain relief, apply ice packs. Local anaesthetic may be required. Symptoms are shortness of breath, weakness, muscle cramps or palpitations. CPR and Expired Air Resuscitation (mouth-to-mouth) may be required. An antivenin has been developed in Australia.

• Irukandji Jellyfish
(Carukia barnesi)
The Irukandji Jellyfish inhabits the northern Australian waters in a wide sweeping arc from Exmouth in Western Australia to Gladstone in Queensland roughly from the end of October to early May. Unlike a sting from a Box Jellyfish, a sting by the Irukandji jellyfish is merely a painful irritant with a rash similar to prickly heat. By the time more serious symptoms appear, it may be too late to save a life.

Above: Marbled electric (torpedo) ray camouflaged in sand and rubble. It can give a 500 volt electric shock.

About 30 minutes after being stung, the victim may suffer painful muscle cramps, severe lower back pain, sweating, anxiety, nausea, headache, palpitations, breathlessness and hypertension.

The Irukandji jellyfish's presence is not confined to coastal waters and with bell and tentacles just 2½cm (1 inch) across, it is almost impossible to detect. There is no known treatment other than controlling the symptoms. Wash the wound with vinegar and get the victim to hospital.

OTHER MARINE ORGANISMS WITH TOXINS
Soft corals, the anemones associated with anemonefish (clownfish), and many nudibranchs also contain toxins – do not touch.

Electric (torpedo) rays
These are capable of giving a severe electric shock, anything from 200 to 2000 volts. The main problem here is the possibility of the victim becoming unconscious in the water.

Poisonous to eat
CIGUATERA
Ciguatera fish poisoning occurs around coral reefs damaged by severe storms, shipwrecks, anchors, quarrying, dredging and blast fishing in tropical regions. It is thought that blue-green algae are the first to settle on newly exposed surfaces. The dinoflagellate, *Gambierdiscus toxicus*, produces ciguatoxin. The dinoflagellates and algae are eaten by herbivorous fish and invertebrates,

who are eaten by carnivorous fish, who are eaten by larger carnivores and so on, up the food chain. The toxin is not broken down so it becomes concentrated in fish at the higher levels of the food chain. Most frequently cited are amberjacks and other jacks, barracuda, Red Snapper (*Lutjanus bohar*), Giant Moray Eels (*Gymnothorax javanicus*), Giant Grouper (*Epinephelus lanceolatus*), hogfish, scorpionfish and Saddleback Coralgrouper (*Plectropomus laevis*). Other species implicated are mullet, parrotfish, surgeonfish, wrasse, grunts, Emperor Angelfish and some triggerfish. Pelagic fish are not normally part of the reef food chain, but in some areas tuna will feed around reefs and so become carriers.

Symptoms include debilitating symptoms, profound weakness, temperature sensation changes, pain, and numbness in the extremities, tingling in the arms, legs and lips, headaches and a red itchy rash. In severe cases there is vomiting, diarrhoea, shortness of breath and cardiac arrest. A decrease in blood pressure distinguishes ciguatera from most other forms of food poisoning. Symptoms usually occur within three to six hours of consuming the contaminated fish and may continue for several days and occasionally for years.

Ciguatera can be sexually transmitted from men to women in the

Above: *Red Snapper (Red Reef Snapper) also known as Twinspot Snapper because the young have two light dorsal spots.*

semen. In pregnant women it can cause premature labour and spontaneous abortion. The foetus can be affected, as well as newborns through breast milk.

Several treatments for ciguatera fish poisoning are under investigation. In the early stages, the diuretic Mannitol may prevent symptoms from lingering for months or years, but it does not seem to work if given at later stages.

SCOMBROID POISONING

Scombroid poisoning is caused by the consumption of certain marine fish species that have begun to spoil through poor refrigeration, with the growth of particular types of food bacteria. Fish most commonly involved are members of the

Scombridae family – tuna and mackerel, and a few non-scombroid relatives – bluefish (*Pomatomus saltatrix*), Dolphinfish (Dorado or mahi-mahi) and amberjacks.

Symptoms include redness of the face and neck, palpitations, headache, nausea, diarrhoea, anxiety and hypo- or hypertension.

If the patient has minimal symptoms, reassurance and observation may be the only treatment necessary, otherwise administer oxygen and monitor cardiac function as required. Administer activated charcoal if the victim is presented within 30-minutes of consumption and a large amount of fish was ingested. Antihistamines and bronchodilators can be used in hospital emergency care.

PUFFERFISH (FUGU) POISONING

Pufferfish and Porcupine Pufferfish are extremely dangerous to eat. Pufferfish livers, intestines, skin and ovaries contain the neurotoxin tetrodotoxin, one of the most dangerous toxins known to man. The level of toxicity is seasonal and, in Japan, Fugu is only served from October to March.

Tetrodotoxin shuts down electrical signalling in nerves by binding to the pores of sodium channel proteins in nerve cell membranes. Its name derives from *Tetraodontidae*, the scientific family name of the pufferfishes, some species of which carry the toxin. Although tetrodotoxin was discovered in these fish, it is actually a product of *Pseudoalteromonas haloplanktis tetraodonis* bacteria, which live inside them, as well as inside some other sea creatures.

Tetrodotoxin causes motor paralysis and occasionally respiratory failure. Although victims have fixed dilated pupils and are paralysed, the senses of the victims are often

intact, they are aware but unable to respond. 160,000 times more potent than cocaine and 500 times stronger than cyanide, pufferfish extract is used for voodoo in Haiti and West Africa, where there are well-documented cases of people appearing to be dead (and certified dead) recovering after burial. Recovery is natural but slow.

Taken in tiny quantities however, the toxin cuts down cravings in the

Right and top right: Black Blotched Porcupine Pufferfish. The flesh of pufferfish (Fugu) is considered a delicacy in Japan. Prepared by chefs specially trained and certified by the Japanese government to prepare the flesh free of the toxic tissues. Despite these precautions up to 50 cases of tetrodotoxin poisoning are reported each year from eating Fugu.

Fish poisoning in general

brain by calming signals in the hypothalamus, the section of the brain that co-ordinates the senses and controls feelings of addiction. This has led to incorporating it in a drug, which is undergoing trials as a pain-killer.

Monitor carefully and get the victim to hospital. Victims may require endotracheal intubation for oxygenation and airway protection because of muscle weakness and vomiting. Cardiac dysfunction may require support. Activated charcoal, if administered within 30 minutes of ingesting the poison, will reduce the concentration of the toxin.

The word tetrodotoxin is derived from the order of fish, *tetraodontidae*, which means four-toothed. Four very strong teeth, almost fused together, form a beak-like structure that is used to crack shells for food. Tetrodotoxin has been isolated in at least 14 families including gobies, cone snail stings, crabs of the *Xanthidae* family, starfish of the *Astropectinidae* family, Blue-ringed Octopuses, at least three families (*Buccinidae, Bursidae, Terebridae*) of marine snails, toadfish, some algae, a flatworm and Ocean Sunfish as well as some land animals.

Above: Hawksbill Turtle meat is poisonous. Large marine animals such as Giant (Napoleon) Wrasse, large tuna, dolphins and whales, are often old enough to have accumulated dangerous amounts of natural mercury.

Several other toxins are concentrated by marine creatures. Sharks often concentrate dangerous amounts of vitamin A in their livers and gonads. In polluted areas shellfish can harbour cholera and hepatitis A. All fish and shellfish are dangerous to eat when there are Red Tide plankton blooms. Local hotels, resorts and fish

markets usually know which fish to avoid. Visitors are most at risk if they eat fish that they have either caught themselves or bought direct from an unscrupulous fisherman. However, fish poisoning is the exception rather than the rule.

Fish that cut

SURGEONFISH

Surgeonfish have sharp fins called 'scalpels' on either side of the caudal peduncle, which they can use against other fish, with a sweep of the tail. Territorial, they occasionally use them against divers. Wounds should be cleaned and treated with antibiotic cream.

NEEDLEFISH

Do not try to remove a needlefish beak. If the fish remains attached to the embedded beak, cut it off. If the beak has broken off under the skin, press gently but firmly over the wound to control bleeding. Take the victim to an emergency medical facility for removal of the beak and evaluation of possible deep tissue damage.

Diving in freshwater

Lakes, quarries, dams, canals and slow-flowing rivers, are likely to carry infections such as Weil's disease (Leptospirosis) and, in countries where it is endemic,

Above: Surgeonfish showing its yellow scalpel below the caudal fin. It is used against other fish with a sweep of the tail. These scalpels are often covered in toxic mucus. Occasionally they use them on divers when defending territory such as the algae on a permanent ladder.

Bilharzia (Schistosomiasis). Where there is sewage there is a high chance of gut infection.

Doxycycline is an effective prophylactic for Weil's disease. Schistosomiasis is now easily treatable, but you must inform your doctor if you think you have been exposed to infection.

TRAVELLING TO DIVE

If you are new to diving, any exotic destination will please you and a poor dive master may appear to be an expert to be looked up to. Unfortunately some dive masters are overworked, while others lack knowledge of marine biology or have the wrong personality. Resorts catering primarily for novices may not satisfy experienced divers.

A fit diver who doesn't carry a camera and likes fierce currents, will enjoy a different destination to someone with a more leisurely disposition. Remote resorts and smaller live-aboard boats are likely to turn off the electricity generators at night so you may require quick chargers to keep up with battery charging.

The only way to get some idea of whether an operator is any good is to speak to a friend who has been with them recently.

Before you depart

Passport, visa, vaccination and health certificates, money, travel and diving insurance, any prescription medications and C-card, should be in your carry-on baggage with other essentials such as cameras, film, diving computers, prescription masks and spectacles. Airlines are known to lose or delay baggage.

Make sure that you have the necessary batteries, the correct chargers for the destination's voltage and hertz (cycles) and the correct electrical plugs to fit.

Your passport should be valid for six months longer than the expected length of the trip and have at least six empty pages. If you carry local banknotes, these should be clean and unmarked (not written on). Have photocopies of all paperwork, spare passport photographs for local permits and your driving license if you intend to hire a vehicle. Travel and medical insurance must cover diving activities, the cost of the use of a recompression chamber and repatriation by air ambulance in an emergency.

Travelling with diving equipment within most airlines' check-in baggage limit of 20kg (44lb) is a problem. Some airlines will allow an extra 10kg (22lb) for divers on presentation of a

Above: A fishing boat converted to a ferry leaves Perhentian Besar, the largest of the Perhentian Islands, Malaysia. Divers often favour destinations such as these with empty beaches and jungle walks.

C-card and if it is possible to reach your destination via the USA with an American airline that has more sensible baggage limits based on size, then it is best to do so. Where flights on small aircraft are involved the baggage limit may be 10kg (22lb). Groups travelling together should ask the airline for an extra baggage allowance in advance. You can usually get a better deal

TRAVELLING DIVER'S CHECKLIST

Take everything you need, but only what you need.

- Clothes and wash kit for surface use
- Mask
- Snorkel
- Fins
- Regulator with submersible pressure gauge (contents gauge or Manometer) and alternate air source (octopus)
- Buoyancy Compensator Device (stabilizing jacket).
- Weight belt and weights if not provided by the operator
- Compass
- Diving knife and shears for cutting monofilament lines and nets. (Some airlines no longer allow diving knives even in checked baggage.)
- Two diving computers or one diving computer with a watch, depth gauge and tables as a back up
- Wet suit, Lycra skin or dry suit
- Line reel

- Delayed deployment or other surface marker buoy or flag
- Whistle or powered whistle
- An old CD for use as a heliograph
- Waterproof lights, chargers and an electrical multi-fitting travel adaptor plug
- Diving log book
- Mask anti-misting solution (liquid detergent works just as well and is cheaper!)
- Slate and pencil or other form of underwater communication
- Swimming costumes
- Sunglasses
- Spare prescription spectacles if worn
- Wet bag for diving gear
- Dry bag or case for paperwork, cameras, medics, wash kit etc.
- First aid kit
- Towel if not supplied at destination.

on scheduled flights than on charter flights to the same destination because you can threaten to fly with another carrier.

Live-aboard boat skippers prefer diving bags or rucksacks for easy stowage, but they do not stand up well to airport baggage handlers and airport thieves spot them for containing expensive equipment. Lockable wire mesh covers for bags are heavy. Pelican Cases are also prime targets for airport thieves. Shabby cases are better. Find out what equipment is available for hire at your destination so that you

can minimize your checked baggage. However, at third world destinations rental equipment may be in poor condition and fins and wet suits are often too small for large Caucasians.

Spares kit

- Mask and mask straps
- Fin straps and buckles
- Knife straps and buckles
- Wire ties – large and small
- Spare regulator mouthpiece and the correct wire tie
- O-rings for anything that uses

them, including a few for the scuba cylinder valve to regulator fitting
- Fishhooks for removing difficult O-rings
- Removal tool for camera O-rings
- Flat and Phillips (cross-head) screwdrivers
- Pliers
- Circlip removal tool
- Adjustable wrench
- Crescent wrench where necessary
- Allen (hexagonal) keys
- Silicone grease

- Paper towel
- Spare bulbs for lights
- Spares of all necessary batteries and chargers
- Insulating tape or self-vulcanizing rubber tape
- A spare high-pressure hose and a spare mask (if possible)
- An electrical multimeter (for serious photographers only)
- special spanners to re-assemble regulators (they travel best when disassembled).

Travelling diver's medics

The slightest ear or sinus infection can ruin a diving holiday, especially in a remote area or on a live-aboard boat. Being prepared can save your vacation. Many divers travelling to a live-aboard boat assume that they do not require malaria prophylactics because they will spend 99% of their time at sea where mosquitoes do not exist. However, it only needs one mosquito bite in an airport to transmit the disease and there is always the chance that aircraft or boats are delayed, forcing divers to spend extra time at risk on land.

The correct antimalarial should be taken where necessary. Mefloquine (Larium) may have side effects that are not good for divers. Doxycycline (Vibramycin) taken daily can be used short-term, but not during pregnancy or by children. It can cause photosensitivity, so be careful of strong sunlight. Dengue fever is also transmitted by mosquitoes, but in daylight. It is an increasing problem, so make sure that you carry a good insect repellent. When sleeping in a closed room, mosquito nets, knockdown sprays or heated vaporizing repellents are safer than mosquito coils.

Ear infections can be a problem (*see p167*) so take precautions. Masks that keep the ears dry are now available (*see p48*). Most divers carry drops that dry out the ears, decongestants, antihistamine cream, sunscreen and sunburn lotion, lip-salve, anti-diarrhoea medicine, rehydration salts, antibiotics, seasickness remedies and insect repellents.

Most decongestants and seasickness remedies can make you drowsy and should not be taken before diving. However, where it is available legally and without prescription, Sudafed decongestant is long acting and does not cause drowsiness, in fact it causes one to be more awake.

Above: *Expensive or fragile equipment that cannot be taken as carry-on luggage, should be packed in cases that can stand up to airport baggage handlers*

TRAINING AGENCIES

Some of the better-known dive training agencies

Nowadays most agencies cover all diving disciplines. What is most important is the instructor, not the agency.

ANDI – American Nitrox Divers International. www.andihq.com
International headquarters in Freeport, New York, USA.

BSAC – British Sub Aqua Club. www.bsac.com
Based in Ellesmere Port, Cheshire, UK.

CMAS – The World Underwater Federation (Confédération Mondiale des Activités Subaquatiques). www.cmas2000.org
Headquarters in Rome, Italy.

HSA – Handicapped Scuba Association. www.hsascuba.com
Headquarters in San Clemente, California, USA.

IAHD – International Association for Handicapped Divers. www.iahd.org
Based in the Middenmeer, Netherlands (Holland).

IANTD – International Association of Nitrox and Technical Divers. www.iantd.com
World Headquarters in Miami Shores, Florida, USA.

IDEA – International Diving Educators Association. www.idea-scubadiving.com
Headquarters in Jacksonville, Florida, USA.

IUC – Ireland Underwater Council, or Comhairle fo Thuinn (CFT). www.scubaireland.com
Headquarters in Dun Laoghaire, Co. Dublin.

NASDS – National Association of Scuba Diving Schools. (Merged with SSI in 1999)

NAUI – National Association of Underwater Instructors. www.naui.org
Headquarters in Tampa, Florida, USA.

PADI – Professional Association of Diving Instructors. www.padi.com
Headquarters in Rancho Santa Margarita, California, USA.

PDIC – Professional Diving Instructors Corporation. www.pdic-intl.com
Headquarters is in Scranton, Pennsylvania, USA.

SAA – Sub Aqua Association. www.saa.org.uk
Head office in Maghull, Liverpool, UK.

SDI – Scuba Diving International. Refer to TDI

SSAC – Scottish Sub Aqua Club. www.scotsac.com
Head office in Glasgow, Scotland, UK.

SSI – Scuba Schools International. Merged with (NASDS) 1999. www.divessi.com
Headquarters is in Fort Collins, Colorado, USA.

TDI – Technical Diving International. www.tdisdi.com
Headquarters (also sister company SDI) in Topsham, Maine, USA.

YMCA SCUBA – Young Men Christian Association Scuba Programme. www.ymcascuba.org
Headquarters in Chicago, Illinois, USA.

OTHER IMPORTANT AGENCIES

DAN – Divers Alert Network. www.diversalertnetwork.org
The Divers Alert Network is not a training agency but a worldwide diving safety and data collecting agency for diving accidents. DAN was founded in 1980 as the National Diving Accident Network, with a two-year NOAA and NIOSH grant to Dr Peter B Bennett of the FG Hall Hyperbaric Center at Duke University Medical Center in Durham, North Carolina. DAN changed its name to 'Divers Alert Network' in 1983. It is a non-profit organization supported by membership dues and donations. In return, DAN operates a 24-hour emergency hotline, a diving medical information line, conducts diving medical research and members receive a number of benefits including an insurance programme, emergency medical evacuation assistance and related courses.

NOAA – National Oceanic and Atmospheric Administration. www.noaa.gov
Created in October 1970, the NOAA is a consolidation of many component organizations, including the United States Coast Survey established in 1807, the United States Weather Bureau established in 1870, and the United States Commission of Fish and Fisheries established in 1871. The NOAA is a science-based agency with the responsibility to predict changes in the oceanic and atmospheric environments and living marine resources, and to provide related information, and services to the public, industry, researchers, and other government agencies.

Adjustable buoyancy life jacket (ABLJ) – Jacket-style buoyancy compensator device (BCD).

A-flag (Alpha flag) – A blue and white International Code flag: a diver in the water, other craft keep clear.

Air embolism – See Arterial gas embolism.

Algal bloom – A sudden spurt of algal growth that can indicate changes in local water chemistry.

Algorithm – A process or set of rules for calculation or problem solving, especially with a computer.

Alternate air source (supply) – Additional regulator second stage for emergency use by another diver (see octopus).

Arterial Gas Embolism (AGE) – Gas bubbles from the lungs enter the blood stream via burst alveoli. The bubbles can block blood flow to critical parts of the body, usually the brain or heart.

Artificial reef – Artificial structure (ships, cars, etc.) placed on the ocean floor as hard substrate for sea life to colonize.

ATA – see Atmospheres Absolute.

Atmosphere – The average pressure of the atmosphere at sea level. A unit of pressure of 14.7psi or 1 bar. The pressure underwater increases by one atmosphere for every 10m (33ft) of depth.

Atmospheres Absolute (ATA) (underwater) – The sum of the atmospheric pressure and the hydrostatic pressure: the total weight of the water and air above divers.

Backpack – Frame that holds one or more scuba cylinders on a diver's back, either directly or as part of a BCD.

Balanced valve – A valve controlling the passage of high-pressure gas in such a way that the gas pressure does not affect the force needed to operate the valve.

Bar (unit) – A unit of pressure, 10^5 newton per square metre, approximately one atmosphere.

Barotrauma – An injury related to pressure.

Bends – Term used for decompression sickness due to sufferers bending the affected limb to ease the pain.

Bezel – A rotating collar round a watch to show elapsed time on a diving watch.

Blast fishing – A destructive fishing technique using explosives to kill fish.

Bottom mix – Ratio of gases in a diver's scuba cylinder planned for use at the deepest point of the dive.

Bottom time – Time elapsed from leaving the surface until commencing the ascent. This is the time required for decompression calculations.

Bounce Dive – The diver turns around to ascend immediately after reaching maximum depth.

Breathing loop (rebreather) – All the internal areas within which the diver's breathing gases flow, including the counterlung, scrubber, breathing hoses and the divers lungs.

Buddy breathing – Two divers sharing a single air source.

Buddy line – A short line between two or more divers to help them maintain contact in limited visibility or when they cannot contact their boat cover.

Buoyant ascent – A rapid emergency ascent following the inflation of a buoyancy compensator device or dry suit.

Caisson Workers Disease – Decompression sickness (Caisson Workers suffered from it).

Carbon dioxide cartridge – Small cartridge of carbon dioxide (CO_2) for one-off inflation of BCD at the surface.

Certification card (C-card) – Identification card as evidence that the diver has passed certain performance standards of a recognized training agency. Some dive operators also want to see a diver's logbook to check experience.

Chart datum – The plane from which heights and depths are measured. A level below which the tide rarely falls.

Chase-boat – A boat following the surface marker buoy or exhaust bubbles of divers on a drift dive.

Ciguatera – Poisoning that results from eating fish that have eaten a certain type of algae or their predators.

Compartment – A theoretical division of the body with an arbitrarily assigned half-time for nitrogen uptake and elimination. In designing decompression tables the body is divided into a finite number of compartments for the purpose of making calculations.

Compressor – Multistage pump used to fill cylinders or storage 'banks' with compressed air or other gases.

Console – Unit attached to submersible pressure gauge for a collection of instruments to be mounted together.

Contents gauge – Submersible pressure gauge that indicates the amount of gas in the cylinder by its pressure.

Coriolis Effect – The deflection of the path of a body due to the earth's rotation, to the left in the southern hemisphere and to the right in the northern hemisphere.

Counterlung – Sealed flexible bag that inflates as the diver exhales and deflates as the diver inhales. In acting as a storage area for the diver's breathing gases, the positioning of this bag within the breathing loop can greatly affect the breathing effort.

Dead air space – The space containing air in the respiratory system where gaseous exchange does not occur (nasal passages, pharynx, trachea, etc.)

Decompression schedule – A specific decompression procedure for a given dive profile, normally indicated as a depth for so many minutes. The schedule can be computer generated or obtained from decompression tables.

Decompression dive – Dive that requires one or more decompression stops to release dissolved gases in a controlled fashion.

Decompression sickness (DCS) – Condition caused by the rapid release of pressure on ascent, nitrogen (or helium) in the blood and body tissues forms bubbles that can block the circulation.

Decompression stop – Pause the ascent to allow the excess nitrogen (or helium) in the body to dissipate. When not mandatory it is called a safety stop.

Decompression table – Table of times and depths used to calculate the limits of safe diving and decompression stops.

Demand valve (DV) – Another name for a regulator because it only supplies breathing gas on demand.

Density – The compactness of a substance expressed as its mass per unit volume.

Diluent (rebreather) – The gas used in a closed circuit rebreather to make up volume in the breathing loop as the diver goes deeper and the gases in the loop are compressed. The gas used could be air, Nitrox, Trimix or Heliox.

DIN fitting – Extremely reliable regulator to scuba cylinder valve fitting which encloses the O-ring so that it cannot 'burst'.

Dioptre – A unit of the refractive power of a lens that is equal to the reciprocal of its focal length in metres.

Direct-feed – (Also power-inflator), a one-way valve connected to a low-pressure hose, which enables a supply of gas from the first stage of the regulator to inflate the buoyancy compensator device or dry suit.

Dive marshal – Person in overall charge of diving expedition (British term).

Dive master – Person in overall charge of diving expedition (American term).

Dive planner – Table of times and depths used to calculate the limits of safe diving, particularly on multiple dives.

Dive profile – Graphic representation of times spent at various depths.

Dive timer – Timing device activated either manually or when submerged to show elapsed time of a particular dive.

Diving logbook – Record of dives that also acts as proof of the types of dives accomplished since qualifying.

Drift diving – The tide-stream or current moves the diver along. The movement is often faster than swimming unaided, but the diver is not fully in command. Good surface cover is essential.

D-ring – D-shaped stainless steel ring located on the BCD straps or fitted to the weight belt, used to make reliable connections with other equipment.

Dump valve – A valve used to vent gases from dry suits or BCDs.

Dynamite fishing – See blast fishing.

Ebb tide – An outgoing tide, water level falling.

Echo sounder – An instrument for measuring the depth of water by timing the echo off the bottom or a wreck from a pulse of sound originating within the echo sounder.

Elapsed time – Time elapsed since leaving the surface.

Emergency cylinder – Small cylinder fitted to many BCDs for emergency inflation.

Enriched Air Nitrox (EANx) – Mixture of oxygen and nitrogen that has more oxygen than is found in normal air.

Environmentally sealed regulator – Regulator with the first stage sealed to keep out water and sediment. If the sealing unit is filled with a liquid that freezes at a lower temperature than water it will help prevent ice build up in cold water.

First stage – The section of the regulator that reduces the pressure of the gases in the scuba cylinder to a pressure that the second stage requires.

Flashlight – The American name for a torch – a battery-powered light source.

Flood tide – Incoming tide, water level rising.

Fluorescence – Absorbing light of a short (invisible) wavelength and emitting light of longer (visible) wavelength. The substance appears to be unnaturally bright.

Flutter kick – Leg stroke characteristic of crawl swimmers.

Free ascent – A diver surfacing rapidly in an emergency, forcibly breathing out all the way to avoid a burst lung.

Frog kick (modified) – The ankles are rotated so that the tips of the fins point outwards. The feet are moved apart, then the bottoms of the fins are kicked quickly together.

Fully-closed circuit rebreather – See Rebreather.

Gerry line – See Granny line.

Granny Line – A floating line running the length of the boat from the mooring line or anchor line to the stern platform or hang-bar.

Gunwale – The upper edge of the side of a vessel.

Halocline – (in oceanography). Relatively sharp change in salinity of the water column with depth.

Hang line – A horizontal line or bar rigged beneath the boat for divers to hang onto during decompression stops.

HeliAir – Breathing mixture of helium and air, the latter made up of oxygen and nitrogen. The same three constituents are also found in Trimix, the difference being in the way the gases are mixed. Trimix is blended by a three-way mix, first by decanting helium and oxygen into the scuba cylinder and then topping up with air via a conventional compressor. HeliAir is blended by filling the scuba cylinder with the desired amount of helium and then topping up with air. This is used to eliminate Nitrogen narcosis and to control the effects of oxygen toxicity, by eliminating the nitrogen and reducing the amount of oxygen in the breathing mix.

Heliox – A breathing mixture of gases consisting entirely of helium and oxygen. To eliminate Nitrogen narcosis and to control the affects of oxygen toxicity, by eliminating the nitrogen and reducing the amount of oxygen in the mix.

H-Valve – Scuba cylinder valve with two outlets for two regulators. There are two valves with one scuba cylinder connection. Allows the diver to turn off one valve if that regulator free-flows and still be able to use the rest of the air in the cylinder. An H-valve is designed so that it can be used to connect to a manifold by removing one of the valves and adding the interconnecting manifold tube.

Hyperbaric chamber – A pressure chamber that provides recompression treatment for decompression illness (DCI) and Hyperbaric Oxygen Therapy (HBOT) for carbon monoxide poisoning, osteoradionecrosis and other wounds and infections.

Ingassing – Absorption of a breathing gas by tissues.

Jon line – 2m or 4m (6½ft or 13ft) length of strong line, 25mm (1-in) tape or bungee cord. Connected to the diver with a karabiner (snaplink) and the other end has a spring clip to lock round rope, anchor chain or shotlines with one hand.

J-Valve (reserve valve) – Outdated type of scuba cylinder valve used before submersible pressure gauges (SPGs) were standard scuba equipment.

Kit – British term for dive gear.

K–Valve – Simple non-reserve on/off valve scuba cylinder valve.

Littoral – Intertidal; between low and high tide.

Loraine Smith Effect – See Oxygen Toxicity.

Lubber line – The reference line on a compass.

Manifold – Hollow, heavy-duty crosspiece with an isolating valve in the centre that connects the two valves of twin scuba cylinder systems.

Monofilament cutter – Designed to cut through monofilament line or netting (monofilament tends to stretch).

Mouthpiece – Section of a regulator or snorkel which fits into the diver's mouth.

Multilevel diving – Spending time at several different depths on a single dive.

Nematocyst – A specialized cell in the tentacles of coral, jellyfish or other coelenterates (*cnidaria*), containing a barbed or venomous coiled thread that can be projected in self-defence or to capture prey.

Newton (unit) – The unit of force that, acting on a mass of one kilogram, increases its velocity by one metre per second every second along the direction in which it acts.

Nitrogen narcosis – A condition affecting divers' mental processes caused by excess nitrogen in their body tissues. The effects of Nitrogen narcosis on divers are similar to their being drunk and increase with depth.

Nitrox – Refer to Enriched Air Nitrox.

Non-decompression stop dive (no stop dive) – Dive that does not require decompression stops.

Normoxic – The normal mixture of gases found in the atmosphere.

O/O$_2$ – Oxygen.

Octopus rig – A second regulator second stage that is attached to the regulator's first stage and used for sharing air with another diver. By convention it is coloured yellow.

0-ring – Synthetic rubber ring that fits in a groove and is used to form an airtight or watertight seal.

Outgassing – Elimination of gas from the tissues when the ambient pressure is lowered.

Oxygen clean – Clean of combustibles such as oil and grease to allow use with high-pressure oxygen.

Oxygen toxicity – Physiological damage resulting from breathing higher-than-normal partial pressures of oxygen. There are two primary types of oxygen toxicity. Long exposures of elevated partial pressures of oxygen results in The Loraine Smith Effect or Pulmonary Oxygen Toxicity, as the primary damage is to the lungs and airways. The other type of oxygen toxicity results from short exposure to high partial pressures of oxygen and is called The Paul Bert effect or Central Nervous System Toxicity (CNS Toxicity) and is characterized by convulsions.

Partial pressure – Pressure of a particular gas within a mixture of gases. Partial pressures are commonly represented as pp, followed by the atomic symbol of the gas, so the partial pressure of oxygen would be written as ppO$_2$.

Paul Bert Effect – Refer to Oxygen Toxicity.

Perfusion – The delivery of oxygen and nutrients to the body tissues and the elimination of waste products by the circulation of the blood.

Photic zone – The vertical zone in the ocean extending from the surface to that depth permitting photosynthetic activity.

Pony bottle – Small scuba cylinder with its own regulator, strapped to a diver's main scuba cylinder for use in decompression or emergency.

Port (camera housing) – Window through which the camera lens takes the picture.

Port (scuba regulator) – Threaded openings in the first stage that feed the high-pressure submersible pressure gauge and low-pressure units such as the second stage, octopus, direct feed, etc.

Port side (vessel) – The left-hand side of the vessel when you are facing the bow.

Power-inflator – Refer to direct feed.

pp – Partial pressure.

psi – Pounds per square inch.

psia – Pounds per square inch absolute.

Rebreather – A self-contained device used to recirculate and regulate breathing gases for the purposes of extended diving times and quiet operation. In a fully closed-circuit rebreather this is accomplished by chemically removing carbon dioxide (scrubbing CO$_2$), and adding oxygen as necessary to maintain a constant partial pressure of oxygen. This type of rebreather does not release any gases from the unit except under the conditions of ascending from depth. The advantage of this system is the greatest possible use of the oxygen carried, the disadvantage is the added complexity of the electronics and mechanics in the unit. In most semi-closed systems a portion of each breath is released to the water, the carbon dioxide is scrubbed from the remaining gases and a similar portion of new breathing gases are injected into the system.

Recompression chamber – refer to hyperbaric chamber.

Refraction – The rays of light are bent as they pass from one medium to another of different density. Refraction occurs at the interface between the air in the diver's mask, the glass and the water. The refracted image of an underwater object is magnified, appears larger than the real image, and seems to be positioned at a point ¾ of the actual distance between the object and the diver's mask.

Regulator – (Demand valve) Mechanism which reduces the pressure of the gases in the scuba cylinder to the pressure of the water surrounding the body at the level of the diver's lungs so that the gases can be inhaled.

Rescue tube – Highly visible surface marker buoy in the shape of a tube or sausage only deployed when required.

Reserve valve – see J-Valve.

Residual nitrogen – Amount of absorbed nitrogen that is

estimated to remain in the diver's body after a dive.

SafeAir – A mixture of air enriched to between 22 and 50% of oxygen copyrighted by ANDI.

Safety stop – See decompression stop.

Scatter (light) – Scatter occurs when individual photons of light are deflected or diverted when they encounter suspended particles in the water. Scattering also occurs in air, but is of greater importance underwater because light is diffused and scattered by the water molecules themselves, by all kinds of particulate matter suspended in the water and by transparent biological organisms.

Scombroid poisoning – Food poisoning caused by the consumption of scombroid and scombroid-like marine fish species that have begun to spoil with the growth of particular types of food bacteria when not properly frozen.

Scrubber or CO$_2$ scrubber – The part of a rebreather that removes carbon dioxide (CO$_2$) by passing it through a chemical that absorbs it.

SCUBA – An acronym for Self-Contained Underwater Breathing Apparatus.

Scuba cylinder valve – The valve on the scuba cylinder, which is attached either to the regulator or the compressor.

Second stage – The section of the regulator, which further reduces the pressure of the gases from the first stage to the ambient pressure of water level with the diver's lungs so that it can be breathed through the mouthpiece.

Semiclosed circuit rebreather – See rebreather.

Shotline – A weighted line marking an object on the seabed or providing a guide for divers during descent or ascent.

Slack water – The period of still water around the turn of the tide, especially at low tide.

Species (in sexually reproducing organisms) – A group of genetically related organisms, usually similar in physical appearance, that actually or potentially can interbreed and are reproductively isolated from other groups.

Stabilizer (stab) jacket – Another name for a jacket-style buoyancy compensator device (BCD).

Starboard side (vessel) – Right-hand side of the boat when you are facing the bow.

Stern – Back of a boat.

Surface marker buoy (SMB) – Floating buoy used by divers to mark their position.

Symbiosis – Two dissimilar organisms living in close physical association in which each benefits the other.

Tag line – See trail line.

Tetrodotoxin – The most serious type of fish poisoning that is the result of consuming the wrong parts of pufferfish and some other species.

Thermocline – The intersection between two layers of water that are of distinctly different temperatures.

Tissue (human) – Parts of the body with specific characteristics, such as muscle, bone, or cartilage. The term is also used to refer to any part of the body with a specific half time for absorbing and eliminating nitrogen or even a theoretical compartment.

Trail line – A floating line trailing from the stern of the boat when the current is strong. Divers can hold onto this line while waiting for their buddy or the ladder to clear and can pull themselves to the ladder when it is clear.

Transits – Bearings taken by lining up two objects – usually fixed items such as buildings onshore.

Trimix – A breathing mixture of gases most often composed of oxygen, nitrogen and helium. Used to eliminate Nitrogen narcosis and control the effects of oxygen toxicity, by eliminating the nitrogen and reducing the amount of oxygen in the breathing mix. The proportions of each gas are changed according to the requirements of the particular dive plan.

Visibility – Underwater visibility is defined as 'The estimated distance at which you can easily discern a diver' – it should always be measured horizontally.

Walls – A reef wall that is near to the vertical and may be overhanging or undercut.

Windward – The side that faces the prevailing wind.

Y-Valve – A scuba cylinder valve with two outlets for two regulators. There are two valves with one scuba cylinder connection to allow the diver to turn off one valve if that regulator free-flows and still be able to use the rest of the air in the scuba cylinder. The two valves are arranged in the shape of a Y.

Zodiac – A brand name for an inflatable or rigid inflatable boat (RIB) that has become generic.

PHOTOGRAPHIC CREDITS

All photography by Jack Jackson, with the exception of the photographers listed below and/or their agencies.
(Copyright rests with the photographers and/or their agents.)
Key to Locations: t = top; b = bottom; l = left; r = right; c = centre. (No abbreviation is given for pages
with a single image, or pages on which all photographs are by the same photographer.)

AB = Andy Belcher
IOA = Images of Africa (www.imagesofafrica.co.za)
GS = Geoff Spiby

PA = Photo Access
PH/AK = Peter Hemming/Arctic Kingdom
SL = Stefania Lamberti